The American peril

Shipping Comb°

E PLURIBUS UNUM

A MORGANATIC MARRIAGE.

THE LATEST AMERICAN DO(D)GE WEDS THE ATLANTIC WITH A 'RING."

[*from* Punch, *30 April 1902*

THE
AMERICAN PERIL

Challenge to Britain
on the North Atlantic
1901-04

VIVIAN VALE

Manchester
University Press

Published by
Manchester University Press
Oxford Road, Manchester M13 9PL, U.K.
51 Washington Street, Dover, N.H. 03820, U.S.A.

Vale, Vivian
    The American peril.
    1. Great Britain—Foreign relations—United
States 2. United States—Foreign relations
—Great Britain 3. United States—Foreign
relations—1901–1910 4. United States—
Foreign relations—1901–1909
    I. Title
    327.41073   E183.8.G7

ISBN 0-7190-1718-1

Library of Congress cataloging in publication data

Vale, Vivian
    The American peril.
    Includes index.
    1. Great Britain—Commercial policy—History—
20th century 2. North Atlantic Region—Commerce
—History—20th century 3. Shipping—North
Atlantic Region—History—20th century 4. North
Atlantic Region—Strategic aspects—History—
20th century 5. Competition, International.
    I. Title
    HF1533.V35 1984   382'.3'0941   84-9683

ISBN 0-7190-1718-1

Filmset by J & L Composition Ltd. Filey, N. Yorkshire

Printed in Great Britain by
Butler & Tanner Ltd, Frome and London

Contents

Foreword

That historical milestones may sometimes be landmarks is an aphorism as applicable to the shipping industry as to any other economic enterprise.

During the Falklands campaign, in spring 1982, the container ship *Atlantic Conveyor* was hit and sunk by enemy missiles. Already twelve years old, she had been commandeered for military supply service in the South Atlantic from her owners, Cunard, of whose parent company, Trafalgar House, Lord Matthews was chairman. Throughout July 1982 negotiations as to compensation, replacement, and so on, proceeded between him and representatives of the Departments of Treasury, Industry, Trade and Employment, later joined by Defence. Under the Prime Minister's chairmanship, Cabinet members also met top executives of British Shipbuilders, one of whose subsidiaries, Swan Hunter, were hopeful of building a replacement for the lost vessel on Tyneside.

Swan Hunter's tender was reported to be priced nearly 50% above that of the South Korean yard which Cunard had previously in mind for the work. Little fuss had been made when, not long before, the P&O line had decided to place their order for a new cruise liner – a project twice as valuable – with a Finnish yard. Yet now considerations of security, employment and patriotism combined to induce the British government to urge that *Atlantic Conveyor*'s replacement be built in Britain. Lord Matthews accordingly pressed Cunard's claim for a governmental subsidy to bridge a financial gap variously estimated at between £15 million and half that figure. Some tough and sophisticated bargaining ensued.

At this point the Ministry of Defence entered the picture. As Secretary of State it was John Nott's belief – though one not necessarily or unanimously shared by the Admiralty – that the late campaign in the South Atlantic had emphasised the value to the Royal Navy of large container vessels requisitioned from the mercantile marine; especially of the *Atlantic Conveyor* class – not just a large container but designed also for flexible ('roll on, roll off') carriage of vehicles and break-bulk cargo. Her successor might be modified (e.g. with strengthened steel decks) so as to make military conversion easier. The Ministry, proposed Mr Nott, might contribute significantly towards a vessel so convertible, if built in a British yard. To make that possible, the financial package eventually assembled by the government was to contain a number of elements sufficient in the aggregate to ensure the order for Swan Hunter.

This episode is touched on here because no greater contrast could be imagined with the circumstances surrounding those almost parallel transactions of eighty years earlier – in the North, not South, Atlantic – which are central to the ensuing chapters. First, the aforementioned financial package of July 1982 comprised an element of compensation (£10 million) to Cunard for the lost vessel; a Ministry of Defence subvention, with military needs in mind, of £4 million; 30% of the cost of replacing it, in the form of export credits plus an intervention fund grant covering 15% of the sale price; together with the benefits accruing from the home shipbuilding credit guarantee scheme (allowing 80% of the contract price repayable over up to eight and a half years at a fixed interest rate of 7½%). Moreover, British Shipbuilders continued to receive government subsidies (for 1981–82 to the tune of £150 million) to minimise their trading losses. By contrast in 1900 only one of these elements, the subvention for merchant vessels specially adapted for naval use, had been operative and relevant.

Secondly, the financial operation of July 1982 attracted comparatively little surprise or comment; a front-page mention in one issue only of each of two or three leading dailies, with a leader in *The Times*, before suffering relegation to the hinterland of the financial pages. In the Commons the parliamentary opposition, through Michael Foot, was so far in accord with the government as to press them urgently to a generous settlement before Parliament rose for the summer recess. In the 1900's Parliament and press had been rent with discord over an issue seen in black and white as free trade versus protection.

The following chapters attempt to explain how certain maritime and financial episodes of the early 1900's eventuated and why they were viewed, against a background of British–American–German rivalry, as presenting the government with certain issues of principle. How those issues were resolved still affects national trade and security today.

In the making of this book, thanks are due to the Secretary of the Cunard Steam-Ship Company for permission to quote from two volumes of the Company's archives, and to the Warden and Fellows of New College, Oxford, for leave to reproduce extracts from volume 40 of the Milner Papers. Professor Charles Wilson, of the University of Cambridge, and Professor Francis Hyde, late of the University of Liverpool, kindly read the work in an earlier draft but bear no responsibility for its shortcomings. The University of Southampton granted me sabbatical and special leave to complete it in the USA.

V.V.
May 1984

CHAPTER 1

The threat of the trusts

This book purports to be about a challenge. And familiar as we are today with the spectacle of America in Britain's place, some effort of the imagination is needed to recapture the pristine excitement with which our great-grandfathers first beheld and responded to the challenger. The more watchful and prescient of them, truly, had long been warning against the event. Gladstone himself, as his century moved into its third quarter, observed of the rising United States that

> It is she alone who, at a coming time, can and probably will wrest from us our commercial supremacy. We have no title: I have no inclination to murmur at the prospect. If she acquires it, she will make the requisition by the right of the strongest and best. We have no more title against her than Venice or Genoa or Holland has had against us.

Indeed, back at the mid-century, in the very year when Britian was orgulous with the Great Exhibition, some authorities could be heard confidently predicting that 'the superiority of the United States to England is ultimately as certain as the next eclipse'. And in a sense, of course, this weighing of the New World against the Old goes as far back as the era when Adam Smith foresaw the commercial centre of gravity within the British Empire of his own day as fated ultimately to move westward. In the same strain of conjecture Lord Rosebery was inviting the students of Glasgow University in 1901 to contemplate with satisfaction 'the seat of Empire ... solemnly moved across the Atlantic' and a 'British Federal Parliament sitting in Columbian territory'.[1] The difference was that many more people now thought such a transit neither unlikely nor remote.

Yet when the issue came to be joined, neither nation seemed wholly aware of what was at stake or fully apprised of the other's true strengths and weaknesses. It was as though a layer of mutual incomprehension had first to be peeled away. Intensely Anglophile though he was, the future Secretary of State John Hay in 1894 reported back to Henry Cabot Lodge from London:

'If it were not so offensive, the ignorance of people over here about American politics would be very amusing'; and Lodge in his turn had occasion to tax the British with 'a state of ignorance about the United States', and our newspapers with giving her less coverage than they gave Holland or Belgium. Moberly Bell, the first manager of the London *Times* to visit the United States, did not do so until 1901. About the same time our first resident newspaper correspondent there, G. W. Smalley, went over but was not to be joined in Washington by any regular colleagues until World War I. Small wonder that when, for instance, feeling ran high over European intrusion into Latin America in 1896 Bryce had to confess to Theodore Roosevelt that 'not one man out of ten in the House of Commons even knew there was such a thing as a Venezuelan question pending'. As a future head of the American Department of the Foreign Office afterwards confessed, in these years 'Britons seldom condescended to transatlantic politics'. So when at the turn of the century the challenge was thrown down, the British public not surprisingly overestimated, as we shall see, the threat confronting them. But correspondingly, some intelligent and cosmopolitan Americans were over-hasty in proclaiming the decadence of Edwardian Britain. 'England is sad – to me very sad', wrote Brooks Adams to Lodge in 1900. 'Like you I hope she may revive, but I admit my hope is faint ... I fancy England will grow gradually more and more sluggish, until at length, after our day, she will drop out of the strenuous competition of the new world which is forming'.[2]

Despite the pessimists, however, this lact of precise mutual knowledge was not to prevent – indeed, it may have encouraged – a climate of opinion highly conducive to *entente* between the entrenched and the rising power. As the nineteenth century drew to an end in Britain, it was truly remarkable how many of her public men professed, often vociferously, their belief in the need for greater Anglo-American amity. This new and enthusiastic advocacy of *rapprochement*, surviving all territorial collisions between the two countries – Venezuela, Nicaragua, Alaska, Liberia – assumed, according to one Anglo-American historian, 'so deep and historic a significance' that it 'must indeed take first rank ... among the decisive events of modern history'.

2

Partly it was a matter of sentiment. Gladstone in old age had acknowledged something 'conventionally termed the Anglo-Saxon race'. And now many prominent Britons confessed to being permeated with a spirit they variously identified as 'pan-Anglism', 'Anglo-Saxonism' or 'patriotism of race', and a desire to promote and foster a 'union of the English-speaking peoples'. Prominent advocates of some form of transatlantic association, political or cultural, were to be encountered in all walks of our public life. Among statesmen and political notables were A. J. Balfour, Haldane, Dilke, Campbell-Bannerman, Asquith, Grey, Rhodes and, above all, Joseph Chamberlain; among men of letters could be numbered Kipling, Henley, Conan Doyle, Walter Besant and Alfred Austin. Pro-Americanism pervaded elder historians like J. R. Green and Lecky, contemporary chroniclers like Sidney Low, but equally the rising left personified by Sidney Webb, H. G. Wells and Bertrand Russell. It waxed particularly strong within those who personally knew both sides of the Atlantic, including ambassadors present and to be – Bryce, William Herbert and Cecil Spring-Rice. True, notions of the optimum degree of Anglo-American *entente* showed a fine gradation, from friendship to alliance to fusion. The legalist Dicey and the young politician Winston Churchill, for example, concurred in pressing for a common citizenship while dismissing any suggestion of political absorption. But if leading Britons of that day viewed *rapprochement* variously, most of them agreed that the need for it was there.

In tone advocacy ranged from the brash to the subtle. At one extreme was to be found a journalist who straddled the Atlantic. To the reporter and editor W. T. Stead it seemed self-evident that

'the true line of England's destinies lies in her uniting herself to the United States of America and forming part of a great federal union of the English-speaking states of the world ... It is a plain duty which we have got to accomplish, and that right speedily, unless we are to be undone ... There is no other alternative'

save 'our ultimate reduction to the status of an English-speaking Belgium'. 'We could, of course', he reassured his readers, 'keep the Union Jack as a local flag'.[4] . Stead's *bête noire* was what he called the rampant jingoism of Joseph Chamberlain –

an outlook he regarded as at the opposite end of the spectrum from his own. But in fact Chamberlain, with whom our succeeding chapters will be much concerned, is an interesting study in the nuances of Anglo-Saxonism. Blessed with an American third wife, personal experience of Washington and frequent private communications therefrom, he had in May 1898 uttered his celebrated plea – well received in the USA – that 'the Stars and Stripes and the Union Jack should wave together over an Anglo-Saxon alliance'. There was much in America he admired, from her protective trading arrangements down to her local party organisations. Some qualified adoption of the former by Britain he advocated with increasing urgency: the latter he directly imitated when organising his Birmingham caucus. Not for nothing did Gladstone once describe him as the most American of English statesmen. Yet one must recall that Chamberlain's earlier conception of a new epoch of (as he put it) 'aggregation, not segregation' would have included Germany too in 'a new Triple Alliance between the Teutonic race and the two great branches of the Anglo-Saxon race'. Only when his proposal was met in Reichstag and press with indifference or hostility did he turn to a narrower Anglo-Americanism, one which did not necessarily imply anything more formal than 'temporary alliances for extraordinary emergencies'.[5] And it must in any case be allowed that a more fervent courtship of the United States would have carried British politicians too far ahead of public opinion.

At social and cultural levels, too, this *rapprochement* was beginning to make itself felt. A number of organisations were springing up which bore such titles as the Anglo-American Association (1871), the Anglo-American League (1898) and the Pilgrims (1901): or the Atlantic Union (1900) created by Besant, whereby Britons might extend hospitality and entertainment to their visiting American congeners – mainly professional people and chiefly in London. Most such initiatives originated on this side of the Atlantic and proved short-lived: few were made from the further side, where pockets of Anglophobia lingered on. Yet reciprocal warmth was by no means lacking there. The naval strategist Captain Alfred Thayer Mahan, for instance, was ardent for exploring 'The Possibilities of an Anglo-American Reunion', whereby 'mutual understanding of common interests and common traditions' might girdle the globe.[6] The Scottish-born industrialist Andrew Carnegie, despite his low opinion of monarchic forms, preached the gospel of 'the Reunited States'. So desirable an amalgam would of course include Canada too.

To account for this seeming era of mutual good feeling historians have on the whole preferred to point us toward common material interests. Victory in her recent conflict with Spain had brought the United States transmarine dependencies which promised to align her with Britain as imperial power and colonial administrator. An instinctive feeling of sympathy between old and emergent world powers is therefore posited. The latter's new territorial possessions are seen as lending weight to that body of American domestic opinion less unfavourable than heretofore towards the British Empire as such. Correspondingly British imperialists, who had of late come under fire from native critics, felt themselves reinvigorated and reinforced by a sympathetic resonance on the other side of the world. After the Spanish-American war such Britons had gone beyond official disinterest to press the USA to annexe the Philippines. For this, the neutrality subsequently observed by the United States throughout Britain's embarrassing South African embroilment appeared as benevolent reciprocation. Evidently the complications of international politics were making it easier for us to perceive the value of American goodwill. Certainly, through nearly a decade around the turn of the century Republican imperialism beyond the sea seemed to coincide with and reinforce Conservative imperialism (and that of Grey-ish Liberals) in this kingdom. A new and joint *imperium*, involving the United States in the *Pax Britannica*, was welcomed not only as securing our rear – and in the Far East as well as the Atlantic British naval policy now postulated continuous friendship with the USA – but as signifying that custodianship of the world's peace rested in an Anglo-American hegemony.

Before the first year of the new century had ended, moreover, the United States was to gain a new master to whom such views had long been meat and drink. Pupil of John W. Burgess at Columbia, himself the postgraduate author of a *Naval History of the War of 1812*, correspondent of the British naval authority Willian Laird Clowes and enthusiastic reviewer of Mahan, President Roosevelt did not envisage his country's responsibilities as being limited to the Pacific only. Rather he saw her amicably conjoined with the other 'civilized' powers for the purpose of ensuring orderly governance and rising prosperity to all 'the waste places of the earth'. Though rejecting notions of racism, Roosevelt preserved unshakable faith in the superior civilisation, in the more mature political and social institutions, of 'the so-called white race' (as he termed it in his Romanes lecture of 1910 at Oxford). While professing abhorrence of 'militarism' and 'imperialism', he and his friends undoubtedly viewed their country's acquisition of overseas empire as the climax of their philosophy. In his eyes the civilising duty of the United States, as a nation providentially advantaged, was 'not a matter of regret, but pride'. Believing this onus to lie particularly upon the English-speaking peoples – for in ideas and culture they lay closest together – it was with British leaders such as Chamberlain and Balfour that, even before his entry to the White House, Roosevelt had discussed the possibilty of some kind of Anglo-American alliance. 'I think the twentieth century', he confided to Spring-Rice, 'will still be the century of the men who speak English'; and, more candidly, that together Britain and the United States could 'whip the world'. In vain Bryce warned him that American institutions were 'quite unsuited to the government of dependencies'. Only in his latter years was Roosevelt to waver in his belief about the relationship of democracy to empire.[7]

While it is probably true to say that Roosevelt thought and felt in terms of physical power more than of economics, regarding both as the servant of higher values, yet the connection could not be ignored. The future President who swallowed whole Brooks Adams's study of *America's Economic Supremacy* naturally saw the need to create a market for her expanding productivity as one good reason for keeping her flag flying over the Philippines. It would be hypocritical too to pretend that in the economic expansion of their Columbian cousins the British themselves had nothing at stake. Monetarily we had given a very considerable hostage to their prosperity. For decades past, many bank agents and financial promoters in the United Kingdon had, like the ill-fated house of Barings, specialised in raising British capital for American development. At the start of the twentieth century the United States was furnishing about half Britain's income from overseas investments, which probably represented more than one-third of all our investment outside the Empire itself. By 1914 the worth of British-controlled enterprises in the USA would be estimated at about $600 million. Much of this capital lay in American railroads, whose fluctuations kept British and other European speculators continuously apprehensive. Cynics indeed have hazarded the guess that Britons' cordiality toward America fluctuated according to the profitability of their money there. Certainly, not the least of the duties of a banker like J. P. Morgan was to soothe the nerves of the Old World's investors in the New.

No comparable degree of American money had yet appeared in Europe. Until 1914 the predominant direction of capital flow was to continue to be westward. The pattern of the United States' overseas investment, heaviest in Canada and Mexico, can have given her imperialists little satisfaction. Throughout the 1890's many Americans, of whom Brooks Adams, Albert Beveridge and Mahan are but a few examples, urged their nation in vain to shed its republican distinctiveness and compete globally with Britain and Germany. But with the new century the picture was beginning to change, and herein lay a threat to the new-found amity. Americans having now opened up their own land to the last bourne of westward settlement, the same internal forces and native energies which were driving them toward external territorial expansion would make for trade expansion also. As Mahan prophesied, 'Whether they will or no, Americans must now begin to look outward. The growing production of the country demands it'.[8] Their rapidly expanding industries required new outlets. In 1895, at about the time Mahan made his prognosis, the annual value of all United States exports was just passing the £200 million mark and within ten years would roughly double: in 1898 it already exceeded the value of imports. This new commercial threat, if such it was, impinged first upon the United Kingdom, to which alone the annual value of American exports between 1890 and 1900 was multiplied more than twofold – from £10·3 million to £21·3 million over the decade. By the latter year 27% of our imports by value were coming from the USA. American-owned manufactories established by then in Europe probably did not exceed one hundred in number, and most of them small (though most of them, also, in Britain). While American investment in this country, from consols to tobacco firms, began at this juncture markedly to rise, the proportion of her imports from us (about one-fifth in 1900) as steeply declined; so that at the opening of the new century the United Kingdom's adverse trade balance with the USA exceeded £100 million.*

What was more, the new challenger was beginning to seek export markets in the areas that overlapped with our own. The pressure of this expansion was felt not only in adjacent Canada, where current negotiations for a possible Canadian-USA commercial reciprocity treaty were sorely worrying the mother country. Its impact was beginning to be observed in New Zealand, the West Indies and South America, and to be perceptible even in Africa and the Far East. British consular agents, not primarily or habitually concerned with trade promotion, signalled their warnings from all round the globe into London. There a free-trade government was not seriously concerned with either the balance or future growth of national commerce. Yet, spurred by the American example, the Board of Trade, stronghold of *laissez-faire*, was sufficiently moved for the first time to set up a Commercial Intelligence Board.

Although Britain's capital and investments were still immense, her volume of overseas commerce unrivalled, and the Edwardian expansion of her trade little short of miraculous, yet to a nation long accustomed to undisturbed predominance the changing situation gave ground for worry and soul-searching. When at the turn of the century the national self-confidence seemed to falter, anxiety became focused on the USA's penetration of our domestic market. If not in value, yet in suddenness, this phenomenon assumed the appearance of a sustained assault. Though the main tide of Anglo-American amity did not slacken, a strong contrary current began to set in, with the threat of choppy water in the reaches ahead. A spate of warnings in books, pamphlets and periodicals aroused the British public to the imminent peril of what, said one of our leading industrialist, Sir Christopher Furness,

* For statistical evidence of change in volume and direction of USA foreign trade during the last ten years of the nineteenth century, see Table (a) at p. 247 below.

for want of a better term may be called the American invasion, which has created so vivid a sensation and apprehension of the Old World... Europe has been appalled by the sight of America bursting her bonds and stepping armed *cap-à-pied* into the arena as an industrial giant of almost irresistible power, with the openly proclaimed determination to conquer the world's markets and gain universal commercial supremacy.[9]

Rhetoric as high-pitched as this had only a few years earlier been directed against Germany. But if there were truth in it, must not the British be doomed in the not-so-long term to commercial subordination, to become hewers of wood and drawers of water to their transatlantic supplanters, patching and repairing what they had made? Americans, complained one of our most popular newspapers,

are selling their cotton in Manchester, pig-iron in Lancashire and steel in Sheffield. They send oatmeal to Scotland, potatoes to Ireland, and our national beef to England... Supremacy in some of our great industries seems to have gone from us for ever. We have slept while our commercial rivals went ahead. [10]

'Wake Up, John Bull', cried W. T. Stead repeatedly; and the alarm clock that aroused our national effigy was labelled 'Made in America'.

Was the commercial emergence of the USA really, as Stead claimed, 'the greatest political, social and commercial phenomenon of our time'? Certainly there seemed much to justify her young President's boast that America had 'just begun to assume that commanding position in the international business of the world which we believe will more and more be hers'. Already by the end of the old century she had outstripped Britain as the world's greatest coal-producing country. In all types of mining, indeed, her engineers were – as in South Africa, where Cecil Rhodes had just appointed an American as his chief consultant – threatening to displace British. Even more marked was the USA's new-won supremacy in iron and steel production. Though cheap German steel, hardened by a Krupp process, was the mainstay of British naval construction, for civilian uses America was now our greatest competitor. In 1884 we had been producing nearly twice as much pig-iron as the United States. When fifteen years later the situation was precisely reversed, the change-over represented a growth of 300% in US output compared with 23% here. The rise during the first two years of the new century in the value of our imported American steel cargoes was tenfold. While the South Wales tinplate industry languished, Cardiff's docks in a single month of 1901 received 20,000 tons of American plate. The new and gigantic US Steel Corporation indeed, thought one of our ironmasters, was now facing our native steel and iron trades with the stark alternatives of 'incorporation or extinction'. With bridges and viaducts of standard pattern America was capturing orders in Canada, India and British Africa. The International Harvester Trust of Chicago was covering Australia and New Zealand with its products. In watches and firearms, carpet sweepers and passenger lifts, America was seriously challenging British markets at home and abroad. At the international exhibitions in Paris (1900) and Glasgow (1901) the Americans displayed the excellence of their own machinery and machine tools before the eyes of the whole world.

By then their competition was also being felt in cotton and in textiles. Englishwomen began to appear in American-style blouses or 'shirt-waisters'. Our biggest manufacturers of sewing thread, J. & P. Coats, were being forced into alliance with United States competitors, the whole amalgamation of half a million spindles then securing a world dominance in that market. In boots and shoes, again, America's presence was becoming conspicuous. Although her machine-made footwear had been reaching us regularly since the late 1870's, its quantity suddenly more than trebled between 1898 and 1900, until by 1902 some three-quarters of a million Britons were American-shod. In quite a different field, it was under United States patents that the new printing, typesetting and distributing machines patented by Messrs Hoe of New York were ousting the older British models from our national presses. New American circulation methods, startling to the denizens of Paternoster Row, were being ruthlessly applied in British periodical and book markets. Even in foodstuffs our rivals were forcing an entry at certain points – from the so-called Meat Trust, newly moving into Smithfield, to Messrs Horton's ice-cream and Messrs Styles's soda-water parlours, now becoming a familiar sight in central London. The earliest of Messrs Heinz's fifty-seven varieties were reaching our dining tables, handy tablets from the American pharmacopeia our medicine chests.

By such highly miscellaneous imports was signified America's rivalry in the old trades. But a more disturbing feature of this, our first experience of the *défi américain*, was the lead she seemed to be establishing in the new. For instance, we had ourselves made the earliest practical telephone instruments. But neglect to acquire world patents now left us dependent for supplies on firms such as Western Electric of Chicago, to whom in 1901 the Post Office was obliged to award a very large contract for the equipment needed rapidly and in quantity. In our government and business offices the only serious competitor with the American £20 Remington typewriter was a Canadian model. The new portable folding cameras ('You press the button and we do the rest') were all coming from Eastman-Kodak of New Jersey.

American technology, however, made its most remarkable inroads in the field of public transport. Here the problem it raised for us was not simply one of fighting off a competitor in the world export trade of steam locomotives, carriages and trucks. George Westinghouse's achievement in alternating current and air brakes was already known to some of our main-line companies. In 1899 Westinghouse established a British subsidiary at Trafford Park, where a great industrial estate was erected with astonishing speed. It was alleged that within a few years most of the machinery at the King's Cross railway works was of American design. A sharper threat was the new American electric traction now appearing in many of Britain's big cities. The latest street tramcars, their motors and generating equipment, came from firms like Macartney McElroy & Co. of New York, from whom the Glasgow city corporation re-equipped its public system. A transatlantic firm even outbid the local authority for the contract to maintain the cable cars on Highgate Hill. By 1902 it was estimated that between one-half and two-thirds of the motors in our trams were American. In an older sphere of transport, the Erie Canal Traction Co. secured concessions for operating some 5,000 miles of inland water in Great Britain and continental Europe.

Above all else in the transport field, the building or conversion of London's underground railways threatened to become an

American province. The Central London line, opened in July 1900, went for its equipment (including the new multipolar generating plant) to General Electric of New York, for its lifts to the Sprague Elevator Co. American-trained officials became chairmen of the Central London and the Metropolitan & District railway companies. The streetcar king of Chicago, Charles Tyson Yerkes, won contracts for building the projected underground stretches of line from Holborn to Finsbury Park and for the Brompton–Piccadilly tube. In the autumn of 1900 Yerkes submitted a competitive tender for electrifying the Metropolitan District Railway. His newly founded Metropolitan Electric Traction Co. drew up a private Bill and laid it before Parliament, so that if he won the contract the work could begin at once. Though Yerkes successfully outbid his rivals (including his fellow Americans, the J. P. Morgan Co.), he faced opposition from the District shareholders, who supported their directors' preference for the European (Ganz) system of electrification as against the 'continuous current' system advocated by Yerkes. Though he assured the parliamentary committee he would seek to obtain all he needed from British sources, Yerkes did not muffle his criticism of British traction design and methods. When the Board of Trade, as arbitrators, decided in favour of his system, he immediately gave the contract for powerhouse machinery to Westinghouse at Trafford Park. His offer to buy the District Railway outright was, however, rejected, as was his attempt to supply electricity through his own company.[11]

To Londoners in particular the American presence was symbolised by the great blocks of office buildings, with their steel frames and sandstone fronts, now rising on Holborn Viaduct and elsewhere in the capital to house the representatives of our commercial competitor. But his products might meet the consumer's eye anywhere in the United Kingdom. As a long-forgotten journalist of that day expressed it,

'In the domestic life we have got to this: The average Briton rises in the morning from his New England sheets, he shaves with 'William's" soap and a Yankee safety razor, pulls on his Boston boots over his socks from North Carolina, fastens his Connecticut braces, slips his Waltham or Waterbury watch in his pocket, and sits down to breakfast. There he congratulates his wife on the way her Illinois straight-front corset sets off her Massachusetts blouse, and he tackles his breakfast, where he eats bread made from prairie flour (possibly doctored at the special establishment on the Lakes), tinned oysters from Baltimore, and a little Kansas City bacon, while his wife plays with a slice of Chicago ox-tongue. The children are given 'Quaker' oats. At the same time he reads his morning newspaper printed by American machines, on American paper with American ink, and, possibly, edited by a smart journalist from New York City.

He rushes out, catches the electric tram (New York) to Shepherd's Bush, where he gets in a Yankee elevator to take him on to the American-fitted electric railway to the City.

At his office, of course, everything is American. He sits on a Nebraskan swivel chair, before a Michigan roll-top desk, writes his letters on a Syracuse typewriter, signing them with a New York fountain pen, and drying them with a blotting-sheet from New England. The letter copies are put away in files manufactured in Grand Rapids.

At lunch time he hastily swallows some cold roast beef that comes from the Mid-West cow, and flavours it with Pittsburg pickles, followed by a few Delaware tinned peaches, and then soothes his mind with a couple of Virginia cigarettes.

To follow his course all day would be wearisome. But when evening comes he seeks relaxation at the latest American musical comedy, drinks a cocktail or some Californian wine, and finishes up with a couple of 'little liver pills' 'made in America'.[12]

And à propos of the little liver pills, the new American advertising methods gave great offence when at one point Messrs Carter used the White Cliffs of Dover as a billboard.

Just how much of all this was really nonsense could not have been evident at the time. And even today we still lack any painstaking industry-by-industry study from which to assess the relative impacts of transatlantic competition at this period – where it was most damaging, where it was most stimulating, and where it merely filled a vacuum: though Professor Saul for one has suggested how we might set about it.[13] And as to *why* American manufacturers were so successfully competing in certain British markets, conjectures differed even among those Britons (and there were many at the time) who crossed the Atlantic, singly or in teams, for the specific purpose of inspecting American industrial methods at first hand. Certainly a great deal of popular anxiety here was, if not misplaced, at least exaggerated. Journalistic rumour grossly inflated, for instance, the number of American sewing machines we imported: the output of either of two British firms, Singer or Wilcok & Gibbs, was greater than the quantity of all imported machines, from whatever source, combined. An American offensive against our bicycle trade was repelled. A British lift-making firm, R. Waygood & Co., absorbed its American rival here, the Otis Elevator Co. The sum total of all electrical apparatus imported in 1901 was less than what was bought in that year by one city, Manchester, alone. Of machine tools we imported, most in fact came from Germany. Where certain American products – watches or footwear, for example – reached us in quantity, the wholesale nature of this output did not much affect our demand for the good quality native, hand-made, articles. Sir John Clapham has pointed out how American competition in the hosiery trade compelled British manufacturers to 'ruthless scrapping' of obsolete machinery. In footwear, indeed, the threat of competition from the machine-made article was sufficient to revitalise a branch of British industry which had somewhat stagnated; while in electrical goods the American invasion pointed our own manufacturers to an unfilled need. Within little more than ten years Westinghouse's British subsidiary was to be taken over by Vickers. Transatlantic threats served to reinforce the appeal of such counter-organisations as the 'British Made League', the 'Union Jack Industries League' and the 'Imperial Industries Club'. As to overseas markets, offical figures were drawn upon to make the point that the USA's present shipments of manufactured articles must be doubled before they approached the German, and nearly trebled to come near the British export trade; so that (as one economist inferred) 'the notion of overwhelming all Europe by the boundless production of America is, for all the purposes likely to concern any one now living, the most fantastic figment of the imagination'. Other statisticians cushioned us in the comfortable belief that what had lately appeared to be a fall in our exports was in fact accountable for by a fall in world prices.[14]

Yet apprehension died hard about the likelihood of the USA's inheriting the world markets Britain had built up, and much introspection was devoted to diagnosing the malady. Some saw it in excessive external regulation of our industries. What handicapped the young electrical business, for instance, was alleged to be the grandmotherly restrictions imposed by the

Board of Trade. What put our extractive industries at a disadvantage, it was complained, were the heavy rents and royalties exacted in a situation where minerals were not owned by those engaged in working them. Many complained of excessive rail freight charges. 'Our railways', declared one Fabian economist, 'are as much an incubus as an aid to our industry ... To nationalisation it must come if we wish to maintain the trade and commerce of the country'. Others again drew attention to the expensiveness of our patent laws to the young inventor – £100 for examination of the merits of a claim, as against the equivalent of £7 in the USA. For the lag in our new industries, one reason proffered was the under-investment at their heart: at their periphery, municipalities (and especially the LCC) were accused of enforcing shortsightedly low wage limits in their contracts for, e.g., transport and electrical work. But one must observe that equally in old industries (like cotton) there was a reluctance to finance re-equipment, and that wages on the railways tended to be strictly frozen by custom.[15]

Other explanations of the Americans' industrial thrust looked to their native enterprise, such as the entrepreneur's freer access to capital, or to the distinctive United States technology with its standardisation of engineering designs and methods, relying on interchangeable parts and on specialised machinery rather than on the specialist worker. Also held up for British emulation were America's greater encouragement of technical inventiveness by ease of patenting; higher development of the art of work management and flow; more accurate techniques for handling cost data, etc; and better methods of advertising, merchandising and distribution of goods, so as to create a greater 'social depth' (as the modern economist would say) of demand for its standardised products. 'If we are a nation of shopkeepers', observed the *Daily Mail*, 'then the United States are a nation of commercial travellers'. Much was made of the restless energy and push of the American businessman, disposed to 'lick creation' and divinely discontented with the mere *status quo*, unflagging in his search for improved machinery and methods, treating his workers with 'intelligent liberality' over piecework, his sole criterion being profit. 'Trade in America is esteemed a calling; here it is looked upon as a means to a life devoted to games and sport, and to entering a circle of social distinction'. So wrote Furness, whose own mode of life, however, provided a standing refutation of this view. 'We need', urged Lord Rosebery in 1901, 'to be inoculated with some of the nervous energy of the Americans'.

Still other kinds of explanation of the transatlantic challenge in manufacturing pointed to the American operative himself and to his working conditions. His better technical education was admired. His labour-saving machinery, his freedom from customary restrictions on earnings and from social stratification, his greater output and higher wage levels were envied. Even the drier climate was cited as one reason why the migrant European toiled more energetically and productively over there. Comparisons with the British labourer were all too often unfavourably drawn. 'The British trade union', it was said, 'instead of being an organisation for the protection of labour against the tyranny and opposition of capital, is really an organisation for the restraint of labour and the fettering of capital'. A notable series of articles in the London *Times* of 1901 charged that a deliberate trade union policy of ca'canny or 'spreading the work' was eating the heart out of British prosperity. Though this charge was partially rebutted by the Webbs and others, they could not deny that some unions were unreasonable in their opposition to members working as hard and fast as they could. British critics found their objections to this 'neo-unionism', as some called it, reinforced by the unfavourable comment of visiting American industrialists. When Charles Schwab, future head of the newly formed US Steel Corporation, visited England in 1901, much publicity was given to his warnings that British iron and steel production was being hamstrung by 'the unreasonable rules of the trade unions'. 'The difficulty with labour unions today', Schwab was later to tell the US Industrial Commission, 'is simply whether the masters will surrender the control of their works to the men'. Naturally, some British trade unionists feared imitation of what was regarded as the typical attitude of the large American employer who (it was believed) scrapped a used-up worker as unhesitatingly as he discarded an obsolescent machine. 'Americanisation' of labour became a bad word among some of our trade unionists, who deprecated 'hustle' in working methods, often reportedly to the neglect of such minimum safety standards as

State law might lay down. Reports of transatlantic brutality and violence when workers confronted 'the trusts' received wide notice over here. Against the profitability of the American worker's higher output had to be weighed the reported danger of 'scientific management' by efficiency experts such as F. W. Taylor. The relatively low, though growing, degree of genuine unionisation in the United States was noted, as was the current campaign of employers and civic authorities there for the open shop.[17]

Enough has now been said to show how widely various were the diagnoses of Britain's commercial malaise at the turn of the century. On one point, however, most observers were agreed — that the chief carriers of the American industrial threat were agents to be described, generally and indiscriminately , as 'the trusts'. This new economic species was believed to breed and thrive in the warm and hospitable climate of United States protectionism. So long as the tariff's sheltering wall tempered the blasts of foreign competition, so long would native American industrialists be tempted to reduce domestic competition also by a policy of what President McKinley called 'benevolent assimilation'. Hence, it was inferred, the current American trend towards industrial giantism by way of amalgamations and absorptions. And now, it seemed, these omnivorous creatures, the trusts, having exhausted the forage of their native habitat, were emerging to raven on European pastures also.

Hence the alarm which spread at this junction to all sectors of our economy. The British industrialist, if (as most often) a free-trader, complained of being handicapped in the fight against the trusts by excessive governmental regulation. If (more rarely) a protectionist, he demanded greater government help. As for our trade unionist, already on the defensive against the fire of the efficiency critics, he was inclined to fear for union organisation if the management methods of the American trust-masters were imitated over here. A correspondent of the *Daily News* voiced the anxieties of many fellow workers when he saw 'the Peril of Trusts' to lie in their 'forcing British captains of industry in self-defence to resort, not only to the latest machinery, but to the latest extravagance of commercial tyranny'. Indeed, one historian of the British labour movement sees the transatlantic trust bogey as helping to hasten our trade union leaders at the turn of the century towards the formation of their own Labour Party. This possibility cannot be ignored, though it is noteworthy that some sections of British socialism or Marxism actually welcomed the new phenomenon from the belief that (in H. M. Hyndman's words) 'these trusts will bring us socialism quickly'. And not all our trade union officers who visited the United States at this period thought the relative condition of her workers economically unattractive.[18]

Were contemporaries correct in describing the tariff as the mother of trusts? Certainly such a parental link existed in the USA. Yet it must be allowed that in both English-speaking countries general economic trends had lately been conducive to consolidation. This development in Britain, though on nothing like the American scale, was not negligible. Between 1898 and 1906 it revealed itself in such trades as dyeing and calico printing, in soap and cement, or even when in 1901 Elder's came together with Fyffe's to combine production and transport in the banana trade. Much more remarkable, however, had been the recent combination in coal, steel, iron and shipping. In the north-east Sir Christopher Furness was the connecting link between the South Durham Steel Co. (1898), the Weardale Iron & Coal Co. (1899), the Hartlepool shipbuilding and graving dock business of Furness Withy & Co. (1891), the Wilson and Furness Leyland Line (1896) and the million-pound marine engineering firm of Richardson's Westgarth & Co. (1900). The practical outcome here was a great horizontal complex wherein one of the world's largest marine engineering concerns was coupled, by overlapping investment and directorship, to about 20% of Teesside shipbuilding, to coal mining and distribution, steel production, and freight and insurance brokerage. Furness also had considerable holdings in Armstrong Whitworth & Co. Other comparable concerns who were simultaneously expanding their empires included the Sunderland Iron Co., Dorman Long, and Vickers Son & Maxim at Barrow. Shippping was linked to oil interests by the newly grown Shell Transport & Trading Co. In shipbuilding the year 1903 saw Laird of Birkenhead amalgamating with Cammell of Sheffield in an enterprise which two years later bought half the ordinary shares of Fairfield (originally John Elder & Co.) on the Clyde. Before long Cammell Laird, Fairfield and John Brown were between them exercising an internationally unassailable 'community of interest'. Of consolidation in the world of pure shipping at this period the following chapters will yield examples enough. It was scarcely surprising that some men of public eminence, such as Lord Bryce and Sir Robert Giffen, were calling for industrial consolidation in Britain to be statutorily regulated.

Evidently this consolidation had not been called into being by American competition specifically. Indeed, few Britons really understood much of the detailed nature of the American trusts. Lord Rosebery's proposal was a good one, that the London School of Economics should put on a special course on that topic. 'Popular opinion', observed the *Quarterly Review* in 1904, 'looking only to capitalisation, dubs any organisation of large capital a "trust"'.[19] In historical fact, at least three distinct patterns had emerged successively in the USA.

The earliest of these was the pool – an informal agreement between a number of companies engaged in supplying a competitive product or service, having in view the regulating of prices and/or dividing up of markets or earnings by mutual consent. This device first attracted public notice in the case of the railroads; whether over (for example) the allotment of freight, agreement of carriage rates, or purchase of rails. But much the same procedure was resorted to for the voluntary limitation of output among American manufacturers of, e.g., spirits, salt, cordage or barbed wire; and the shipping pool, ring or 'convention' was becoming (as we shall see) in the second half of the nineteenth century a familiar phenomenon. Since, however, no such agreement was enforceable at common law, but depended on the temporary self-interest of the parties to it, it tended to lack durability. Hence the need for an arrangement which would provide for effective overall supervision.

This need was in due course supplied by the trust properly so called, a device which involved no surrender of identity or ownership by the participators. What was normally done was for the latter to create a small body of trustees and assign to it all their respective stocks together with the power of voting them. The trustees then proceeded to evaluate the properties comprised in the new combination and to issue trust certificates against stock, on the basis of which profits were divided. This device, with which a Pennsylvania lawyer, Samuel Dodd, is usually credited, thus not only secured centralised direction of policy but, since it possessed neither charter nor legal identity, circumvented any existing legislation that forbade any one corporation from holding stock in another. The *locus classicus*, indeed exemplar, of this instrument of potential monopoly was the Standard Oil Trust, formed by Rockefeller in 1879, wherein nine trustees 'exercised general supervision' and voted the stock of forty companies who together controlled 90% of the oil refining business of the USA and 90% of its pipelines. Standard Oil's secret was not finally revealed until a public investigation of 1888; meanwhile some dozen of these large aggregations had made their appearance – in cottonseed and linseed oil, in sugar, lead and tobacco, and among the distillers and cattle-feeders (the so-called Whiskey Trust). By this means tightly integrated structures achieved virtual if temporary monopolies over which, since they were not themselves corporations, no legal control yet existed.

Yet trustee agreements were matters of record; and it was on this ground that they were before long moved against at common law in a number of successful suits in state courts – against cottonseed oil (1887, Louisiana), against sugar (1889, New York), and against Standard Oil itself (1890, Ohio). So the trust proper was to prove a short-lived expedient. How could it avoid revocation of its charter under the so-called Sherman anti-trust act? The answer was to be found by a New Jersey lawyer, James B. Dill, who in 1889 had advised his state's government to amend its corporation laws in such a way as to permit any one corporation within its territory to hold the stock of another. In 1896 New Jersey's law was further liberalised to allow any such corporation to purchase the shares and bonds of any other corporation, whether chartered in New Jersey or any other state. In New Jersey, accordingly, there came to be incorporated *inter alia* the American Sugar Refining Co. (1891) and the Standard Oil Co. (1889). The expedient was imitated promptly by four, and later by another two, states.

So by the end of the century American trusts were dissolving and being reformed as holding companies, each of which was designed to perform exactly the functions of the trust supplanted but to enjoy legal immunity. The promoter would secure from a state a charter of incorporation for his company, which by a serious of agreements would then proceed to acquire either the whole or a majority of the stock of other companies. In return it gave its own shares, or part cash. Since potential vendors could be better persuaded to participate if offered more for their stock than its current market value, the tendency was for the holding company to inflate the value of its own stock, involving over-capitalisation of the new corporation. This was not necessarily deleterious. If consolidation improved business or reduced ad-ministrative costs, it was legitimate to capitalise the increased net profits in the form of additional stock, which would therefore not necessarily be water. The capitalisation of US Steel in 1901 exceeded by $300 million the total amount of the capitals of the constituent companies, yet the corporation and its underwriters throve. On the other hand overcapitalisation in the following year of the US Shipbuilding Co. was over-optimistic and led to disaster. In either type of case it was the preferred stock that represented the corporation's real assets and was therefore the real investment security. Common stock was usually thrown in as a bonus to facilitate the amalgamation, remaining (as its recipients understood) essentially a speculative security, usu-ally very low and subject to fluctuation.

The holding company's entire assets, then, were composed of interests in the capital stocks of the constituent companies, for whom it performed at law merely a trustee function. US Steel, for example, owned the stock but not the physical properties of its components. In practice, exchange of its shares for those of its constituent companies brought its officers power to elect the latter's directorates and thus to centralise control of the entire structure. (In the case of US Steel this included control of over a hundred steamships on the Great Lakes and half a dozen size-able railroads). The new single organisation might then be in a way to capture the greater part of the market. Yet its separate components might retain their corporate identities, brand names of goods, etc., and thus perhaps conceal for a while from the public the magnitude of the operation.

To those Europeans who did not understand the ingrained America habit of 'capitalising ahead' on the most sanguine estimates of future growth potential, these new consolidations were as suspect as awesome. Britons who took alarm at the relatively minor promotions of a Henry John Lawson or an

Ernest Terah Hooley were naturally aghast at the freedom with which American bankers underwrote the sky-scraping aggregations of the New World, seemingly raised on little but scrip. Still painfully fresh in investors' minds, too, were the pioneer generation of American promoters – the Goulds, Huntingtons and Russell Sages, mismanagers on principle who for personal gain had wantonly created what Veblen called the 'disturbance of the industrial citizen'. Was this not precisely what Henry Demarest Lloyd and others had been warning the world against throughout the 1880's and '90's? A shrewdly devised strategy of capitalisation and recapitalisation appeared like an alchemic process, leaving at each successive stage a few million dollars at the bottom of the crucible for someone. Could Europeans really be expected to believe that this kind of economic growth was a natural process and not a conspiracy of the 'millionaire Molochs'?.

Vindication at law of a major holding company in the sugar business, by the Supreme Court in its E. C. Knight ruling of 1895, showed plainly enough that such monopolies had little to fear from federal prosecution.[20] Between that year and 1903, therefore, this type of consolidation swiftly penetrated American commerce. The census enumeration of 1900 found 185 industrial combinations whose total capitalisation of $3 billion represented one-third of all capital then invested in the manufacturing activites of the United States. Although those corporations which could be described as very large constituted only 0·8% of the list, they controlled approximately 40% of all capital invested in manufacturing enterprise. According to that census, half a million industrial establishments in the USA made a gross product valued at $13 billion. Only 8% of them were corporations, but these accounted for 60% of the value of the gross product and were particularly prominent in iron and steel, food pulps, chemicals, metal and metal products, liquors and beverages. About half such combinations had been effected in the eighteen months immediately preceding June 1900. Thereafter the very great call on aggregated capital for further consolidations, especially in railroads, was seen to be straining the resources of some of the principal banks and banking houses. Later consolidations tended to appear in new industries, whose chief concern was alleged to be not the creation of monopoly pure and simple so much as the perfection of economies arising out of large-scale operation. Within a few years, too, the investing public began to show a decline in confidence and the Department of Justice to cast around for means of more rigorously interpreting anti-trust legislation. So there was some falling off in the formation of combines and some retrenchment by banks, until by 1904 the market had a distinctly bearish tone. But that is to anticipate.

The promoter of a holding company was apt to take the bulk of his commission in the form of a large slice of the consolidation's stock. As the promotional function came increasingly to be filled by the investment banker – who alone had the resources to complete the overarching edifice of American capitalism – so financial leadership came to dominate industrial. The new class of promoter was not a rags-to-riches man. J. P. Morgan's career, for example, originated not in American industry but in the financial support of the City of London. In sharp contrast to the earlier generation of speculators and pirates he was born into the purple of the new finance capitalism, being the son of the Junius S. Morgan who, as partner and then sucessor of his fellow countryman George Peabody in London, had since the 1850's done so much to open up the New World to and with the capital of the Old. Having spent ten years as his father's agent in New York, John Pierpont in 1871 set up himself and his partners there as Drexel Morgan & Co., private bankers. Throughout the 1880's and '90's this investment house had more-à-more found itself serving as principal agent for the receivership, reorganisation and recapitalisation of those many American railroad companies who, along with their hapless stockholders, had suffered sorely – and in the bankruptcies and depression of 1893–97 dramatically – from a period of reckless promotion. Morgan himself was no railroad man but the head of a general staff, a skilled financial surgeon, and withal an incomparable reassurer of European investors. His work of rehabilitation had by the end of the century made 'Jupiter' Morgan the financial controller of over 55,000 miles of American railroad – or more than the total mileage in Great Britain and Germany combined – and the virtual dictator of peace terms to warring financiers of lesser stature. It also gave, and for years was to continue to give, the House of Morgan a unique authority *vis-à-vis* the federal government during periods of difficulty or crisis for the US Treasury. And it made New York one of the great money markets of the world.

How ubiquitous and versatile was Morgan's influence the opening years of the new century were now to behold. For one thing, the unexpectedly protracted resistance of the Boers in South Africa necessitated the novelty of British borrowing on Wall Street. The greater part of this loan was underwritten by the J. P. Morgan Co., whose head would henceforward have a double reason for making his annual visit to Europe and to his town house in Prince's Gate. Secondly, the year 1901 saw the coping stone laid upon his imposing edifice of railroad consolidation in the form of the Northern Securities Company – a gigantic holding corporation with $400 million capital, signifying the merger forced by its architect upon the rival railway magnates Edward H. Harriman and James J. Hill. In the following year, by means of diplomatic pressure upon the coal operators, Morgan directly aided the new President, Theodore Roosevelt, to settle a national strike in the anthracite industry. But most formidable of all Morgan's achievements in the British industrialist's view was to be his creation in 1901 of US Steel. Having bought out Andrew Carnegie at the latter's price of $450 million he concentrated his country's chief banking and industrial resources into the world's first billion-dollar corporation, controlling 70% of the iron and steel industry of the United States. Thus did her bankers consolidate America's first industrial revolution. Henceforward, as Morgan proceeded to apply his doctrine of 'community of interest' by the creation of trusts in other fields also, to European eyes his image as creator and conservator was to become, however unjustly, overlaid by that of predator and monopolist. It was the Washington correspondent of the London *Times*, George W. Smalley, who remarked that about such figures

> Englishmen have formed a notion of their own ... They have seen much of Mr. Pierpont Morgan, and they seem inclined to suppose all great financiers to be, in manner as in fact, masterful, dominating, huge in physique, born rulers of other men.

But in hailing him as a Napoleon or Cecil Rhodes of finance, or at the very least a John Law, it must be conceded that British popular jounals were doing no more than following certain sections of the American press.[21]

It was not, however, through any instrumentality of Morgan's that the trusts were to make their initial and alarming impact upon the ordinary British citizen. Rather, it was in the homely but ubiquitous context of his local tobacco retailer that he first espied the lurking American menace. The episode in question deserves more attention than it has yet received.

In 1890 five major cigarette manufacturers in the United States, including W. Duke & Sons of New York and Durham, North Carolina, had combined to form the American Tobacco Company. James Buchanan Duke was its president and the chief director of its policy. The company's prosperity was initially based on its exclusive American right to use the most modern (Bonsack) cigarette-making machine: but its subsequent growth proceeded by way of a series of combinations with, or absorption of, other tobacco concerns, whom it systematically undercut. By 1897 the American Tobacco Co. not only controlled 90% of the country's cigarette industry but had secured a dominating position in the plug tobacco business also. This latter branch it handled from 1898 on through a subsidiary, the Continental Tobacco Co. – like its parent company grossly overcapitalised by European standards.[22]

For various reasons, however, the last few years of the nineteenth century saw a sharp falling off in American (though not in European) consumption of cigarettes, and a corresponding swing of fashion towards the cigar. The ATC therefore developed its polices along two lines. Firstly, it turned its attention to the cigar business. By purchase of a number of existing cigar-making concerns it organised in January 1901 the American Cigar Co., of whose capital stock the ATC and the Continental Tobacco Co. between them held 7%. By advertising lavishly and selling at a loss this newly found concern soon came to control about one-sixth of the USA's cigar output. Secondly, the ATC looked swiftly to the enlargement of its foreign business. Already it possessed subsidiary companies in Australia and Canada and controlling interests in two large firms in Germany and Japan. By 1900, moreover, the export of its own American-made cigarettes represented one-third of the company's production. In June 1901 the combination raised fresh capital by resorting to the device of a holding company, which acquired nearly all the common stock of the ATC and

Continental Tobacco Co., and issued its own 4% bonds in exchange. The cash proceeds – reputedly $30 million – from sale of the new capital stock were then made available to finance new undertakings abroad. About one-sixth of it was earmarked for expansion in Britain, where a London depot had hitherto sufficed the ATC for its sales outlet.

In the late summer of 1901 'Buck' Duke landed at Liverpool. By the end of September he had acquired for his combination, at a cost of over $5¼ million, substantially the whole of the outstanding stock of Messrs Ogden, a Merseyside concern producing nationally popular pipe tobaccos and cigarettes. He was reported to have also approached, with similar abruptness, Gallaher, Cope and John Player & Sons.

The shock that ran through the British tobacco world at this incursion was the greater because Ogden's had recently been doing particularly well and had just moved into a new main factory. This very expansion, however, had left them short of capital. Both in their offers and their threats therefore – as Ogden's chairman explained – the Americans proved irresistible. Our native manufacturers, moreover, had just received another grim warning. In 1896 the Diamond Match Co. of America had built in Liverpool a large match factory, equipped it with the most modern machinery available, and spent heavily in pre-empting sole patent rights on improved models. The leading British firm in that field, Bryant & May, which had till then been paying comfortable dividends of around 20%, was quick to feel the draught, slow to react. By 1901 it had no commercial alternative but to sell out to the Americans. The absorption of Bryant & May was an object lesson not lost upon British manufacturers in a closely related trade.

This time the cisatlantic reponse was prompt and unequivocal. On 1st November thirteen firms – of which W. D. & H. O. Wills, big even by international standards, was by much predominant – amalgamated into the Imperial Tobacco Company (of Great Britain & Ireland) Ltd, which issued its prospectus the following February. Its authorised capital, share and loan together, of £17½ million signified the biggest commercial property heretofore incorporated under the Companies Acts. The new British combination at once made two moves to repel the American invader. First, it safeguarded its own retail outlets by entering

into a restrictive agreement with Britain's largest chain tobac-
conists, Salmon & Gluckstein Ltd, to whose preference shareholders it guaranteed in return an annual dividend of 10%.
Secondly, the ITC circularised *all* the 300,000 or so tobacco
retailers in the United Kingdom with a bonus-sharing offer
(part lump sum, part by distribution of ITC's net profits) in
consideration of their signing an undertaking not to stock the
products of the ATC (Ogden). The war was on. Ogden retaliated
with a counter-offer of bonuses, distributable quarterly over the
next four years, to retailers in return for their simple promise
not to sign the ITC circular. At the same time it cut the prices of
its most popular brands and introduced 'free gift' coupons.

From the duel which followed, the retailers, had they organised themselves more efficiently, might have emerged as *tertius
gaudens*. In the outcome, however, the British company was to
achieve victory within little more than a year. Not only did it
successfully defend home ground – its own profits rising as
steeply as Ogden's fell off – but indeed carried the war into the
enemy's territory. In the summer of 1902 Imperial announced
that it had bought a number of large factories, warehouses, and
land for further building in Richmond, Virginia, where it credibly threatened to begin its own manufacturing. After Ogden's
had paid out two quarterly bonuses Duke capitulated. Twelve
months of bitter conflict ended in the signing of a treaty whereby the American combination agreed to cease its activities in
Britain and to sell Ogden's to Imperial, who for their part would
abandon plans to enter the United States save for the annual
leaf-buying. A demarcation of overseas markets was agreed
between the contestants, reciprocal rights in each other's
brands were exchanged, and peace was restored.

The episode of the tobacco war, though transient in itself,
produced two notable effects. It encouraged business in the
inference that even the large American trust was far from
invincible if counter-combination were promptly and energetically resorted to. 'If the Imperial Company', concluded the *Daily
Mail* after the smoke of battle had cleared, 'has achieved a
victory, it will have demonstrated that the terrors of American
competition vanish when boldly faced'. Secondly, it was the
confrontation over tobacco which first brought the sense of
economic danger home to the British public at large – not to the

smokers alone, but to everyone who could read a newspaper. Alongside the rivalry of bonuses and the gift coupon schemes had appeared a plethora of dramatic advertisements. The ITC's appealed widely to patriotism against 'the American system of Trust Monopoly and all that is implied therein'; while cartoons like those inserted to boost the sales of Phillips's 'Guinea Gold' depicted Uncle Sam kidnapping Britain and crushing her working men. Thanks to Duke and his colleagues, therefore, public nervousness was already at its height when the first warnings of a far greater threat from the west began to loom.

This was the purchase by an American steamship combination, backed by the J. P. Morgan Co. as bankers and subsequently styled the International Mercantile Marine Co., of a very large quantity of British passenger tonnage plying in the North Atlantic. The British concerns bought up in swift succession included the celebrated Leyland and White Star lines; and at one stage the sole remaining major British company there, Cunard, was also thought vulnerable to purchase.

Whereas the American challenges to Britain of this period in other fields, such as tobacco, precipitated straightforward trade duels in which a *laissez-faire* government did not interest itself directly, this new and formidable menace on the high seas possessed certain unique and important features which require an extended study to assess. It appeared, first and foremost, to present a direct threat to that maritime ascendancy which was the historic and indispensable basis of Britain's world position. 'A shiver of apprehension', wrote one journalist typical of his time, 'ran through the whole of the British nation', for 'when the invaders attack our shipping they touch our most sensitive nerve'.[23] As the extent of the threat unrolled itself, alarm and apprehension spread from the commercial community to the public at large, until at last it became clear to all that the USA, not Germany, was to be our principal trading competitor of the new century. Indeed, when the American combine proceeded to associate with itself the two great German shipping lines, a double jeopardy revealed itself in the linking of our nearest commercial rival to our most ostensive political foe.

Unprecedentedly, therefore, and at a very early stage of its development, the Atlantic challenge drew in the British government as a vitally interested party. The matter was to go at least four times to the Cabinet and involve five major departments of state in long and intricate negotiations. Into these discussions certain other matters beside trade were inevitably injected. How would American ownership and control of so large a slice of our mercantile marine affect our food supplies, and indeed our whole national safety, in time of war? Those vessels seemingly to be lost to the Americans included some of our fastest, upon which the Admiralty relied for naval auxiliaries and (as in the current South African war) transports; and much of Britain's mercantile marine, of whatever speed, had traditionally served as a source of wartime manpower. This crisis, as it was on all sides felt to be, of maritime and naval security provoked a long-due review of our national defence at sea which bore upon, and in a marked degree accelerated, the controversial reforms of Sir John Fisher.

In another important respect, too, the furore aroused by American initiative in the Atlantic was immediately to contribute to national controversy on the hither side. By abruptly reviving demands for reciprocal protection it brought to what in retrospect we see as its climax the whole passionate debate over the free trade/protectionist issue. Fluctuations of the American tariff were, of course, always narrowly watched from these shores, where from time to time it impinged uncomfortably upon certain areas of industry. But now, and most sharply, opinion in this country became polarised. 'Free trade', observed one commentator in 1902,

> is coming up for trial ... The dramatic suddenness with which the cream of our Atlantic shipping trade has been wiped out of existence and the threat which lies in the Shipping Trust to increase the price of our food and raw materials are bound to stir up the nation, and to open the eyes even of the most self-complacent Free Trader. Great Britain is getting a lesson. It will probably be a very expensive lesson, and consequently it will be taken to heart.[24]

Of the nationwide debate thus precipitated, one of the committees set up by the government in consequence – the parliamentary Select Committee on Steamship Subsidies – was to provide the main institutional forum. The outcome was a limited success for those who demanded modifications in official policy. For it compelled the government into an agreement with Cunard which marks both the first breach in its traditional *laissez-faire* and the foundation of its modern policy, and that of other nations, in shipbuilding subsidisation. Changes so considerable require that we pay heed in some detail to the events which brought them about.

NOTES

1 W. E. Gladstone: 'Kin Beyond Sea', in *Prose Masterpieces from Modern Essayists* (1886), p. 350; *Economist*, 8 Mar. 1851; W. T. Stead: *The Americanisation of the World* (1901), pp. 152 and 542.
2 J. Hay to H. C. Lodge, 30 Aug. 1894, *Lodge MSS.*, Bryce to T. Roosevelt, 1 Jan. 1896, *T. Roosevelt MSS.*, Brooks Adams to Lodge, 14 Oct. 1900, *Lodge MSS.*, all quoted in H. J. Beale: *Theodore Roosevelt and the Rise of America to World Power* (1956), pp. 82, 84 and 450; Lodge to A. J. Balfour, quoted in Blanche E. C. Dugdale: *Arthur James Balfour* (1936) I: 226; Lord Vansittart: *The Mist Procession* (1958), p. 318.
3 L. M. Gelber: *The Rise of Anglo-American Friendship* (1938), p. 1.
4 Stead: *op. cit.*, pp. 151–3, and *Review of Reviews* 26:41 (1902).
5 J. Chamberlain in *Scribner's Magazine* 26: p. 675 (Dec. 1898); among popular analyses of Anglophobia in Germany at this period, see *Contemporary Review* 81:13.21 (1902).
6 A. T. Mahan, 'The possibilities of an Anglo-American reunion', *Northern American Review* 119:551–63 (1894).
7 T. Roosevelt, quoted in Beale: *op. cit.*, pp. 70, 81 and 152n.; Bryce, 'The policy of annexation for America', in *Forum* 24:391–2 (1897)
8 Mahan: *The Interest of America in Sea Power* (1897), pp. 21–33.
9 C. Furness in *Pall Mall Magazine* 26:362 (1902).
10 F. A Mackenzie: *The American Invaders* (1901), pp. 5, 6 and 12.
11 F. Sprague, 'The rapid transit problem in London', *Engineering Magazine* XIV (Oct. 1901); C. Rous-Martin, 'British locomotives abroad', *Page's Magazine* 2: 499–507 (1903); Stead, *Review of Reviews* 24:99–108 and 322–4 (1901).
12 Mackenzie: *op. cit.*, pp. 59–61.
13 S. B. Saul, 'The American impact upon British industry, 1895–1914', *Business History* 3:19–38 (1960).
14 S. E. Moffett, 'The American invasion', *New Liberal Review* 2:114 (1902); anon. in *Fortnightly Review* 70 (Oct. 1901); H Morgan-Browne, 'Is Great Britain falling into economic decay?', *Contemporary Review* 79:492–502 (1901).
15 Furness, 'How British trade is handicapped', *The World's Work* 1:81ff. (1902); H. W. Macrosty in *Fortnightly Review* 71:150 (1902); Stead: *The Americanisation of the World* (1901), p. 150; E. M. Lacy, 'The Americanisation of British electrical equipment', *Empire Review* III (May 1902).
16 G. W. Steevens: *The Land of the Dollar* (1897), p. 252; Furness

in *Pall Mall Magazine, loc. cit.*, p. 365; C. C. Townsend, 'The American industrial peril' *Contemporary Review* 92:562–7 (1902); E., Leveasseur; *The American Workman* (1900), p. 6; E. Verney: *American Methods* (1904); W. R. Lawson: *American Finance* (2nd edit., 1908), pp. 247–9.

17 A. H. Thwaite: *The American Invasion* (1902), p. 18; *Times*, 'The crisis in British industry', 18 Nov. 1901 *et seq.*; Clement Edwards, 'Do trade unions limit output?', *Contemporary Review* 82:113–28 (1902); Macrosty, 'Trusts and the workman', in GFTU *Annual Report* for 1901; B. A. Taylor in *Northern American Review*, Aug. 1901; A. Mosley, 'The Americanisation of British trade unions', *The World's Work* I:318–22; Mackenzie: *op. cit.*, pp. 127–8.

18 *Daily News*, 5 April 1902; H. M. Pelling, 'The American economy and the foundation of the British Labour Party', *Economic History Review*, 2nd series 7:1–17 (1955).

19 *Quarterly Review* 198: 189 (1904).

20 *US v EC Knight Co.*, 156 US 1 (1895).

21 G. W. Smalley: *Anglo-American Memoirs*, 1st series (1911), p. 271; see also the 2nd series (1912), pp. 221–40. Smalley was also for a time a contributor to the *New York Tribune*. In articles of this period on Morgan, compare the similarity of content between Maurice Lowe in *The World's Work* I:672–5 (1902); R. S. Baker in *McClure's Magazine* 17 (Oct. 1901); E. S. Machen in *Cosmopolitan* 30 (June 1901); S. E. Moffett in *Pall Mall Magazine* 23 (Feb. 1902); and J. B. Walker in *Cosmopolitan* 34 (Jan. 1903)

22 For fuller particulars, see US Commissioner of Corporations: *Report on the Tobacco Industry* (Washington, DC, 1909).

23 Moffett, 'The sovereignty of the seas', *New Liberal Review* 4:104 (1902).

24 O. Elzbacher, 'The American shipping trust', *Contemporary Review* 82:75–6 (1902).

CHAPTER 2

American genesis

The train of events which now concerns us began to be laid in 1892 with the death of the Liverpool shipping magnate Frederick R. Leyland. Briefly familiar to the British public from his notorious dispute with Whistler over the painting of peacocks on the drawing-room door of his Prince's Gate mansion, in the international shipping world Leyland had been continuously eminent since 1876. That was the year when he had founded his business by purchase of the Bibby Line, trading to the Mediterranean, to which he had later added services from Liverpool to Boston. Freighters provided the bulk of his fleet, and live cattle and general cargo the greater part of his revenue. This thriving enterprise was after its founder's death transformed, through the agency of the London financier H. Osborne O'Hagan, into a limited company, Frederick Leyland & Co., with Sir Christopher Furness, the industrialist, as chairman and another light of Liverpool shipping circles, Walter Glyn, as managing director. Although the bulk of Leyland's property, in shares and otherwise, had been left to his daughters and sons-in-law, the largest single holding of the new ordinary and preference shares had been acquired by John Reeves Ellerman, of 12 Moorgate Street.

Son of a German father but adopting his mother's British nationality, and barely thirty years old at the time of this purchase, Ellerman had risen fast. An accountant by training, he had developed his capital in breweries, both English and American; and his approach to shipping was financial rather than executive – enterpreneurial in a sense comparable with, say, Harriman's attitude toward American railroads. With O'Hagan's help he secured a directorship in the reconstituted Leyland company, and by gradual acquisition of most of its ordinary shares rapidly assumed control of its policies. Before long he had displaced Furness in the chairmanship and ousted the last remaining family representative, G. R. Leyland, from the board of directors in favour of his own nominee. Professional relationship and goodwill were nonetheless preserved: and when in 1896 the London interests of the company were temporarily hived off to help form the Wilson & Furness-Leyland Line, for handling mostly cargo to Boston and New York, Frederick Leyland & Co. held one-third of its shares and Ellerman and Glyn made two of its directors.[1]

Though possessing none of the maritime expertise of a Leyland or Furness, Ellerman correctly judged the future in store for passenger liners. Greatly expanding the Leyland company by purchase and merger, he made from 1897 onward repeated though unsuccessful approaches, as we shall see, to the Cunard company, and in 1900 was laying plans to buy the West Indies & Pacific Steamship Co., whose fleet of over 97,000 tons, built and building, plied to the West Indies and the Gulf of Mexico. The prosperity of the enterprise, already manifest in the regularity of its dividends and the high market rating of its securities, was further revealed when on 28th March 1900 it was again reconstructed and re-registered as Frederick Leyland & Co. (1900) Ltd, with a share capital of £2.8 million. Possessing nearly 100,000 tons of shipping and earning in that year some £200,000, the new company issued a further £2½ million worth of debentures to debenture holders in the old company, and was seen from its latest prospectus to own more than 99% of the capital of the Wilson & Furness-Leyland Line Ltd.

At this juncture it was becoming clear in what particular new direction Ellerman's ambitions were pointing him. Early in 1900 reports were beginning to circulate that Leyland were seeking to acquire or control one of the very few American-owned steamship concerns in the North Atlantic trade. This was the Atlantic Transport Co., founded in 1882 as a cargo and cattle line from Baltimore, but which, with the backing of the Baltimore & Ohio Railroad, had entered the passenger trade at the same time as it opened a New York terminal in 1892. With the outbreak of the Spanish-American war the United States government had bought the company's entire fleet for troop-ships: but these had been almost immediately replaced out of the Wilson & Furness-Leyland Line's New York tonnage, and further steamers had been added since. As a holding company, the Atlantic Transport's current American operations were limited to storage and lighterage at its base in Baltimore harbour. But it possessed two subsidiaries in Britain, sailing under the red ensign. One of these, the National Steamship Co., was indeed small: but the other, the steadily prospering Atlantic Transport Co. Ltd, owned sixteen foreign-built steamships aggregating over 114,000 tons and a nominal capital of £2 million.

Acquisition of this Baltimore enterprise would yield clear advantage to Ellerman. Between his north-crossing line to New York and his projected West Indian and Pacific line to the Gulf, it would add a middle line to give Leyland complete coverage of the United States' east coast. In late 1899 or early 1900, therefore, he entered into negotiations with the American who owned both the Baltimore holding company and more than nine-tenths of the Atlantic Transport Co. Ltd's 50,000 shares, Bernard Nadal Baker.

A Baltimorean born and bred, the forty-six-year-old Baker had early abandoned his prospects in the family chemical business in favour of shipping and affiliated interests in Pennsylvanian coal mining and distribution. Like other American businessmen of stature he held miscellaneous financial directorships, enjoyed international connections (not least as American agent for the Hamburg-America line, with Albert Ballin, biggest name in German shipping) while gracing a variety of philanthropic and cultural positions, including a trusteeship of Johns Hopkins University. To Baker, as to Ellerman, it would have been clear that in the booming Atlantic trade increased capital was urgently required for the building of new vessels. A merger with Leyland, even if it involved his own demotion to the position of that company's Baltimore manager – and Baker's ambitions were not overweening – would not merely make his Atlantic Transport shares exchangeable for Ellerman securities, but thereby bring him the benefit of the plenteous capital to which Ellerman so evidently enjoyed easy access.

Whatever the negotiators' motives, from early March 1900 onwards *Fairplay*, the leading organ of British shipping, published repeated and categorical predictions that the entire fleet of Baker's Atlantic Transport Co., including the new ships currently being built for it by Harland & Wolff, plus its controlling interest in the National Line, plus 'other lines, with which negotiations are now being carried on', were about to be bought by Leyland. Adding the West Indian & Pacific line and 'a fifth considerable fleet', Ellerman would shortly be controlling a huge company with a total tonnage of over 300,000 g.r.t.[2] and a capital of £4.7 million, whose passenger and freight operations would take in the whole eastern seaboard of America from Canada to the Gulf, and the Mediterranean. Informed opinion was later to attribute these confident news items – which did not omit to mention that Leyland's £10 shares had risen in value by 40% over recent weeks – to the inspiration of Baker himself. Baker may also have been behind *Fairplay*'s comment that

> This operation bears out what has been predicted in competent quarters for the last fifteen years or more, and has been gradually going on in various directions, namely that under present conditions of trade, shipping would have a tendency to pass into a comparatively few strong hands. This movement is entirely in accordance with what we are witnessing every day in the combinations which are being formed in our leading trades.[3]

What was the 'fifth considerable fleet'? Presumably Cunard, to whose chairman Ellerman had again on 22nd March written confidentially to say that Leyland had definitely acquired the Atlantic Transport line, were on the point of closing terms with another business, and would shortly be going out to the public with a new preference share issue. Would Cunard be interested in coming in on the terms he had earlier suggested? But Ellerman's proposal was declined by Cunard's board of directors, as was Baker's approach to their New York agent.[4] Baker crossed to Liverpool on 28th March. It may be noted, in view of what follows, that one of his fellow passengers on the same vessel was J. Pierpont Morgan.

Fairplay had prophesied completion of the Ellerman-Baker transaction by 1st May. On the 3rd its startled its readers by announcing that the deal was not, after all, to be consummated. Leyland's purchase of the West Indian & Pacific company did indeed go through, after ratification by Leyland shareholders on 27th May, and at a level much in excess of stock market quotations – £992,000 in cash, equivalent to £62 per share with 30% dividend. But all negotiations with Atlantic Transport came to an abrupt end. The only explanation *Fairplay* could offer at the time was that Baker, 'being advised that heavy responsibility would rest on him if he became a party to the prospectus of the new Company, as settled, was unable to see his way to join the Leyland directorate'.[5] An alternative and much later opinion attributed the debacle to Ellerman's having withdrawn in pique after a public attack on him by a friend of Furness in the *Financial Times*. But Ellerman's own explanation to his shareholders, whether ingenuous or otherwise, was prescient;

> The outlook for freights in the near future is, in my judgement, an uncertain one. We have had prosperous times, and I feel that the near future may bring, at all events for a time, a reflux of bad times, particularly when the tonnage which is usually employed in government transport work, returns to normal employment; in addition to which a large amount of tonnage is building in America for employment in the Atlantic trade.[6]

He was, before all, a financier, with no particular vocational or family attachment to the shipping business.

Failure in the Ellerman-Baker negotiations, however, was but the prelude to a bigger deal, whose circumstances in themselves provide a more plausible explanation of the Leyland *volte face*. Of this larger transaction the prime cause was the ambition of another – one might say, *the* other – leading American shipowner; a man older than Baker, and whose aspirations for his country's place in the North Atlantic trade had been longer maturing. Clement Acton Griscom, a sixty-year-old Philadelphian, had passed all his life and amassed most of his fortune in shipping. Like Baker, he had interests in Pennsylvania transport, but also in New York and New Jersey-centred businesses, including Standard Oil. By politics he was a staunch Republican, perennially and indefatigably lobbying for federal subsidies to shipowners.

The enterprise over which Griscom presided was the International Navigation Company (INC), reorganised and registered in New Jersey in June 1893, which in 1900 possessed a capital stock of nearly $15 million and a funded debt exceeding $8 million.[7] It had been painstakingly accumulated over the years, piece by piece, since 1873, when Griscom had laid its foundation by buying the Red Star line of Belgium, whose British-built vessels plied between Antwerp and Philadelphia. Initiated under the sponsorship of Leopold II and operated through a Belgian subsidiary (the Société Anonyme Belge-

Americaine), direction of Red Star had fallen at an early stage into its debenture holders' hands. In 1884 Griscom had added to his INC the Keystone Line, behind which, as its title betrayed, stood the Pennsylvania Railroad. Since its creation in 1873 Keystone had been operating a Philadelphia–Queenstown–Liverpool service under the American flag, though its fleet had frequently to be augmented by chartered British freighters. After the purchase the INC had retained the line's American registry; and it continued to provide a freight and emigrant service, though unprofitably, under the title of the International Navigation Co. Ltd. Then, two years later, in 1886, Griscom had gone on to buy up and revitalise the old Inman Line, in financial difficulties but possessing two fine twin-screw steamers recently built by J. & J. Thomson on Clydebank, the *City of New York* and the *City of Paris*, the latter of which captured the Atlantic record from Cunard both ways on her maiden voyage. As these sisters found difficulty in entering the Mersey, the ex-Inman fleet had moved its eastern terminal to Southampton. From Keystone and Inman, Griscom in 1893 had formed his new American Line, which also took over the Red Star's Philadelphia service.

Griscom's International Navigation Co. in 1900, then, was like Baker's Atlantic Transport a conglomerate holding company with interests abroad as well as at home; and its three component enterprises worked as a single tonnage, much of it interchangeable, under a common funnel. Unlike Baker's, however, it was closely concerned with, because greatly dependent on, the controversial matters of registration and subsidies. For while Griscom's British and Belgian-registered subsidiaries prospered, his American component did not. Only the US mail contract kept it going, and even so it rarely succeeded in earning the full annual subvention. Lacking adequate renewals, his American-registered fleet fell steadily behind in international competition and ceased to yield dividends on either preferred or common stock. Four of its units, moreover, had suffered from government requisitioning for use in the Spanish-American war of 1898, while others had been transferred to the Pacific to meet the demands of the Klondike gold rush. However, Griscom had in 1892 successfully petitioned Congress to grant, by special and unique enactment,[8] American registration for the *New*

York and the *Paris*, thus rendering his two fastest vessels, though built outside the United States, eligible for federal contract subsidy.

It was this happy circumstance that had enabled him to rehabilitate his American Line in 1893, and now in 1900 contributed to his large expectations for both his country's and his company's future role in Atlantic shipping. This buoyant optimism, unshared by Baker, rested broadly upon three articles of faith – on the continuance of the world shipping boom, on the favourable outcome of a ship subsidy Bill in the Congress, and on his own assured access to native sources for the needful capital expansion.

Certainly the first of these grounds for optimism looked solid enough. After recovery from the depression of the early 1890's, which for shipowners reached a nadir in 1895, the current condition of world shipping appeared, on a short view at least, one of rude health. That the North Atlantic passenger trade was enjoying in 1900 a record-breaking year could be attributed to causes wider than war or the Paris Exhibition. Growth of European liner companies owed much to the rising flood of westward migration – four million voyagers to the New World between 1860 and 1900 – whose rate of flow had not yet reached its peak. Why should not an American company with European footholds take a bigger share of this traffic? As to the eastward journey, the preamble to a shipping measure now lying before Congress was surely correct in holding that 'the profitable employment of the surplus productive power of the farms, factories, mines, forests and fisheries of the United States imperatively demands the increase of foreign commerce'. It doubtless irked Griscom to see the USA's swelling seaborne trade (notably in grain) still dependent upon foreign shippers and schedules, upon the exigencies of European policies and conflicts. She ought on the contrary to be in a position to take advantage of the general boom, especially at a juncture when the biggest European shipping power had temporarily withdrawn an immense quantity of tonnage from trade in order to meet the transport and logistic demands of war in South Africa. If Griscom could increase his share of such an outlet, and at the same time salvage the low fortunes of his American-flag component, he might kill two birds with one stone – an enterprise that would show overall profitability.

To such optimism the news of Baker's projected sell-out to Leyland must have come as a heavy blow. If realised, it would entail further concentration of American shipping in British hands at a juncture when Griscom read the signs as favouring deliberate movement in the opposite direction. Consummation of the plan would gravely set back the possibility of any combination of resources among American shipowners of the nature Griscom desired. Indeed, it would leave him isolated as the only one of them remaining engaged on any scale in the North Atlantic trade. Griscom's determination to avert and reverse the Ellerman-Baker transaction does much to explain why by the end of 1900 rumours were circulating – though 'all the principals mentioned seem to deny the allegation concerned'[9] – of a huge American-owned shipping combination about to absorb not only International Navigation and Atlantic Transport but Leyland and other British lines as well. In April 1901 rumour became a factual statement which burst like a bombshell upon the international shipping world and upon Britain in especial. To understand how this diplomatic revolution came about, however, requires a somewhat lengthy explanation of American maritime conditions at this juncture.

America's transition from sail to steam, like that from wood to iron, took place several decades behind Britain's, and then only partially and sluggishly. One reason for this delay was the navigation monopoly enjoyed by native ships in her coastwise trade, which greatly protected sail against competition from the steam tramp. Her steamships were initially developed for river and lake navigation only, where the level of freight rates was usually adequate to maintain returns on capital. Elsewhere their only profitable use remained until the 1890's confined chiefly to North Atlantic freight. Until the end of the century, sail predominated in the USA's foreign trade, and even in the years immediately preceding World War I accounted for roughly one-third of the American flagships thus engaged. Faced with so limited a demand, American shipyard owners were understandably reluctant to turn over to steam. Though the pioneer William Cramp had built his Philadelphia yard for this purpose in the 1870's, by the end of the century only three more yards of note had managed to establish themselves on the Atlantic coast. By the first year of the new, Cramp himself was in such low water as to lend credibility to a rumour that he was selling out to Vickers Sons & Maxim of Britain.

A second cause of this tardy conversion was that for American builders the cost hurdles were dauntingly high. Freight charges on iron ore from the newly opened ranges of Minnesota, and on coal from the Ohio valley, made raw materials and fuel costly at the seaboard. The USA lacked coaling stations abroad; and maintenance of coal supplies even over the longer coastwise trade routes was problematic. As for iron and steel and their products, these were, despite the tariff, usually cheaper to import from Europe. Obviously the coming of steam raised shipbuilding out of the handicraft level. The new industry required costly components and elaborate assembly plants. For boilers, turbines, propellers, generators and other essential items, close contact with heavy industry was clearly necessary, and the new yards therefore tended to become narrowly localised. Shipbuilding, a delicate infant, was long to remain in thrall to the lusty primary industries and their magnates. One of these latter, indeed, the Germano-American Charles M. Schwab, in 1901 went so far as to promote a shipbuilding trust within which the Bethlehem Steel Co. would actually be embodied. Though the project collapsed amid some public scandal,[10] it was entirely consonant with the American situation. Shipbuilders' prices and wage levels were virtually determined by those prevailing in heavy industry generally and, protected as the latter were from international competition, soared high. Their economic power virtually unimpaired by anti-trust legislation, the new steel corporations were able to impose their own price levels on the entire industry; to discriminate by regions; and even to dump ship steel abroad, the nascent US Steel Corporation selling in Belfast at three-quarters its home price. Such practices were highly detrimental to native shipbuilders, who greatly resented the steel trusts and their masters. At the same time the tariff effectively prevented a poorly protected home maritime industry from importing foreign steel or its products extensively. Labour, too, was formidably expensive. American wages, which drew men across from Britain's coalfields, iron foundries and the Clyde, had the effect of raising the American shipbuilder's labour cost levels, according to the type of yard and vessel, to between 50% and 100% above Britain's.[11]

Overall, the costs of ship construction in the USA at the start of the twentieth century could be reckoned at between 37% and 43% more than in the United Kingdom. One concrete illustration may suffice. In 1901 Bernard Baker's Atlantic Transport Co. took delivery of four 16 knot cargo-and-passenger steamships each of 13,000 g.r.t. Of these, two had been built at home by the New York Shipbuilding Co. for $1,846,000 apiece, and the other two at Belfast by Harland & Wolff to the identical specifications at $1,419,210 each. At about the same time Baker's line placed orders for four 12 knot freighters of 8,000 g.r.t. at home and two further identical vessels in Belfast: the respective prices per vessel were $534,000 and $436,000.[12] The aggregate cost differential for those two sets of transactions might be expressed at about 30% of the British figure for the large vessels and 36%–50% for the freighters. Even a nation of 80 million, if it uses its tariff to raise prices so substantially above world level, must wave its own merchant marine goodbye.

In a circular fashion, moreover, high and rigid costs further depressed demand for American-built steamers. Native yards were slow to develop either high specialisation or wide versatility. Hence any one variety of ship – steam tramps, for instance, which were turned out in their hundreds by specialised British yards – could not be so economically produced by an American yard that might be required to lay down a battleship one month, a liner the next, then a cargo boat, a tugboat, etc. Low demand, again, kept skills low and American shipbuilding technically backward. When the Pennsylvania Railroad ordered ships from Cramp it stipulated that he first make an extended survey of recent innovations of design and practice in Europe – where he took the opportunity to study *inter alia* compound engines of the early Elder type. Correspondingly, what foreign visitors – an engineering team from Britain, for example, or the Chief Constructor of the German Navy – found most to admire in Cramp's own Philadelphia yard in 1902 were improved processes applicable to the construction industry as a whole, not to shipbuilding in particular. The new machines whose operation Cramp's men were sent over to Southampton to demonstrate were pneumatic riveters for general use.

Small wonder that, weighing all such handicaps, the American shipowner preferred to buy his fleet abroad. True, he faced a legal obstacle in that federal law denied American registry to any vessel which had not been built, or rebuilt or repaired to at least three-quarters of her valuation, within the United States. Nevertheless, a great and growing amount of foreign-built tonnage plying under flags of origin, chiefly British, was in fact owned and controlled by Americans whether as shareholders in limited companies, mortgage holders, or contracting manager-owners. Investment of this kind had risen so steeply that by 1901, after the purchase of Leyland, the 672,500 ton American-controlled foreign flag fleet of 136 steamers was approaching in size the 880,000 ton American-flag fleet in the overseas carrying trade.[13] Investors willing to accept the political risks involved included small individual shipowners and large liner operators, capitalists seeking to deploy large funds more profitably, railroad executives and rising industrial firms like the United Fruit Co.

This preference, coupled with the failure of many of her yards following the financial catastrophe of 1873, had had a deplorable effect upon figures of America's home-built tonnage during the 1870's and 1880's. Midway through the latter decade construction fell, and remained, below the million-ton mark. By 1900 it was estimated that the total such tonnage employed in foreign trade was under 827,000 g.r.t., of which only 341,000 was power-driven – statistics which underlay the circumstance that less than 12% of the nation's imports and hardly more than 6% of her exports (both measured by value of cargoes) were carried in American bottoms. Four years later the promoter of a Bill in Congress to set up a Mercantile Marine Commission pointed out that not a single American-registered ship plied regularly to Germany, Scandinavia or the Netherlands. The commission when established was told in its very first year (1905) that American yards had not laid the keel of a single steamer for use exclusively in foreign commerce since June 1901, and that only one such now rested on native stocks. Witnesses spoke of 'severe depression' and 'disaster' in the industry: while Britain, with twelve times the ocean-going steam tonnage of the USA, was doing about 60% of all the latter's foreign carrying. But for federal mail subsidies, indeed, the native fraction would have been even less.[14]

So much for the builders' plight. To American shipowners and operators, too, the new maritime economy, ever expanding in pace with technological development, brought its problems. Steam fleets were costly, exacting high overheads and requiring rapid turn-round. Economies of scale could be secured only by a large volume of traffic, and was increasingly seen to entail corporate ownership. In a world where great nations pursued rival policies in transport, trading and naval affairs, no country's shipowners could expect to escape competition. This was an age when the major European powers (as well as Japan and Canada) were establishing networks of contract services along the principal trunk routes of ocean commerce where speed was a matter of prestige as well as efficiency. The era of mercantile nationalism and subsidy struggles was about to open. Its keenest winds might be tempered somewhat by devices of mutual co-operation shipping rings or 'conferences', designed to avoid ruinous rate wars and ensure some stability of operation. But all such co-operative arrangements to divide traffic according to agreed schedules were necessarily evanescent as relative opportunities changed, and were invariably denounced by critics as tending to foster monopoly and artificially high rate structures.[15] For American shipowners, handicapped by high costs, something more than voluntary self-regulation was needed, and they looked for subsidy or other concessions to a government insufficiently aware of the new age that was dawning.

But Washington found itself under pressure from a number of directions. The shipbuilders, whose interests (as we have seen) clashed with the steelmasters', wanted firstly a selective reduction of the tariff on imported shipbuilding materials and components. Several Congressional committees had indeed recommended partial exemptions for such commodities, but unavailingly until very recent years. More than this, the builders claimed some governmental favour for their infant industry equivalent to the tariff protecting American manufacturers in general. Home building being costlier under conditions which

held them in subordination to the steel industry, they wanted
bounties; and as an offset to the cost of bounties, some
builders claimed to have calculated that the United States by
carrying its own commerce in its own ships would save up to
$200 million. Meanwhile they pressed successfully for the
continuance of their monopoly of building for the coastwide
trade.

In alliance with the shipbuilding lobby was to be found the
young United States Navy, stressing the demands of national
defence for more ships to be native-built and native-manned;
together with a miscellany of mercantilist and nationalist
elements crying the country's need of self-sufficiency in steam
carriage in circumstances where, as in the South African war,
other countries had to withdraw theirs. With her recently
acquired possessions in the Caribbean and far Pacific, the
United States as a colonial power bore fresh burdens of communication and defence. The Spanish-American war had
demonstrated the desirability of being able to bring under the
American flag auxiliary vessels of a type convertible to naval
use.

The shipowners and operators, too, jealously opposed any
move to admit foreign-built vessels to the coastwise trade,
whose relative importance was the more enhanced as
America's foreign-trade fleet declined. To that extent they
spoke in unison with the builders. In other respects, however, Congress had heard from the nation's shippers a very
different tale, and one that was corroborated by many
American producers for the long-voyage trades. They argued,
correctly enough, that it was so much cheaper to buy foreign-
built than American steamers that even their present unsatisfactory position *vis-à-vis* Britain and other maritime
powers could only be maintained by continuing to purchase
abroad. The shippers had therefore for some years been demanding that the government adopt a 'free ship' policy, i.e.,
relax or repeal the current federal law, dating back to 1792,
which restricted American registration to the narrow categories of vessel we have already noted. The Lynch committee
of 1896 had been told bluntly by the packet operators that if
relief were not soon granted they might be compelled to transfer their entire fleets to the British flag. The committee had

indeed recommended some moderate bounty for the operators, as against a larger one for the builders,[16] but neither had been gratified by legislation.

To the latter's objection that a free-ship policy would cripple native yards, and thereby impair the nation's economy and defence, the operators produced several answers. First, that evidence of this was lacking, since these yards were as yet producing few steam vessels for foreign trade anyway. Second, in their Congressional testimony the operators cited the extensive capital investment by Americans in foreign ships (which we have noted) as the true index of demand. Indeed, they said, American capital would be even more abundantly invested in British ships were it not for the cumbersome and protracted methods of English law in transferring stock in British-registered ships. There was plenty of idle capital seeking such investment; and the fact that transfers of stock could be made in the USA at any time by simple endorsement would greatly facilitate the release of such capital in native-registered shipping. Thirdly, the anti-protectionist lobby pointed to European experience as evidence that this demand when released would so support an expanded home shipbuilding programme as to enable the United States to accumulate a large mercantile marine inexpensively. Great Britain had flourished since she repealed her own registry law in 1849. In Germany, where it was permitted to purchase from Britain without automatic forfeiture of native registry, a free-ship policy was markedly stimulating indigenous construction.

In federal bounties American owners and operators had felt little confidence hitherto, and an abortive Postal Subsidy Act of 1885 had done nothing to change their mind. Yet the prolonged fall in the nation's foreign trade tonnage – dropping again by nearly one-third during the 1880's – now inclined them perforce to think that only by allying themselves with the builders in pursuit of a subvention could they hope to arrest the decline. This demand they supplemented with the complaint that the present manning standards required for American registry proved much too expensive in operation. By 1890, then, some realignment of pressures was observable, whereby yards and shipping lines combined to mount a new and determined assault on Capitol Hill.

Effectively, Congress was being forced to confront urgent but by no means novel problems of national mercantile policy. A number of alternative solutions might be pursued. First, it might opt simply to prolong its existing *laissez-faire* attitude towards both foreign and domestic shipping in international trade, continuing to benefit from the subsidies and other encouragements of European powers towards their own respective shipping lines, somewhat as the United States continued passively to benefit from the Royal Navy, whose presence signified the Pax Britannica. Yet acquiescence in foreign registry for the bulk of its oceanic shipping was by the 1890's becoming irksome to the mounting sentiment of nationalism, as signifying America's dependence upon other nations both in peace and war.

Or, secondly, the federal government might resort to protection by retaliation. That is to say, it might choose to impose discriminatory duties against foreign-borne cargoes or allow rebate to American-borne. Though some pressure was periodically generated in favour of such a course, it never became seriously feasible. For thereby America would have denied herself much of the indispensable benefit of foreign services while inviting almost certain retaliation, as conflicting with an international reciprocity policy already somewhat breached by her 'hands off' protection of her own internal and coastwise navigation. A system of rebates, moreover, would be either impossibly elaborate or, if simple and general, insensitive because operating without regard to distance travelled or value of freight carried.

Thirdly, Congress might instead allow itself to be persuaded by shipowners to open American registry to more American-owned vessels built abroad. Evidence repeatedly given to its committees, from the Lynch committee of 1869 onward, laid bare the plain economics of the situation – that only by means of foreign purchase could shippers keep down their costs, raise efficiency, and provide the necessary margin for expansion. Yet these committees were not convinced that a free-ship policy could of itself provide the whole answer to America's need to ensure successful *international* competition. Moreover, protectionist patterns were so deeply ingrained in Congressional thinking that all such committees usually ended by recommending policies more solicitous for the builders than the operators: and this was to remain the case until 1912. Meanwhile, could American registry be made more attractive – by a bounty, for instance, to offset the higher costs entailed in meeting the higher manning standards that such registration required?

Many paths, including the free-ship issue, appeared to be leading Congress in the 1890's toward some form of subvention. But mention of subsidies immediately raised a host of complicated and contentious questions. Some committee members were willing to accept without reservation the whole of the shipbuilders' and operators' case, and to attribute uncritically the greater maritime success of other countries to this form of aid. Yet many more Congressmen questioned the wisdom of any general ship subsidy. How would it be administered? If a vessel could run practically in ballast and still draw a bounty, ships would multiply in no proportion to national need but simply to qualify for subvention. Bounties, once introduced, would grow with what they fed on. Their effect was held to be temporary and their influence debilitating, as fostering undue dependence on Washington, where lobbying for appropriations from the public fisc would magnify corruption. Above all loomed the cost of unselective subvention. France, it was pointed out, was by 1900 paying over $8·5 million annually on that score, while Britain's support of her marine postal transport alone cost her Treasury the equivalent of $6 million a year. Even to meet the by no means general subsidy proposed by one Bill before Congress in 1901 would, calculated its critics, burden the US. Treasury to the tune of $40 million – a figure in their eyes unjustified on grounds of efficiency.

Would a policy of qualified and selective subvention prove more politically feasible? If so, in what form – a bounty from the federal treasury to enterprises which enlarged the national economy, or a payment for services directly rendered, such as mail-carrying? Sailing ships, which predominated in number, wanted the former: but sail was of little value in wartime. The objectively best course would have been for Congress to supplement foreign shipping services by selective encouragement of carefully chosen native lines. Unfortunately, the only North Atlantic precedent for this had been doubly unsatisfactory. Congress had used the subsidy not to complement foreign operators, but to try to warn them off. And it had provided no safeguard against operational inefficiency.

This *locus classicus* of misapplied public aid followed a Congressional enactment of 1845 directing the Postmaster General to go to tender for carriage of American overseas mail. In thus imitating the example of the British Admiralty, Congress had been animated by no desire to improve communications or foster native packet operators, but by considerations of international rivalry and misconceived self-protection. Tenders were not easy to elicit. But in 1847 it authorised the Secretary of the Navy to contract with the shipowner E. K. Collins for mail carriage between New York and Liverpool at $385,000 p.a., a sum roughly equivalent to the £80,000 the federal government had been paying the British North America Co. (Cunard) for its weekly translantic service. Congress stipulated that the new vessels required by the Collins line should be built in the United States.[17]

But inexperience on both sides seriously underestimated the cost of special construction – ultimately almost $3 million for four liners. Within a year Collins had to apply to Congress for a loan and permission to delay inauguration of his service. In 1851 Congress agreed to waive interest. Even with this help, and with many British sailings to New York in suspense during the Crimean War, the line never looked like paying dividends. Its new paddlers were over-elaborate and, though remarkably fast, pressed beyond their safe limit. The fleet suffered two tragic disasters. Its dramatic duel with Cunard, whose ships it outclassed in everything save cargo capacity, to attract more passengers entailed highly extravagant working. While a British select committee were preparing to recommend the reduction of mail subsidy wherever possible, Congress was obliged to increase that to Collins by some 80%, or almost double what the US Post Office had been paying Cunard for the same service.[18]

Economic nemesis had followed. In 1855 President Pierce vetoed a Bill for continuing the extra subvention. Three years later the legislature terminated all mail contracts and Collins collapsed. The shipbuilder Cramp was later to blame the fiasco on superior backing given Cunard by the British government.[19] But in truth this first American experiment in shipping subvention had been based on erroneous principles and unaccompanied by any attempt comparable with the British Admiralty's to insist on its most economic deployment. The episode had cost the United States Treasury $14 million, had given the Washington shipping lobby a bad name and aroused scepticism as to whether Congress had learned anything from its experience with similar abuses in railroad construction.

The Collins affair was nevertheless noteworthy as revealing the first clear division of Congress over shipping policy along regional lines. The maritime-minded and protectionist east had supported it: direct payments from the US Treasury, according to the Republicans, together with strict maintenance of the navigation laws, would raise the low demand for a home-built mercantile marine. Their national platform of 1896 came out in favour of federal subsidies, as did McKinley in his letter accepting the presidential nomination. Yet such were the suspicion and hostility of south and west, seeking as always the cheapest outlet for their produce, that any such subvention stood condemned in their eyes as merely one more sop to the eastern industrialists. Were not American shipping lines in foreign trade mere adjuncts to the corporate economies of the railroad companies who respectively sponsored them? Would not the latter's indulgence in discriminatory rate wars ensure that any federal shipping subsidy would practically, if indirectly, be diverted to line their own pockets? The pattern prevailing in Congress had been for many years one where Republicans demanded subsidy, while most Democrats countered with demands for free ships. Between the two, American navigation policy had long lain becalmed.

Despite the Collins debacle, however, by the late 1880's the protectionists were coming to feel the climate changing in their favour. In the Senate they were now led by the assiduous James G. Blaine, Republican, of the seaboard state of Maine, who with some backing in the State Department pursued a project for overseas trade expansion (though chiefly with South America) through subsidies to steamship builders and operators. After another special committee had reported, the protectionists appeared to have won some ground by the introduction in 1890 of a subsidy measure designed to help the slow freight carriers. The

Frye-Farquhar Bill proposed a general bounty of 30 cents per gross ton for each thousand miles sailed by American-registered vessels of over 500 tons employed in the United States foreign carrying trades. A second Bill with the same sponsorship would establish by competitive tender a number of short-term mail contracts with owners of fast liners flying the stars and stripes, payment to be on a scale rising to $6 per mile. But no free-ship concessions were offered – sure sign that Washington was not yet coming to grips with the basic economic problem.

In the teeth of attacks led by the democratic Senator Vest of Missouri, both these Bills passed the Senate by large majorities. Opposition in the House, however, with the Speaker's connivance killed the tonnage bounty. The mail subsidies reached the statute book only after they had been made inflexibly applicable to all foreign-trade American vessels and routes, and their value cut to a figure too low to attract many bids.[20]

Nevertheless, it was the Merchant Marine Act of 1891 that gave Griscom cause for optimism. For it opened the way to the special Act by which Congress agreed to admit to the American register (as we have seen) his two newly bought but British-built greyhounds, the *New York* and the *Paris*, making them eligible to receive the new American subsidy in lieu of the British mail subvention forfeited upon their purchase from the Inman Line. President Benjamin Harrison duly raised the American flag over them; and in return Griscom undertook to order for his new American line two similar vessels to be built in the USA. The Cramp shipyard, of which Griscom was a director, in 1894-95 constructed the *St Louis* and the *St Paul*, of 19–20 knots and 11,630 g.r.t., at a price about 30% above what they would have cost from a British yard. Despite setbacks, the four vessels attracted an aggregate mail subsidy of $644,800 from the federal government until World War I; and down to 1923 more than half the total laid out in United States postal subventions was earned by the American Line.

Congress's special favour to Griscom was politically feasible because agreeable to both builders' and shippers' lobbies. This item apart, the Act of 1891 remained unfruitful. The American Line contributed vessels for the Spanish-American war but, carrying little freight, did not 'expand commerce' within the meaning of the Act's preamble. All attempts to extend subsidies under Cleveland's second administration came to nought. A tariff Act of 1890 had moved iron and steel plate for ship construction on to the duty-free list, which another such Act of 1894 further extended to include all shipbuilding materials. Pressure for a free-ship law failed when Democrats from the seaboard states deserted their party colleagues on the roll-call.

In 1898, however, the Republicans captured both Houses, which they were to hold with scarcely a lapse until 1910, and the protectionist tide again flowed strongly. President McKinley and his successor repeatedly urged a subsidy programme upon the legislature, in the belief that the swelling exports of American manufactured commodities would be still further increased thereby. Theodore Roosevelt as Assistant Secretary of the Navy was particularly receptive to the philosophy of Captain A. T. Mahan, which held that

> Ships and cargoes in transit upon the sea are private property in only one point of view, and that the narrowest. Internationally considered, they are national wealth engaged in reproducing and multiplying itself, to the intensification of the national power.[21]

Moreover the volume of warship construction, begun in the 1880's, increased until the US Navy became the most important customer of native shipbuilders, who by the Navy Act of 1886[22] were required to use only domestic materials in naval building. Although the biggest spurt was to come under Roosevelt's presidency in 1901–05, with the authorisation of ten battleships, the government's building programme had already in the 1890's acquired a regularity and momentum which promised to be the salvation of native yards.

Another drive for State subvention was signalled when, in 1898, Senator Mark A. Hanna tabled a Bill proposing general subsidisation of American-flag vessels in the foreign trade according to a scale of bounties of seemingly unlimited scope. This failing, the offensive was maintained through the concerted strategy of a group which included Griscom, Cramp and the US Commissioner of Navigation, Eugene Tyler Chamberlain, strategy being directed in the Fifty-sixth and succeeding Congresses by Blaine's successor in this role, Senator Frye, also from Maine. In December 1899 Frye introduced in the Senate, and Representative Payne in the House, a measure purporting 'to provide for ocean mail service between the United States and foreign ports, and the common defence; to promote commerce; and to encourage the deep-sea fisheries'. Because the Frye-Payne Bill, which the Senate's Committee on Commerce took up in the following February, was more limited in scope and cost than Hanna's, and since Frye was the committee's chairman, its expectation of life was rated higher. Because its provisions closely influenced the conduct of Griscom and his associates, and therefore the course of events in 1902 with which we are chiefly concerned, they deserve notice in some detail.

As amended after reintroduction in the Fifty-seventh Congress,[23] they stood in 1902 as follows. All American-flag vessels of 1,000 g.r.t. and over engaged in foreign trade would qualify for a subsidy of, at maximum, 15 cents per gross ton carried. This general navigation bounty would be limited to sixteen voyages a year and reviewed after five years. It was calculated to represent the difference – perhaps 30% – in operational costs between American-built vessels sailing under the American flag and corresponding British-built vessels flying the British. In addition, mail subsidies were proposed per gross ton for every 100 nautical miles' carriage, but steeply graded according to the class (i.e., size and speed) of the vessel, which must be suitable for conversion into an auxiliary naval cruiser. These special rates for fast steamers of native construction were designed to give them, down to a speed of twelve knots, a pronounced advantage over their British rivals. To be eligible for either type of subsidy, vessels must be officered and (at any rate for the first two years of the contract) crewed entirely by American citizens. Owners must within five years of accepting subsidy build in the United States tonnage aggregating 25% of their tonnage already subsidised. A foreign-built vessel sailing under the American flag, where Americans on 1st January 1900 owned a majority interest in it, would be entitled – and here was the first small but (for Griscom and his like) significant concession to the 'free shippers' – to 50% of the corresponding full subsidy.[24] At the time the Frye Bill was originally tabled, it was reckoned that about 255,00 g.r.t. of American steam (plus 554,000 of American sail) tonnage would have been eligible for the full subsidy, and some further 315,000 g.r.t. of American-owned but foreign-built vessels, if brought under the American flag, for the 50%.

For Griscom and the few other American shipowners in his class the stakes on a successful outcome of the Frye Bill were high indeed. Though its proposed general subsidy benefited cargo vessels in some measure, it was readily seen that the bounty was so graduated as to confer on the fastest passenger liners some three times the sum it offered freighters. Maximum bonus was reserved for vessels in the first grade of the Bill's schedule, i.e. those of 10,000 g.r.t. or more and capable of making twenty knots; and these Griscom's line was almost alone in possessing. Together with the 50% subsidy for his British-built vessels flying the American flag, he stood to gain some £350,000 p.a. – perhaps sufficient to pull the American-flag component of his International Navigation Co. out of the red. In addition there would be the earnings from mail carriage. The British press was quick to observe that under the Bill the American Line 'gets over $500,000 for carrying about half as much of the US mail as is carried by the Cunard Co., to whom the United States government pays only about $200,000'. It was pointed out also that a mere seven ships of the Cunard fleet alone, had they been American vessels, would have received for the year ending 30th July 1900 $645,738 in speed subsidy and $431,175 in mileage subsidy. 'Such a subvention,' calculated *Fairplay*, 'would be sufficient to pay a dividend of 13·46% on the whole of the share capital' of the Britsh company, and this by employment of only a fraction of its fleet.[25]

Naturally it was this very onesidedness of its prospective benefit that drew most fire upon the measure from Democrats of south and west. Between 80% and 90% of the nation's agricultural exports, they observed, went out in ordinary freighters: passenger steamers, who would do best under the new proposals, carried less than 10%. Senators Clay, Vest and Spooner had no difficulty in showing where the Treasury bounty would actually go – not to native shippers but to eastern capitalists and builders. Attention was drawn to the recent and sharp rise in home steel prices following the formation of US Steel. What need had such giants of public subvention? Democrats were not placated when at one point in the debate Frye declared that subsidy 'is only another name for protection'. Some of them went so far as to accuse Republicans of pressing the Bill in order to mobilise the support of shipping interests for their projected Nicaragua canal scheme.

Typical and most eloquent of the opposition was Senator George Turner from the far western state of Washington. The Frye measure he described as 'not taxation but spoliation ... socialistic, ... a lawless, piratical raid ... on the Treasury of the United States', It could not possibly achieve its ostensible aim. For shipbuilders were not going to give shipowners the benefit of this bounty if they could help it, and would simply raise their prices, thus reducing the volume of orders to native yards. It had not been shown that a single new ship would be built there as a result of the Bill. As for national defence, the government could build amply to its own requirements for a quarter the sum proposed to be given away. The farmers, on whose behalf he spoke, did not care what flag their produce sailed under. 'What we want and need is cheap ships,' and must be free to buy where cheapest.[26]

In the Bill's favour its promoters urged that it would gain for the country 'a measure of maritime independence corresponding with our industrial and agricultural independence'. Its supporters claimed that it would eventually put the United States' mercantile marine in a competitive position *vis-à-vis* the British, would give her an auxiliary navy second only to the latter's, and in so doing would incomparably stimulate and expand her native shipbuilding. These claims had the advocacy of two successive Presidents, the Commissioner of Navigation and the Secretary of the Treasury. Among favourable committee witnesses for the shipping fraternity, Griscom himself warned sharply that if the measure were not passed, his American Line could not long continue under the American flag on present terms. Bernard Baker issued a similar public warning, on behalf of his Atlantic Transport Co., in the *New York Times*.[27] Auguries for the Bill's long-deferred passage were good after the Senate Committee on Commerce had again reported it out favourably in January 1902; and by March it had cleared the Senate with gratifying speed.

Returning now to Griscom in particular, it will be evident from this somewhat lengthy digression that two of his three grounds for optimism in 1902 about the future of American shipping did not lack semblance of solidity. The country's export trade was booming; and Congress at last appeared to be taking seriously a subsidy Bill that would make his International Navigation Co. one of the principal beneficiaries. What of his third hopeful prospect – assurance of access to a bigger source of native capital than heretofore? To expand and augment his company Griscom would require considerable backing from quite a large financial concern whose means were beyond the resources of Philadelphia.

Here, by another happy coincidence, a channel had already been cut which was to lead Griscom to the biggest American financier of all. Confident that Washington was moving at last towards a wider subsidy policy, he had early in 1899 sought the means of expanding his American Line with six new vessels, each at least as large as any it already possessed.[28] The bankers to whom he turned were the private Philadelphia house of Drexel & Co., who floated a mortgage bond issue on the INC's behalf. Two of the new security holders were the Philadelphian transport magnates Peter A. B. Widener and William L. Elkins, who both at this point joined the INC's board of directors. Drexel & Co. were the Philadelphia subsidiary of the J. P. Morgan Co. Morgan himself, having recently (as we noted) crossed the Atlantic in Bernard Baker's company, may be assumed to have already had at least an inkling of the latter's plans. What is certain is that Morgan turned a sympathetic ear to Griscom's more positive scheme for a consolidation of American-owned lines augmented by purchase of one or more British. Six months of three-cornered discussion thereafter between Griscom, Morgan and Baker led by the end of 1900 to an agreement whereby Griscom's International Navigation would merge with Baker's Atlantic Transport in a combine which would also include two other (at present unspecified) shipping companies. J. P. Morgan Co. would advance funds for the enlargement of Atlantic Transport's operating tonnage by new vessels. Of these, some would be built in the USA, but a number of them – the new *Minne–* series, largest and fastest freighters of their day, but with some excellent passenger accommodation – by Harland & Wolff at Belfast. All (it was assumed) would be eligible, either in full or half, for the subsidy that Congress –

and there was great confidence about this – would soon be enacting.

Early rumours about the new syndicate represented Morgan himself as its guiding genius.[28] In fact, the principal responsibility for this novel and bold move rested with the shippers themselves, Morgan's role being confined to that of banker, advancing cash for the new ships, easing the syndicate's passage by his contacts in the United States and abroad, and arranging to market a proportion of its preferred stock ($75 million worth in all, at 6% cumulative).

The risk involved cannot at this stage have appeared to him great. If the subsidy Bill duly passed, the future of the American-owned ships in the combination seemed assured. If it failed, Morgan could expect to enjoy a lien on the new vessels as security and on the profits of the four consolidated lines as support for the new issue of preferred stock. Once the Morgan partners had agreed, in December 1900, to supply the indispensable support, Baker left for London to reopen negotiations with Ellerman, but this time in the presence of J. P. Morgan junior and in the role of prospective purchaser, not seller.

It was through the publication of Ellerman's circular letter of 29th April 1901 that Leyland shareholders, the British public and the shipping world at large first learnt not only of the American trust but of the identity of one of the additonal lines proposed to be incorporated into it. At the shareholders' meeting of 7th May it appeared that the trust had at first proposed to buy Ellerman's controlling interest in Leyland stock, of 71,000 shares, at market valuation. But Ellerman, in negotiation with Morgan personally, had raised his price by nearly one-third to £14 10s per share, payable in cash, and had stipulated equality of treatment for all fellow shareholders, with option to sell at this price until 26th May. The resolution embodying these proposals was approved by each class of shareholder – on that, too, Ellerman had made the deal conditional. Thereby J. P. Morgan Co. ultimated acquired, and transferred to the new American combine, 118,463 of £10 ordinary and 58,703 of £10 preference shares in Frederick Leyland & Co. (1900) Ltd. Already Morgan's had become drawn in to a degree beyond their first expectations. Instead of being merely a bank advancing credit and arranging sale of securities, they were now implicated, through their London affiliate, J. S. Morgan & Co., in one of the largest shipping concerns in the United States foreign trade to the tune not of $3·5 million but of $11 million. Ellerman for his part agreed not to engage, directly or indirectly, in the Atlantic trade or trade between Britain and the Continent, for the term of fourteen years.[30] (Thereby, incidentally, he ceased to be a possible purchaser of the Cunard Company). He and most of his fellow directors quitted the Leyland board, their places being taken by several directors of Baker's and Griscom's organisations and – significantly for the future – by W. J. Pirrie of Belfast.

This explosion of news set off, like shock waves, a further chain of speculation in the British press. True, Leyland's Mediterranean fleet was to be excluded from the deal. Nevertheless the forty-four ships about to pass into American possession represented some 277,000 g.r.t. and were the best of its fleet, including as they did the new 14 knot *Devonian* and *Winifredian*, each of 10,400 tons, and the three 12,000 – 13,000 ton vessels currently being laid down. 'Except as part of a far-reaching scheme', reflected *Fairplay*, 'the transaction would be absolutely unintelligible'; and it forecast that Morgan's purchase of Leyland 'is but the beginning of his investments in vessel property'. 'These colossal deals' would soon involve 'four other well-known lines in the North Atlantic trade'.[31] Other guesses were that the Leyland fleet would shortly be transferred to the American flag; that Morgan was about to buy the Beaver and Dominion lines also; that he intended to build a number of fast passenger liners to beat anything afloat; and that the Cunard and White Star lines had resolved to combine for mutual protection.

These conjectures subsided: but only to give way to a more serious report which, despite categorical denials, was to resound in the popular British press throughout the winter of 1901–02.[32] Its first appearance seems to have been on 18th September 1901, when the New York correspondent of several British newspapers reported that Morgan was completing negotiations to secure for his American enterprise the controlling interest in the White Star Line. The impact of this information at home can be readily imagined. For White Star (the Oceanic Steam Navigation Co.) was by far the most flourishing British line on the

North Atlantic, one of Cunard's fiercest rivals, and of recent years had been earning about 50% more per gross ton than Baker's Atlantic Transport. It had just launched the world's biggest passenger liner, the *Celtic*, of over 20,000 tons. It was, moreover, in contract to the General Post Office and the Admiralty.

Circumstances lent this dire report some plausibility. The line's great founder, Thomas Henry Ismay, had died in November 1899 – two months after his latest vessel, the *Oceanic*, longest ship in the world, had embarked on her maiden voyage – and some uncertainty attended the winding up of his estate. This comprised the largest single interest, 150 units of the company's stock; and since each unit was of unusually high valuation, there was the likelihood that it would have to be disposed of *en bloc*.

In planning the line's future, the initiative passed meanwhile to the holder of the second largest bloc of the line's securities, William James Pirrie, president of the British Chamber of Shipping and partner and chairman of the important Belfast shipbuilding firm of Harland & Wolff. Ever since 1867, when Ismay had given them a first order for passenger steamers to their own revolutionary design, Harland & Wolff's Queen's Island yard had enjoyed an exclusive and symbiotic relationship with White Star which it was to preserve to the last. It was common knowledge that Pirrie did not see eye-to-eye with Joseph Bruce Ismay, the heir and successor of his father at the head of White Star, on proposals for the line's future development.

How long Pirrie had been in touch with the Americans is not evident. But he had revisited the United States as recently as September 1899; and his recent elevation to the directorate of Leyland, once the latter had passed into Morgan's hands, may be read as signifying a more than nominal connection. His biographer, indeed, credits him with a desire to prevent the proposed Baker-Ellerman deal.[33] Be that as it may, by the spring of 1901, while Morgan, Griscom and Widener were on a visit to Baker in London, it became apparent that Pirrie was acting as agent, self-appointed or otherwise, in negotiations with the Americans.

Because White Star stock had never before been publicly

offered, an established market price did not exist. At the start of the negotiations the Americans offered $24 million in 6% cumulative preferred stock in return for complete ownership of the company. This promised to yield annual dividends not less than those the line had been paying throughout most of the preceding decade. But Pirrie, perhaps with Ellerman's example before him, drove a hard bargain. The basis of valuation finally agreed upon was the line's earnings for the year 1900 (less an allowance represnting the British government's subsidy to White Star for troop carriage during the years of the Boer War) multiplied by ten in order to arrive at the base price. This gave a figure of about $32 million, or one-third more than the Americans' original offer. The White Star owners however, unlike Leyland's, eventually agreed to take a quarter of this in cash, the remaining 75% to be in the preferred stock of the new combine. They were also to be given the opportunity to participate in its common stock, plus a notional bonus related to respective holdings in preferred. Further, the purchasers undertook to allow the sellers a return on the value of their property based on the company's earnings of the last five years, in the form of 6% cumulative preferred; and in addition – which was to cost the purchasers another $7 million – a cash payment to represent fairly the growth in value of their property since 1900.

Notice was published on 30th April 1902 that White Star had entered into a provisional agreement with Messrs J. P. Morgan & Co. 'the object of which is a community of interests between the American, Atlantic Transport, Dominion, Leyland, Red Star, and White Star Lines'. Inclusion of the Dominion Line, chiefly a freight service to Canada and New England operated with consistent unprofitability by two fairly minor companies, was stipulated by Pirrie because (so the shipping world said) Harland & Wolff had built its fleet and now held more of its paper than they cared for.[34] The agreement was submitted to White Star shareholders on 17th May and ratified after a meeting believed to have been long and stormy.

When the terms of the agreement were first published, in a highly condensed summary in the *Times* of 8th May 1902, informed opinion, both financial and maritime, stood aghast at the seeming extravagance of the transaction. They pointed out that the year 1900, upon which the main purchase price was based, had been one of quite unprecedented, and possibly un-repeatable, prosperity for the shipping industry, and therefore yielded a grossly inflated valuation. A White Star stockholder, it was remarked, had only to reinvest his cash receipts from the deal in British government securities in order to get a better return than he had ever received from White Star dividends. What true valuation, then, could be placed upon the new concern's preferred, let alone common, stock? His critics should have know Morgan better. Under Ismay, White Star had in fact been unobtrusively limiting payments in dividends to only some 15% of its earnings. The Americans proposed to raise this to about 70%, which would of course greatly improve the market value of White Star securities. Practically, too, supersession of the old White Star high-denomination shares by smaller units of stock would enhance marketability.

Extravagant or not, the transaction was greeted by British press and public with understandable consternation and dismay. To them White Star had come to symbolise all that was most estimable and progressive in the country's maritime enterprise. It contained some of the fastest British ships afloat – including the *Oceanic*, one of the only three vessels of over 20 knots flying the national flag – and their importance to the navy in time of war was officially recognised. The loss would be not of prestige alone but of national security. In passing into foreign hands, moreover, such lines would be taking their business with them, leaving Britain competitively at a sad disadvantage in the Atlantic. True, 40% of White Star tonnage plied elsewhere – to Australasia, for instance. But that circumstance was of little comfort if it helped to spread American competition to other regions. And what if Cunard too changed hands? Already with their new acquisitions the American combine could be calculated to enjoy possession or control of 114 steamers of British registry, representing 816,364 g.r.t. When to this was added their eighteen non-British steamers, aggregating a further 133,918 g.r.t., it was evident that our rivals had succeeded in compiling the largest commercial armada the world had yet seen, equal in tonnage almost to the entire merchant marine of France and comprising nearly one-third of all dry cargo tonnage then deployed in the North American transatlantic carrying trade.

Worse news, however, was to follow. By summer reports were circulating that the two great German shipping companies, owners of the fastest vessels then on the New York route, had entered into some kind of trading alliance with the already huge American consortium. To British ears such tidings bore strong political overtones. But what concerns us here is the nature of the new German-American association and its commerical potentialities.

NOTES

1 H. O. O'Hagan: *Leaves from my Life* (1929), i, 383–5; Francis E. Hyde: *Shipping Enterprise and Management, 1830–1939: Harrison's of Liverpool* (1967), p. 31; *Fairplay* 34:745 (3 May 1900).
2 Tonnage figures used throughout these pages indicate space measurement in gross registered tons (1 gross ton = 100 cu ft of permanently enclosed space) and bear no relation to displacements, net or deadweight tonnage.
3 *Ibid.*, 34:353, 422, 654, 696 (1 and 8, Mar., 19 and 26 April 1900).
4 See n. 4, chapter 5 below.
5 *Fairplay* 34:741, 831, 918, 987 (3, 17 and 31 May, 14 June 1900); O'Hagan: *op. cit.*, i, 385–6.
6 Quoted in US Commissioner of Navigation: *Annual Report* for 1901 (Washington, D. C.), p. 321. See also Ellerman's letter to the *Daily Mail* of 8 May 1901.
7 *Fairplay* 36:198 (31 Jan. 1901). For a portrait of Griscom see L. Perry in *The World's Work* II (1902), pp. 857–60.
8 27 US Stat. 27 (10 May 1892).
9 *Fairplay* 35:911 (7 Nov. 1900).
10 See E. H. Meade's chapter on 'The US shipbuilding trust' in W. Z. Ripley: *Trusts, Pools and Corporations* (New York, 1916).
11 Report of the US Merchant Marine Commission (1905), Senate Doc. 2755, 58 Congress, 3 Session, *passim*; see particularly the evidence of William H. Cramp in vol. ii, pp. 423–5, of W. G. Sickel, ii, 723, and of B. N. Baker himself, iii, 1873.
12 US Commissioner of Navigation, *Annual Report* for 1901, pp. 23–4.
13 *Loc. cit.*, p. 34.
14 Report of the US Merchant Marine Commission (1905), selectively quoted in Walter T. Dunmore: *Shipping Subsidies* (Boston and New York, 1907) pp. 31 ff.
15 For a detailed and balanced discussion of the pros and cons of shipping conferences at this period see J. Russell Smith: 'Ocean freight rates and their control through combination', *Political Science Quarterly* 21:2 pp. 261 ff. (1906) and Daniel Marx, Jr.: *International Shipping Cartels* (Princeton, 1953), pp. 53 ff.

16 Report of the Select Committee on the Causes of the Reduction of American Tonnage (1870), House of Representatives Report 28, 41 Cong., 2 sess.
17 5 US Stat. 748 (3 Mar. 1845).
18 9 US Stat. 266 (3 Aug. 1848); *Parliamentary Papers* xcv (1852–53) p. 2; 9 US Stat. 621 (3 Mar. 1851); 10 US Stat. 61 (30 Aug.1852).
19 Statement of Cramp to US Merchant Marine Commission (27 May 1904), *loc. cit.*, pp. 453–8, quoting his own article in *North Atlantic Review*, July–Dec. 1902.
20 *Congressional Record*, 51 Cong., 1 sess., 6907–14; 2 sess., 3350 ff., 3504–7, 7186–9, the debate leading to 26 US Stat. 830–2 (1891). See also Griscom's testimony to US Senate, 56 Cong., 1 sess., *Miscellaneous Documents*, vol. 149, pp. 100–9.
21 See J. D. Richardson: *Messages and Papers of the Presidents*, vol. x, 16, 41, 135, 215, 396, 429–430.
22 24 US Stat. 215–6 (4 Aug. 1886).
23 S. Report 201, 57 Cong., 1 ses., pp. 1 ff.
24 *Congressional Record*, 56 Cong., 2 sess., 34:255.
25 *National Review* 39:466 (May 1902); *Fairplay* 36:863 (23 May 1901).
26 *Congressional Record*, 56 Cong., 2 sess., 255, 1335–40, 1607–19; 57 Cong., 1 sess., 2302.
27 *New York Times*, 21 Feb. 1902, letter of B. N. Baker.
28 *Commercial and Financial Chronicle*, 11 Feb. 1899, p. 282.
29 E.g. that in *Fairplay* 36:198 (31 Jan. 1901), though incorrectly relating the rumoured merger to recent deals of the House of Morgan with J. J. Mill (railroads) and J. D. Rockefeller (oil).
30 *Ibid.*, 36:720, 757 and 782 (2 and 9 May 1901).
31 *Ibid.*, 36:820 (16 May 1901).
32 *Ibid.*, 37:481–2 (26 Sept. 1901); *Daily Express*, 15 Oct. 1901; *Liverpool Daily Post*, 16 Oct. and 16 Nov. 1901, 24 Mar. and 26 Apr. 1902.
33 Herbert Jefferson: *Viscount Pirrie of Belfast* (Belfast, n.d.) p. 266.
34 *Fairplay* 41:470 (24 Sept. 1903). For the disposition of T. H. Ismay's estate at his death, and other personal particulars, see Wilton J. Oldham: *The Ismay Line* (Liverpool, 1961) ch. x. Ismay's widow signed the agreement between White Star and the J. P. Morgan Co. on 22 May 1902. For a typical British outcry at loss of the line to America see S. Allingham in the *Nautical Magazine* lxxi (1902), pp. 591–607.

CHAPTER 3

German accession

A partnership of any sort between the American and German shipping worlds at the opening of the twentieth century was, on first sight, an odd development. For to turn, as we now must, from the one to the other is to move between almost diametric opposites. Where the American shipping industry was, both in nature and location, widely if thinly spread, Germany's was extremely concentrated. German competitiveness at sea as the nineteenth century neared its end had become inspissated in the liner trade of the North Atlantic, where the USA had not for decades offered Britain serious rivalry. Whereas the United States marine received little encouragement from Washington, that of the newly founded German Empire was deliberately fostered by Berlin. Again, while ship construction in the USA was the pawn of her heavy industry, in Germany the two operated in harmonious accord.

One important factor making for Germany's concentration of her mercantile marine was plainly geographic. Her single shoreline embraced only two major shipping outlets, the originally sovereign and always rival Hanseatic cities of Hamburg and Bremen. Although by entering the Zollverein in 1888 they had come to terms with Bismarck's empire, their respective steamship companies had already established themselves without government aid, and now between them mustered well over half the new nation's mercantile fleet. On the Elbe in 1847 had been founded the Hamburg-Amerikanische Paketfahrt (Hapag). In that year the Hamburg-America Line dispatched its first vessel, the sailing ship *Deutschland*, to New York. Ten years later the Norddeutscher-Lloyd (NGL) was formed in Bremerhaven, thirty miles downstream from Bremen on the Weser and farthest west of German deep-water ports. In 1860 NGL signed its first mail contracts with Britain and the United States, the latter superseding an agreement entered into fourteen years earlier by Congress's authority with an American contractor. By 1860 Germany's sail fleet had been almost completely superseded by steam, and within another twenty years she made her debut in the transatlantic express service.[1]

A second concentrative influence was the timing of this maritime expansion. It coincided with the commencement of the era of the great liner trades, for which pre-eminently the bulk of Germany's modern shipping was therefore designed. Whereas perhaps as much as 40% of Britain's merchant tonnage was in tramps, such independent enterprises bulked much smaller in Germany's – a structural difference reflected in the high degree of marine ownership in the hands of relatively few companies. Nineteen of these in 1905 reputedly owned and controlled three-quarters of the German merchant fleet, the seven largest of them accounting for 60% of it. If concentration implied solidarity, the young empire of Bismarck was well placed to resist outside competition on the high seas.

Her own competitive strength lay at the turn of the century on the North Atlantic, drawn thither by the vast phenomenon of westward migration. Both Hapag and NGL had found their modern fortunes on the steerage traffic supplied by the efflux, unstaunched till 1914, of emigrants from northern and eastern Europe, for which their respective North Sea ports were the natural outlets. For these two companies of Hamburg and Bremen the imperial government in the early 1890s awarded a valuable concession. It entrusted to them the operation of the special sanitary control stations along the empire's eastern borders, through which must pass the would-be emigrant from central or eastern Europe on his way to the New World. His transit permits across German territory might easily, if unofficially, be made conditional upon his agreeing to make the Atlantic passage aboard a German vessel. Not until 1906 was a comparable Russian shipping line established. German control of shipping agencies in Austro-Hungary, indeed, exerted a strong influence over Italian lines.

Both Hapag and NGL, however, did business of a global nature of which the North Atlantic was only a part. Much of this, particularly in Africa, was related to their country's recent colonial expansion. Neither company loomed very large as yet in the great bulk cargo trades of the world; but, in addition to their steerage traffic, each began in 1880 to concentrate on providing liner services of quality. Their New York services, begun on parallel lines, had thereafter tended to diverge for reasons inherent in their respective geographic locations. North German Lloyd, which was also prominent on Far Eastern and Australian routes, began to specialise in fast passenger traffic. In 1883, under the chairmanship of J. G. Lohmann, it established a weekly express service from Bremerhaven to New York with the single-screw *Elbe*, Clyde-built and the first German challenger via Southampton to British steamers from Liverpool. By 1891 NGL's New York service was twice weekly, and most of its steerage business was being relegated to a subsidiary, the Roland Line. Hapag's strength, by contrast, then lay in slower vessels with excellent first-class quarters and enormous capacity for migrants and freight.

Both companies had raised themselves on a base of British-built tonnage, albeit not necessarily of the most advanced design. Native yards lacked the experience that comes with opportunity. In 1867 the Reichstag had indeed commanded that all German war vessels be built at home, and by the late 1870's Germany's yards were in fact supplying some foreign navies. But little business of importance was put their way by native shipping lines. NGL's founder and first chairman, H. H. Meier, had insisted that all his line's major orders should go to John Elder of Glasgow. Similarly, Hamburg-America looked to Clydeside or Birkenhead, and strong pressure from the imperial Ministry of Marine was required to induce Hapag in the late 1880's to have two large steamers built at home.

That decade nevertheless saw the beginning of a growing alliance of German mercantile with imperial and naval policies, with the adoption of a series of expedients designed to foster native shipping. A tariff law of 1879 had placed on the duty-free list all materials imported for the purpose of shipbuilding and repairing. It was in addition the policy of the Imperial Railways Office since 1895 that preferential rates should be granted by German railways for carriage of such materials, and also to manufacturers exporting goods on through bills of lading. German shippers were thus enabled to quote very low combined sea-and rail rates – a concession reckoned by one British expert in 1902 as giving the German exporter an advantage of £1 per ton over his United Kingdom rival.[2] It was also widely rumoured that German lines employed intelligence agents to identify and attract consigners of goods hitherto shipped in British vessels.

As for the positive subvention, an Act passed at Bismarck's insistence in 1881 provided the first contract subsidy for vessels constructed at home, of which – though it carried no 'bonification' in the Atlantic – North German Lloyd began to avail itself five years later, to the tune of £85,000, for its Far Eastern services. Though reckoned in itself a costly failure, this subvention was in 1898 and again in 1901 raised in scale and widened in scope. In that latter year alone the imperial government was calculated to be spending (including its payment for transatlantic mail services) some £440,470 in order to make its shipping lines competitive with the British (representing a subsidy per net ton of 4s. 6d against the British government's 2s. 2d). Of this figure it was calculable that NGL received in that year an aggregate government subvention of £280,000. Though no part of this was paid directly on account of the company's North Atlantic services, in toto it was estimated by British observers to represent the equivalent of 7% upon its existing capital.[3] Thus seemingly fortified, and possessing a geographical position which gave it the whole of northern Europe, including the British Isles, for its gathering ground, NGL was able to maintain vessels that exceeded the commercially profitable speed by which the operations of British and European lines were governed.

One must not, however, exaggerate the probable financial effect of these various expedients. The quantity of German cargo, for example, moved on through bills of lading was after all relatively minute: shipbuilding materials, it will be recalled, were admitted free of duty into Britain also. This in any case would benefit the builders rather than the operators, and even so would not significantly reduce the high costs of German shipbuilding. As for direct subsidy, during the 1890's this was confined to less than 4% of Germany's tonnage, and any benefit was probably offset by being limited to vessels built at home. Despite a subsidy of 44·3 million marks for its East Asian and Australian services during the decade 1886–96 (a rather higher rate of subvention than P.& O were receiving from the British Treasury in the same area) North German Lloyd made a net loss of 5·25 million marks over these routes during that period.[4] It is noteworthy, moreover, that where NGL was most formidably competitive – in the North Atlantic – it was receiving (a very small mail subsidy apart) no subvention at all.

Yet it would be true to say that these national policies for fostering native shipping, together with extensive construction orders for the growing imperial navy, had by the end of the nineteenth century so successfully induced a climate of maritime expansion as to render Germany's shipbuilders capable of meeting, at a price, most of her needs, whether in warships, express liners or the necessary variety of small craft. Not only was this burgeoning industry, like the American, a highly concentrated affair: unlike the American it was being served by native iron and steel industries, principally in Westphalia and Silesia, in a deliberate and effective way. Technical advances followed. The Vulkan yard at Stettin and the Schichau yard at Elbing, which twenty years earlier had been struggling for recognition, could by 1900 be compared, if not in volume at least in efficiency, with anything in Britain. From 1895 onwards, installations at Hamburg, Bremen, Elbing, Danzig and Stettin were so enormously enlarged and improved as to suggest to the British commercial attaché in Berlin the possibility that Germany might soon be taking the lead in marine engineering.[5] Certainly there was no British equivalent of NGL's new experimental tank for ship models at Bremen.

Stimulation of another kind was imparted by the sharpening contest during the 1890's between the NGL and Hamburg-America. The early 1880's had found the latter lying somewhat becalmed, compelled to watch the Bremen line skim the cream of the saloon business while the Elbe remained inadequate for the new express steamers of the size its rival was rapidly acquiring. Amalgamation with the Carr Line, however, brought Hapag an unconvenanted boon in the person of a young Jew, Albert Ballin, son of a small Hamburg broker. From the first, Ballin's experience had lain in the transatlantic trade, connected as had been his career at the start with an emigration agency which dealt with the American Line in Hamburg. During the 1870's Ballin had also close contacts with Henry Wilding, head of the Liverpool firm representing the American Line in the United Kingdom. In 1886, at the age of thirty, Ballin had been appointed head of Hapag's North Atlantic passenger department, and two years later a member of its board of directors.

Thereupon a revitalised Hapag expanded even more rapidly than North German Lloyd. New services, and new arrangements with British lines, not only gave it a clear ascendancy in the emigrant traffic, but Ballin adopted what may be called the White Star conception of the most profitable type of liner service. Four twin-screw flyers were ordered, to eclipse NGL's best. Paradigm of these was the luxurious *August Viktoria*, from Vulkan in 1889 though extensively remodelled by Harland & Wolff in 1897. She was followed by the *Columbia* from Birkenhead, the *Normannia* from Fairfield on the Clyde, and – best of the four – the *Fürst Bismarck*, also from Stettin. This quartet gave Hapag not only its due share of the German mail subsidy but the best-balanced express service in the Atlantic passenger saloon trade, as to the profitability of which Ballin was thereby able to convince his fellow directors. NGL retaliated with the *Kaiser Wilhelm der Grosse*, first non-British ship to capture the Blue Riband since the ill-fated Collins Line. Hamburg-America's rejoinder was the *Deutschland* (1900), which, though never very satisfactory, carried the trophy to Hamburg: Bremen's riposte came next year with the still bigger and faster *Kronprinz Wilhelm*, victor in 1902. In that year also, Hapag's new docks at Cuxhaven, adequate for the largest liners entering the Elbe, came into regular use.

Although the volume of this maritime growth came nowhere near Britain's, it was nevertheless remarkable. In 1870 it had scarcely been possible to regard Germany as possessing a merchant marine at all – an insignificant steam tonnage of less than 100,000 g.r.t. Yet already by the early 1880's her two chief lines were between them accounting for some 30% of the total westbound passenger traffic on the North Atlantic and rapidly encroaching on the British hegemony there. By 1891 *Shipping World* could plausibly warn that 'Today there is no question that the chief competitor we have on the seas is Germany'. Dominant only in the North Atlantic, she had nevertheless by the end of that decade secured at least a foothold in many other major trading areas also. In the first year of the new century Ballin was able to estimate the size of his company's fleet at about 650,000 g.r.t. – the largest in the world under a single flag and serving the USA and Canada, Mexico and South America, the West Indies, the Pacific coast, Asia and the Mediterranean. Slightly more numerous (when subsidiaries were added), and no less ubiquitous, was NGL's fleet of 150 steamers. Careful readers of *Lloyd's Register* for 1902 could discover that Germany as a whole ranked, by quantity of shipping owned, second only to the United Kingdom, and furthermore that her merchant tonnage had almost exactly doubled over the last ten years. 'For the first time since the age of steam', Sir John Clapham has said of that period, 'there existed a merchant navy which could compare itself with that of England without appearing ridiculous'. 'In point of quality', he added, 'comparison was far from ridiculous'. [6] (After only ten years of the new century had elapsed, Germany's technological advance was to manifest itself in the genius of Rudolf Diesel.) A new great national enterprise was even – index of the changed times! – buying up and absorbing whole British fleets. In 1899 the Holt and East India lines, and in 1900 the Scottish Oriental Steamship Co., had passed into German hands. The new shipping surge, moreover, when translated into figures, could be read as the multiplication of Germany's exports by $2\frac{1}{4}$ in value over the three decades preceding 1902.

Growth of this new rival in size, scope and speed drew dire prophecies from the more chauvinist of British press organs, notably the *Daily Mail* and the *National Review*. Even so orthodox a free-trader as Sir Robert Giffen, respected statistician at the Board of Trade, warned the Select Committee on Steamship Subsidies of 1902 about what must follow from the circumstance that 'subsidised steamers which are really part of the German navy are being nursed on the internal business of the British Empire'. What impact the American combine was to make upon the great free trade/protection controversy in Britain will be for consideration in chapter 6. Suffice it that the tendency of some to link German success to governmental subsidy was not taken lightly by the *Times*, despite a letter of reasoned and forthright denial to its columns from Ballin himself.[7]

Yet in the end a better balanced view was, as we shall see, reached by the majority of the select committee when it reported. Its chairman, Evelyn Cecil, in the summer of 1902 made a personal visit to the East African coast to see for himself how far the subidised German East Africa Line had been able to push trade there. It was observed that even this area, where Germany had a virtual monopoly of direct shipping services, was a far from profitable one for her.[8] Generally speaking, alarm and pessimism were not typical of the British press as a whole, no responsible organ of which seriously supported the thesis of trade war. As for the British shipping world, it was not so much worried by German aims as irritated by German methods of pursuing them. Most British trade journals of the time show a desire for peaceful relations with a commercial rival which still found it prudent to renew annually the 'most favoured nation' status for us and our colonies, whither virtually a quarter of her exported produce was sent. One could not seriously maintain that globally her competition was cutting into our share, which at all points reflected the general increase in world trade recovering, since 1897, from ten years of slump.

True, critics could point out that the rate of growth in German exports, like that of the USA's, was now fast exceeding Britain's; that the visible trade balance between ourselves and Germany was perceptibly tilting in the latter's favour; and that her industries stood accused of dumping abroad and sheltering at home behind high tariff walls which were (it was rumoured) about to be raised again in 1902. Yet Germany remained our second largest (after India) market for exports and re-exports; the greater part of this trade – so lucrative for our own shippers, bankers and commodity dealers – was still carried in British bottoms; and the greater part of our rival's expanding merchant marine (including Hapag and NGL) was insured at Lloyd's of London. All in all, and whatever the jingo press might proclaim, Anglo-German trade was of complementary benefit sufficient to render the prospect of escalatory conflict, mercantile or other, highly unattractive. Palpable competition was confined to particular sectors of our industry at particular junctures. British producers of iron, steel and machinery might support Chamberlain's call for reciprocal protection: our cotton industry would not.

So the cause for *Angst* in certain sections of the press, Unionist as well as radical, was not German maritime expansion *per se*.

Rather, it was the new and peculiarly strident tone of Teutonic competitiveness and, above all, the manner in which it was either linked with a concomitant naval aggressiveness or appeared as part and parcel of a thrustful anti-British diplomatic and political offensive. To understand the ground for British dismay when German maritime competitors (as we shall see) now ganged up with American, it is necessary to study, however summarily, the changed nature of Anglo-German relations in a wider sense as the old century ended.

So long as Bismarck had been at the helm, his attitude towards Britain, if anti-Gladstonian in animus, had remained pragmatic. Concerned though he might be to discredit the 'English influence' within the politics of his new nation, and to that end well aware how popular an anti-British colonial policy was, yet internal unification rather than overseas expansion had always first claim on the Chancellor's attention. This unification we had not discouraged: Gladstone indeed had even welcomed Germany's few colonial bids.

With the accession of Wilhelm II, however, to an office upon which the imperial constitution laid great responsibilities and powers, the context and climate of Anglo-German relations had distinctly changed. To the new Kaiser the pursuit of *Weltmacht* appeared the inescapable consequence of the growth of a national already outstripping France in population and national product, both of which now demanded additional territory and expanded markets. Influenced theoretically by Mahan and practically by the conclusion he drew from the Spanish-American and South African wars and from the French surrender at Fashoda, Wilhelm was particularly jealous of the special niche he believed to be reserved for Britain in American esteem. Willingly he lent his ear to new and aggressive organisations – the Kolonialverein, the Nationalverein and the Verein für Handelsgeographie. Colonial envy was fuelled by resentment against the historical advantage enjoyed by a power which seemed to lie athwart Germany's path wherever in the world – in China, in East or West Africa, in Zanzibar or Samoa – she turned. Anglophobia, chronic in Berlin, had spread and risen to fever pitch during the Boer War, deliberately fostered through the close connection between the government and its Foreign Press Office. From the first Wilhelm had been virtually his own Minister of Marine, shaping a maritime establishment increasingly *königlich und kaiserlich* in aspect.

To implement a highly personal rule the Kaiser had appointed new men sympathetic to his objective of full-scale *Weltpolitik*. They included Bülow, the admirer of Treitschke, as Secretary of State; and notably Admiral von Tirpitz, a bitter Anglophobe with grandiose schemes for using a vastly expanded navy as a 'political power factor' against Britain. If Tirpitz's elevation in 1892 manifested official predilection for a Big Navy policy, his transference three years later to the secretaryship of the Reichsmarineamt was taken to signify that both commercial and naval expansion was motivated by identical considerations of *Machtpolitik*. Under two Navy Laws a programme for rapidly enlarging the imperial battle fleet and its port installations progressed from 1893 to 1903, whereby some £80 million was expended in native yards to the great profit of Alfred Krupp and N. H. Mulliner. (Was Germany, asked the *Times*, preparing for 'a naval Sadowa'?) The first Navy Law of April 1898 provided for seventeen new ships of the line and twice that number of smaller armed vessels. But it was the second Navy Bill of July 1900, envisaging a virtual doubling of her battle fleet, which made German motives clear beyond doubt. Its preamble explicitly linked naval expansion with commercial: and three days after its passage Wilhelm emphasised his patronal interest in the latter by sending North German Lloyd a congratulatory telegram which spoke of imposing 'peace on the water as on the land'.[9]

The objective, risky though it might be, was undoubtedly to hold Britain diplomatically in check by the creation of a potential threat to her supremacy at sea. The emperor's demands for equal entitlement *(Gleichberechtung)* in world trade were to be pursued and if necessary enforced by naval influence *(Seegeltung)*. *Flottenpolitik* was to be an instrument of blackmail. The British Admiralty, ever attentive to technical design, observing that the vaunted High Seas Fleet had sacrificed sailing range to gun power, armour and speed, concluded that the projected armada was in fact intended to menace home waters whose protection was the Royal Navy's first task. German and British naval policies were therefore revealed as logically imcompatible, and an expensive naval race was in prospect.

But just because German statesmen cherished the hope that a big fleet would compel Britain to open up her world markets to penetration, need that notion lead to confrontation in a more extreme form? Correspondingly, must a British movement for tariff reform necessarily entail Germanophobia? Opinion in Westminster and Whitehall was divided. Campbell-Bannerman and Grey warned of the German menace, as did certain prominent naval officers such as Sir Charles Beresford, who was also MP for Woolwich. Others, like Selborne, First Lord of the Admiralty, believed that the only possible alternative to a spiralling naval budget, namely an understanding of some sort with Germany, was not unattainable. Chamberlain as Colonial Secretary especially pressed at first for a German alliance. But when in a celebrated speech at Leicester in late November 1899 he had referred to 'the natural alliance between ourselves and the great German empire', his proposal had been met with apathy from his audience and a 'granite' response from Bülow in a Reichstag so audibly hostile that Edward VII was pressed to cancel a visit by the Prince of Wales to Berlin. So Balfour's Cabinet in 1901 were disinclined to the idea of a formal Anglo-German alliance, the Prime Minister himself remaining concilitory but, like his uncle before him, mistrustful.

These debates about *rapprochement*, it must be recalled, had proceeded in a climate of opinion increasingly sceptical of German goodwill. Officials living or travelling abroad – Spring-Rice in Berlin, Rumbold in Vienna, Sir Henry Drummond-Wolf and Lord Cromer – reported systematic attempts to poison Anglo-American relations. Throughout the South African war it was believed, and not implausibly, that the Press Bureau on the Wilhelmstrasse encouraged its agencies in the United States deliberately to foment pro-Boer feeling there. Memories revived of the semi-official German campaign in Washington to misrepresent the United Kingdom's attitude during the Spanish-American war – mischief which had mortally grieved the venerable British ambassador, Lord Pauncefote. The much publicised fêting by German-American Republicans of Prince Henry of Prussia on the occasion of the latter's naval visit to New York in February 1902 was regarded here with a suspicion surpassed only when in the following June a squadron under the prince's command paid a friendly visit to Irish waters.[10] That the Kaiser himself was an honorary Admiral of our Fleet and an annual visitor to Cowes did not commensurably reassure.

Meanwhile the Reichmarineamt's new and aggressive tone was naturally imparting itself to steamship companies, subject as these were to a uniquely high degree of State supervision: 'government patronage', observed the *Times*, 'is the breath of their nostrils'. Freight and passenger rates could not be changed without reference to the Chancellor. Sale or hire of subsidised merchant vessels to a foreign power, even in peace, was statutorily forbidden. In war they would be legally liable to government purchase or conscription for use as armed cruisers. The *Deutschland* and the *Kronprinz Wilhelm*, in whose design the Ministry of Marine had had a considerable say, were to be so used in World War I, the latter vessel proving one of Germany's deadliest commerce raiders. Attention was already being drawn in the House of Commons in 1902 to their potential speed as auxiliary cruisers, capable of one and a half knots beyond even the 22 knot *Lucania* and *Campania*, Britain's fastest. What, it was further asked by the *Morning Post*, would German engineers and stokers, at present employed in British merchant ships, do on the outbreak of war?

Close to the Kaiser, in an amity personal as well as official, stood Albert Ballin. Ballin is plausibly represented by his best-known biographer as inexpugnably opposed to both his government's subsidy and its Big Navy programmes. Nevertheless, since many of his contemporaries were by 1902 disposed to regard his country's maritime policy as synonymous with his own, it is important to distinguish in what the latter precisely consisted.

Ballin's strategy, remarkably consistent over the years, was one which deprecated government intervention in any form as costly and inflexible, but strove instead for an ever-increasing share of world shipping trade through skilful use of pooling arrangements to his own company's maximum advantage. It was clearly the best method by which to break into a field where Germany was a latecomer. Seeking to avoid rate wars over the emigrant traffic, upon which his line and NGL so heavily depended, Ballin as a first step had in 1886 sucessfully brought pressure upon British steamship companies to get their agreement to the setting up of a clearing house in Hamburg. Despite British compaints of unfavourable treatment, he thereafter pressed forward towards a wider and more comprehensive 'community of interest' whereby in 1892 the two big German lines came together with the Holland-American and Red Star to form the first North Atlantic passenger line pool or conference.[11] Under this the participants allocated westbound steerage traffic between them, pegged steerage rates at a level which could only be altered by collective consent, and arranged to divide profits in a certain ratio. Though its membership fluctuated, this North Atlantic Steamship Lines Association (as it was called) remained essentially the basis of pooling arrangements in that area up to World War I.

From this conference British liners had at first held aloof, objecting that the portion of steerage traffic proposed to be allotted them (14%) was unfairly small. However, after cholera outbreak in Hamburg in 1893–94 had brought the volume of such trade tumbling down, and with it (in a fall of 50%) the level of fares, seven British companies – the Allan, Allan & State, Anchor, Beaver, Cunard, Dominion and White Star lines – joined the pool in the following year despite a still lower allotment of steerage traffic, in return for an undertaking by its Continental members to withdraw from the Scandinavian trade and to reduce the number of their calls at British ports. The Beaver Line, however, quitted it before the century was out, and Cunard in May 1903.

Thus Ballin's strategy fructified; and eventually a complex network of such agreements was, up to World War I, to cover thirty different lines in respect of various classes of traffic on both west- and eastbound routes. The influence of such compacts on the North Atlantic is, however, notoriously debatable. They probably took the keen edge off rate-cutting, but did not prevent periodic outbursts of competitive aggression by one member or another which, within limits, the British signatories could tolerate and even profit by. Possibly pooling shifted the competitive emphasis away from fares and towards services, so that the participants vied with each other in size and luxury of accommodation – an excess which was to rebound sharply (and not least upon the framers of the American combine) once the shipping boom of 1900 was over. The conference system, it is generally agreed, enhanced stability of passenger fares; though these were, in any case, less volatile than freight rates. The profit on steerage moreover being very small, its allocation by fixed quotas may have afforded sufficient guarantee of stability in volume of traffic to allow the transatlantic trade to be built up with more assurance than would have been possible otherwise.[12]

Nevertheless it was this determination of Ballin's to expand the community-of-interest principle which was to bring him into early contact with the Americans. To Baker in 1891 he proposed that the latter's Atlantic Transport Co. should take up shares in Hapag, with representation on its Hamburg board, and that Baker himself should supervise Hamburg-America's New York agency. Ballin's purpose, as he candidly stated, was to obtain for his own company a centre of interest in the United States comparable with that enjoyed by components of the Baltimore enterprise. What he did not feel necessary to observe, but which may be legitimately inferred, was that such an arrangement could incidentally give Hapag a competitive foothold in Britain also, whose shipping played a large though indirect part in the European continental business. Because of opposition, chiefly on financial grounds, from Hapag's directorate this scheme never fully materialised.[13] Baker's Baltimore headquarters, however, did undertake to act as agents for Hamburg-America there; the Red Star component of his company, as we have seen, joined Ballin's pooling arrangement of 1892; and when the latter was renewed in 1899, so did the American Line too (which, since it plied to English ports, partly compensated for the British lines' withdrawal).

Another thread led to Pirrie in Belfast. With him Ballin in 1898 reached an agreement under which Harland & Wolff agreed to keep one slipway in their yards always at Hamburg-America's disposal, and to build for Hapag under a particular type of cost-plus contract. This latter arrangement, by keeping Hapag *au courant* with the most advanced British designs, helped the company to get ahead of its Bremen rival. It would seem to have been Pirrie moreover who, disliking the Baker-Ellerman deal contemplated in 1900, brought Baker and Ballin together in London to discuss possible counter-measures. This meeting in turn may have first aroused Ballin's interest in the proposed American combination, whose attractions for him will by now appear intelligible. An international combine on this scale would provide the logically next step in widening the 'community of interest' he so pertinaciously sought in the Atlantic. And since it included one or more British lines, it might give Hapag – if the Hamburg company also joined – the connections he coveted in the United Kingdom. To these prospective advantages Ballin's biographer adds a third: attainment of Euro-American co-operation in rationalising the Atlantic cargo trade also, so as to make possible advance planning to cope with those fluctuations in eastbound agricultural exports from season to season according to the size of the American harverst and of European demand. Be that as it may, it was in July 1901 – a year when failure of the American maize crop coincided with temporary economic recession in Germany – that Ballin again met Pirrie, in London, and learnt of the latter's negotiations with the Americans on behalf of White Star. At yet a further meeting the two were joined by Bruce Ismay, and it was resolved that Pirrie should go forthwith to New York to intimate, among other things, Hamburg-America's interest in the project. Seemingly, the loose proposal then conveyed was that the American combine should concentrate on transatlantic business to and from the United Kingdom, and the Germans to and from the remainder of Europe.

When rumours of the proposed American combine had first reached Ballin's ears, he had prepared an analytical memorandum for the Kaiser, at the latter's suggestion, in order to put the German position in perspective.[14] The respective total tonnages, built and building, employable in the North Atlantic services he estimated as follows: British lines 438,566, the Morgan combine 430,000, and the two German lines together 390,000 grt. 'The whole transaction', he remarked of the combine,

> will be represented in the light of a big Anglo-American community of interest agreement, and the fact that it virtually concedes to the United States the control of the North American shipping business will be kept in the dark as far as it is possible to do so.

From Germany's point of view the shipping trust, even if backed by Congressional subsidy, did not of itself constitute a threat.

'The real danger ... threatens from the amalgamation of the American railway interests with those of American shipping'. Railroad interests were expected to be particularly well represented on the syndicate, and Morgan's own recorded remarks while in Europe a few months back had shown the way his mind was working:

> According to his estimates, nearly 70 per cent of the goods which are shipped to Europe from the North Atlantic ports are carried to the latter by the railroads on Through Bills of Lading, and their further transport is entrusted to foreign shipping companies. He and his friends, Morgan added, did not see any reason why the railroad companies should leave it to foreign-owned companies to carry those American goods across the Atlantic. It would be much more logical to bring about an amalgamation of the American railroad and shipping interests for the purpose of securing the whole profits for American capital.

Such an amalgamation would expose foreign shipping companies to the possibility of finding their cargoes from the American hinterland cut off – produce representing, on Morgan's estimate, some 70% of total seaborne freight. Since German North Atlantic lines were less concerned with freight than (e.g.) British, they would be less hard hit in such an eventuality: perhaps for that reason, Ballin's memorandrum to the Kaiser did not propose any specific German response.

After Pirrie's return from New York, however, and subsequent conversations with Wilding in Southampton, it was made clear that Morgan felt Hapag's close relationship with the German government made its formal association with the combine inadvisable if not impossible. What instead appeared feasible was an arrangement whereby J. S. Morgan & Co. in London would, through Ballin's personal brokers in Berlin and Vienna, buy a minority interest in Hapag stock on behalf of Morgan himself, Griscom and Widener; this holding to remain as a purely personal investment should full affiliation of the line not be proceeded to. Steps would be mutually taken to reduce competition. But there could be no question of prejudicing the national independence of Hapag, and no American would sit on its board of trustees. Even this limited bilateral arangement, however, when word of it leaked out, raised a storm of anti-Americanism in the German press and the stock had eventually to be resold. Clearly Ballin would need to consider some alternative method of association which would involve wider discussions with other European lines and, inescapably, with the German government.

Between July 1901 and February 1902, therefore, while matters hung fire in New York, Ballin and Pirrie continued their efforts to enlarge the scope of the combine in Europe. By October the outcome of their labours had taken the form of a draft ten-year compact (later considerably altered) providing for a mutual exchange of shares between the American syndicate and Hapag, to be limited – out of regard for German official and public opinion – to the equivalent of 25% of the latter party's joint-stock capital. The combine agreed not to call at German ports and Hapag to avoid such European ports as were served by the American enterprise. An agreement was entered into for pooling the cabin business, consideration of steerage and cargo being deferred.

Once Hapag's board of trustees had unanimously approved the draft, the consent of the German government was sought. The immediate response was a telegram summoning Ballin on 16th October to the imperial hunting lodge of Hubertusstock near Eberswalde, some forty kilometres north-east of Berlin. There, by his own account, Ballin for more than twenty-four hours explained and defended the proposed agreement in detail to the Kaiser and his Chancellor, Prince Bülow, in highly informal surroundings.[15] In the end Wilhelm was persuaded that the proposed agreement would leave the German lines distinct and intact (unlike the British components of the Morgan syndicate, which faced absorption). On this understanding he assented to the scheme with the provision that the interests of North German Lloyd be adequately safeguarded.

To draw his Bremen rival into negotiations with the Americans, however, was no light task for Ballin. Cautious men were now at the head of NGL. When its far-sighted founder Meier resigned in 1888 he had been succeeded in the chairmanship of the company by a bureaucrat, Consul Georg Plate. The sudden death of the enterprising Lohmann four years later had led to the appointment of Dr Heinrich Wiegand as Director General. Both the newcomers were relatively conservative in temper, and initially inclined to scepticism in the face of

Ballin's solemn warning – based on what he probably believed at that juncture to be sound information from Wilding – that behind the Morgan combine, if not precisely within it, stood the big eastern railroad companies. NGL moreover had recently undertaken (as we have seen) very heavy capital expenditure in displacing older units of its fleet with modern, and was in no position to incur heavy financial risk. Nevertheless its top officials were persuaded, albeit with deep reservations, to meet the Americans in London in early November 1901, and then to travel to New York to consider a definitive settlement the following February. A copy of the draft agreements, as jointly negotiated at these two encounters, was supplied to the British Admiralty by one of the parties, Bruce Ismay, representing White Star.

The British government's knowledge of the Germano-American negotiations, however, was before long to be supplemented in a much more intimate fashion. On 19th and 21st May 1902 the First Lord of the Admiralty, Lord Selborne, wrote in some excitment to his ministerial colleagues Joseph Chamberlain, at the Colonial Office, and Gerald Balfour, President of the Board of Trade and brother of the Conservative leader, enclosing 'some remarkable documents' which he had 'acquired confidentially from a new and quite unexpected source'. These proved to be copies of the agreements drafted at the meetings of 6th November 1901 and 15th February 1902, and (in an English translation Selborne had had made) of the letters which on both occasions had passed between Plate and Wiegand on the one hand in London or New York, and their NGL colleagues in Bremen. Textually these drafts differed little from those already supplied by Ismay – a circumstance which, together with their internal consistency, led all three Ministers to accept the accompanying correspondence as authentic also. The source of the information does not appear: that Selborne described them as 'new and quite unexpected' suggests that it was not the British secret service. His translator had not sustained the level lately set by Edmund Gosse at the Board of Trade. Nevertheless these documents, to quote Selborne's opinion, 'throw remarkable light on the whole transaction', yielding the government a wealth of confidential particulars.[16]

And it is chiefly upon them that our reconstruction of the two conferences draws here.

To Ballin's approaches NGL, it seems, were at first cool and sceptical if not hostile. On 5th November 1901 Chairman Plate met Ballin and his Hapag colleague Dr Ecker in London, and over lunch Ballin handed him a copy of Hamburg-America's draft agreement with the American combine. The reason for concluding it, Ballin explained, was not Hapag's lack of funds but 'their desire to avoid the immense sacrifices which opposition to the American Combination would impose upon them, and for which neither the Government nor the banks would find the necessary money'. Their motive was twofold: hope of gain by rationalisation of shipping deployment, and recognition that resistance was futile. Afterwards the Germans adjourned to Pirrie's London residence for a meeting with Griscom, his brother, and Wilding. There the draft was read and quickly approved by both parties. Plate was told that it had already been approved in detail ('although at first violently opposed') by Hapag's board of directors, and that its main tenor was agreeable to Morgan though the latter had not yet seen its precise contents.

Plate insisted that NGL stood unsympathetically towards the whole question of affiliation and reserved their position. He himself had come over with the absolute conviction that such an arrangement was undesirable. The meeting then went to work upon him. Pirrie, for White Star and Harland & Wolff, emphasised the point that rationalisation of shipping was needed to prevent waste. To this end he lauded the scheme as 'magnificent' and 'ingenious'.

> His partner, Bruce Ismay, had declared the whole thing for a swindle and a humbug, but he knew better now ... They were reckoning on obtaining subsidies (from Congress) but had no doubt that also without subsidies would the thing pay well.

White Star (whose annual average earnings for the last few years Ballin quoted to Plate as 26%), by throwing in their lot with the venture, were bowing to the inevitable, having found that 'all' Americans railroad lines with termini at the North Atlantic ports were 'controlled' by the combine. They had indeed – Griscom corroborated – bound themselves in writing to the Morgan enterprise, which Ballin described as 'overpowering', 'irresistible', and commanding enormous resources. As to the future of Cunard, statements seem to have been ambivalent. Ballin 'pleaded for the taking-over of the Cunard line in order to remove every cause for friction'. On the other hand Plate was also told that it and the Holland-America Line would not be discussed at present; alternatively, that they were to be 'starved into surrender'. The general project, he was given to understand, was conceived about eighteen years ago, and the moment to carry it out had now come.

Accepting all this as gospel truth, Plate was as impressed as it was intended he should be. Enclosing a copy of the Hapag-Morgan draft agreement, he wrote back next day to Wiegand 'with a heavy heart':

> It appears from all that is said as if the Combination disposes over enormous means ... We committed a grave mistake by not taking Ballin's communication more seriously ... The ground is so completely cut away beneath our feet that I cannot see how we can defend ourselves.

He confessed to being made 'very uneasy' by the 'undeniable consideration that we would find ourselves in a hopeless position which the care for our shareholders' interests and even perhaps patriotic considerations bid us leave. If our first reaction was wrong, must we not now admit it?[17]

Parenthetically, we may note two small oddities in this long letter of Plate's. One is his recorded impression that 'the leading spirit in this gigantic undertaking is Rockefeller' – an inexplicable misunderstanding. The other is the remark that 'Ballin is the only one who has seen from the first how the land lay – our dear friend Schwab has left us nicely in the lurch': a comment implying that NGL's chief source of information hitherto had been the promotor of the disastrous American shipbuilding trust.[18]

Plate's report had the desired effect of bringing North German Lloyd into the discussions as an interested party. On 13th November Wiegand dined with his opposite number from Hapag in the Kaiser's presence at Potsdam. For a time, it would appear, NGL canvassed a proposal that the two German lines might better defend themselves against international competition on the North Atlantic by persuading the imperial government to set up, with the help of private funds, a corporation somewhat similar to the existing Preussische Seehandlung: but Ballin, viewing State interference as anathema, rejected this outright.[19] In early December, accordingly, representatives of the two German companies came together to something nearer the draft Morgan-Hapag terms. After they had discussed them with Pirrie at a meeting in Cologne, these proposals were ready for joint submission to the Americans in the final negotiations, in New York in mid-February. By then Morgan's arrangements with White Star were being satisfactorily concluded. For a detailed account of these New York meetings we again rely on the purloined copy of the correspondence of NGL's representative. This Wiegand, having crossed the Atlantic in the company of Ballin and Tietgens, chairman of Hapag's directorate, reports back to Plate.

During 13th and 14th February the Germans' discussions were mainly with Wilding, Griscom and his brother, Widener and Baker. The most important session, held in Griscom's office on the fifteenth floor of the Empire Building, was on the morning of the 14th. Here they were joined by Charles Steele, a junior partner of J. P. Morgan Co., 'who conducts this matter on behalf of the firm', and was believed to be simultaneously in negotiation with Pirrie and Ismay. (Steele was later to join the board of the projected combine.) First, gaps in the Germans' information were filled. It was confirmed that the White Star and Dominion lines would be bought by the trust, which would probably be registered in the United States. No figures were yet available as to purchase prices or joint capital. But it was explained that purchase of the two British lines would not be wholly in cash but in shares, both preference and ordinary, in the new trust. Further capital was to be raised by the issue of debentures, 'so as to build new ships under the expected new American subsidies Act'. Ismay (reported Wiegand) had been 'very unwilling to entertain the idea at all, and only did so at last because he had no choice, while Pirrie evidently has joined a combination from which he expects great advantages, with a light heart'.

Less certain was the vexed question of the combine's relationship to the railroad companies, which apparently still awaited Morgan's decision. 'When this is mentioned', noted Wiegand, 'the Americans smile knowingly at each other'. The interest of the Pennsylvania Railroad was obvious, since it owned (so the

Germans believed) the American Line, and would therefore obtain a proportion of shares in the trust. Yet it seemed equally obvious that the Pennsylvania alone would be unable to offer it any substantial economic backing; and

> throughout the negotiations it has never been allowed to appear that any considerable support was expected from the railroad companies, so that we may safely assume that they have definitely dropped the absurd idea that the relations with the railways would appear a dangerous factor to us, influencing our final decision.

Wiegand's relief in turn bred scepticism about the whole American project, 'whose staying capacity I do not even believe in'. For one thing, they had not got the right man to head it in the States (presumably one sufficiently conversant with European shipping matters). 'That Griscom is not the man is evident to all who know him'; and Wilding would have his hands full with the European end. Wiegand suspected, moreover, that an undertaking which hoped to draw its strength from monopoly was inherently committed to an endless series of attempts to suppress competition by buying up potential rivals,

> and in spite of this they cannot prevent new competition from springing up. Consequently the whole develops on a gigantic, monstrous scale, and loses the possibility of uniform direction.

After these first meetings Wiegand reported his mature view of the trust as:

> an ephemeral creation, offering nevertheless for a certain number of years advantages which, in so far as they are not counterbalanced by substantial drawbacks, it is the task of the not yet concluded arrangements to secure.

A half-hour visit to Morgan's house with Griscom and Steele on the following day did not greatly modify this impression, though it threw new light into certain corners. Morgan himself the Germans found 'quiet', 'temperate', of 'calm and sane intellect'.

> He has an energetic face, with clever rather restless eyes dominating the rest of his features ... It seems clear that all Morgan's sea-conquering plans, of which so much has been heard, are nothing but sheer imagination ... According to him he has been forced step by step by circumstances ... It appears that Griscom and Pirrie negotiated first with the German lines in order to bring the matter before Morgan in this wise that we were ready to work with them ...

> Morgan and Steele are clearly not the motive forces, but the people of the American-Atlantic Transport Line *[sic]* who hope to extract themselves from doubtful affairs and to do better by the help of Morgan's influence, and they want our help to this end.[20]

Another point about the final composition of the combine remained to be cleared up. At the negotiations of 13th and 14th February Ballin had 'pleaded very earnestly with the Americans to include the Cunard and Holland-American lines', and at their meeting with Morgan on the 15th he reiterated this plea 'in order to have the whole thing complete'. Ballin's anxiety about Holland-America is intelligible enough. Comparatively small though the line still was, its fleet had doubled in carrying capacity during the preceding four years and now included five twin-screw steamers of the most recent design. More significantly, its location at Rotterdam made it strategically a rival on the same northern trade routes as the big German companies. Joining the Morgan combine would yield Ballin little satisfaction if, having thereby tied his own company's hand by trade agreements and area allocations with the Americans, he were forced to watch Hapag's business undercut by the independent Dutch. He therefore secured from Morgan the concessional agreement, as a condition of Hamburg-America's participation, that Pirrie should be authorised to approach Holland-America (for whom also Harland & Wolff had built) with the offer to buy a 51% controlling interest in the line.

As for Cunard, Steele said that although 50% of its shares had been proffered them from various sides, 'they had not entertained this offer at all, as the idea of buying the line was quite outside their intentions'. Morgan confirmed that:

> originally it had simply been a question of gathering together the interests of the American lines; out of that had grown the idea of including the White Star Line with which he through Pirrie and Ismay already was in very close connection.

Besides, he had not wanted to stir up public sentiment in England against his enterprise. But he added that 'as matters now stood' (i.e. with the accession of German support) 'it might possibly be right to consider this purchase'. Steele opined that it might be best not to take in Cunard directly, but to buy up a majority of its shares 'in order to elect a sensible Board and establish a capable manager of the line'. Morgan concurred; and Griscom remarked that he thought such a purchase feasible if the two German lines were willing to participate in the transaction. 'This shows', commented Wiegand in his confidential report,

> what weight can be attached to the saying that these people have money and to spare ... The money for purchasing the Cunard and Holland-America Lines is apparently not to hand, and they reckon on the assistance of the German lines, yet we were wanted to believe that we were in danger of being bought up lock stock and barrel by the Americans! How different things look, and how they shrink when faced squarely.[21]

In the outcome (according to Ballin)[22] Morgan undertook to pursue negotiations for a controlling interest in Cunard through the intermediary of some British friends at the same time as Pirrie approached Holland-America through its director, Van den Toorn. It was also settled that if the combine duly secured control of these two lines, it should be exercised jointly and equally between the American components and its German associates. No additional companies – unless perhaps a small concern like the Phoenix Line – would be absorbed. And each component of the combine would retain local managerial freedoms, being centralised only in a general control board for certain purposes. 'After this revelation', commented Wiegand, 'there can be no question of a force commanding the seas, such as the combination was supposed to possess'.[23]

After the conventional inspection of Niagara Falls, the Germans before they returned to Europe took part in several further sessions of some interest. One with Wilding and Steele on 18th February dealt *inter alia* with cabin pooling arrangements. More important was a session on the 21st which seemed to clear up the only remaining uncertainty, that of the combine's relationship to the railways. This introduced them to Joyce, the young general traffic manager of the Pennsylvania.

Joyce was able to assure them (reported Wiegand) that, so far from offering discriminatory freight rates – such as those, for instance, the Brewer Line regrettably still obtained from the Baltimore & Ohio – his own company would henceforth be adhering strictly to a policy of equal treatment for all steamship lines, for this, he had found, maximised his own carrying business. Joyce also satisfied the visitors as to his road's limited interest in shipping operations: it amounted to no more than $500,000 worth of bonds acquired several years back when the Pennsylvania sold to the American Line four steamers it had unsuccessfully been operating itself. The Pennsylvania had no shares in the American Line and no influence over its management. Nor for that matter did Widener, a director of that line, hold any office in the Pennsylvania, in which he was merely a shareholder. Still less did the Pennsylvania stand in any special relationship to Standard Oil. More generally, Joyce was at pains to dispel the common European impression that the policy of railroads like his was to develop their own shipping connections as subsidiaries. 'They had again and again', he stressed, 'been convinced that it was best to let the railroads stick to their business and leave the overseas freight carrying to independent steamship companies'. Nor was it the case that railways subordinated the interests of non-American shipping trade to the native.[24]

All this the Germans heard corroborated when they subsequently met A. J. Cassatt himself, president of the Pennsylvania, formerly on the board of Griscom's International Navigation Co., and (they had been warned) 'an extremely independent personality'. His company, Cassatt told them,

> had been asked to join the Combination, but had declined to do so for the reason that, as their policy was based on cooperation with all the steamship companies on an equal footing, they would not give the Combination or any other line preference.

'This declaration', Wiegand commented, 'was given very decisively and does away with a great many mistaken ideas'.

Thus reassured, the German negotiators signed the treaty with the American trust on 24th February before departing for home at the end of the month. Both Bremen and Hamburg delegations represented the outcome as a highly satisfactory one, thanks to the personal sagacity of their respective negotiators. 'We have obtained all we wanted', reported Wiegand for NGL. Besides having carried his company's view on points of detail,

> our independence has been preserved as well as ... unlimited possibilities for independent continued development ... North German Lloyd has preserved all that which constitutes its pride and strength,

and this without having to submit to any outside scrutiny of the present or future conduct of its own internal management.[25] To Ballin it seemed that 'this arrangement will assure the German lines of a far-reaching influence on the future development of affairs'. The new combination, once the Dutch had agreed to sell, would be in a position to neutralise competition from Holland-America through its 51% controlling interest in that line. And the possiblity of exerting the same sway over Cunard appeared to be left open. With Wiegand he addressed a joint telegram to the Kaiser, who in reply signified his reciprocal pleasure by conferring upon Ballin the Imperial Order of the Red Eagle with Crown, second class. The coincidental visit to New York of Prince Henry of Prussia, aboard the *Kronprinz Wilhelm*, was made the occasion for mutual hospitality, including a luncheon presided over by Morgan himself, attended by a hundred captains of American industry, and followed by an entertainment for twelve hundred members of the press.[26]

At the ground of these rejoicings, the newly signed Germano-American shipping agreement,[27] it is now time to look in some detail. Deemed to be made and performed under English law, its terms demonstrated unmistakably that the German companies were not incorporating themselves in the Morgan syndicate – neither party was to acquire, either directly or indirectly, shares in the other – but merely allied to the combine by mutuality of interest. The terms on which profits would be allocated were complex but need only brief exposition here. Reckoning the present share capital of each of the German companies at 80 million marks, each undertook to pay the combine annually a sum equivalent to a dividend on one-quarter of that figure, calculated at the same rate at which each company was currently paying dividends to its own shareholders. Reciprocally, the combine would pay annually to each of the German companies a sum equal to 6% dividend on 20 million marks. If either German company increased its share capital, it would raise its annual payment to the combine by a sum equal to the current dividend on 25% of the capital increase, receiving in return from the combine 6% of that notional one-quarter capital increase.

The 6% fixed interest device owed its origin (according to Ballin)[28] to a suggestion of Von Hansemann, director of the

Disconto-Gesellschaft, who had shown an active concern with the development of the whole matter. It was the one item in the negotiations over which Morgan was inclinded to hold out, ultimately conceding it, so Wiegand claimed, at NGL's insistence. Its advantages to the German associates were clear. It simplified negotiations: the Germans need not trouble themselves with the details of the combine's working arrangements, about surrender values, or about its future prosperity. 'Experience has taught us', said Wiegand, 'that we cannot reckon on earning a higher average than 6% on our shares'.[29] And both his company and Ballin's were thereby insured against the consequences either of the combine's passing its own dividends or of tightening its monopoly in future years. A provision was included for adjusting this formula after five years' working experience.

Equally detailed were the provisions for mutual self-restraint between the two associating parties. Thus the combine undertook not to ply at German ports: reciprocally the Germans would observe certain restrictions on North Atlantic traffic from British ports where their connections were not already established. Their steamers in the North Atlantic trade would not call at any British port oftener than seventy-five times a year in each direction (a figure that Wiegand held out for): the combine's steamers between England and the eastern seaboard of the United States would not call at French ports more than twice a week in each direction, so long as the Germans did not increase their own calls there. It was explicitly stated that these and other minor restrictions were not intended to preclude small alterations in service, but only anything amounting to a doubling of sailings *(Expeditionen)* or the establishment of a new line, or going into a new trade; in which cases either party was to offer the other the option of one-third participation in the increased enterprise.

Though the whole agreement was explicitly an offensive and defensive alliance *(Schutz-und-Trutzbündnis)* against any outside competitor, neither participant was prohibited from entering into agreements with the latter where this was not in competition with the other party. If either party, however, should temporarily need more ships than were at its immediate disposal, the other should enjoy a preferential right to supply them so that all steamers covered by the agreement might be profitably employed before recourse was had to outsiders. Pooling of steerage traffic was continued, and new arrangements were made to pool North American saloon traffic. Here the proposals made by Wiegand at the Cologne meeting with Pirrie were accepted, subject to biennial scrutiny and revision. But pool arrangements were not immediately contemplated for freight. The predictable effect would be to give common control of passenger rates in the North Atlantic, but not of cargo.

Execution of the treaty was to be supervised by a joint committee containing two representatives of the combine and one each of the two German associates. (At a general meeting of the Hamburg-America line to consider what amendments were necessary to the company's statutes, Ballin pointed out that this gave the Germans a voting power equal to all the rest). It was informally understood that all resolutions required unanimity, and that neither German company should be preferred by the combine to the other. Besides keeping the associates in touch and securing an understanding on matters affecting their common interests, the committee was to act as resolver in the first instance of their difficulties or contentions. This failing, recourse in arbitration should be had to a commission, sitting in London, chosen by the directing bodies (*Aufsichtsraths-korporationen*).

If any third party were to seek control of the German companies by offers of majority share purchase, the combine should be entitled to prior consulation with the latter as to the steps to be taken. The duration of the agreement was to be twenty years, with the option of proposing a revision after ten, and of withdrawing at the end of a further year if the revision could not be effected to mutual satisfaction. In the event of either Germany or the USA becoming involved in war, the agreement would be suspended indefinitely.

As for Holland-America, Pirrie's approach with the offer to buy a 51% controlling interest had divided its board of directors, who could agree only an deciding to send a representative to New York to discuss it direct with the Americans. Of the German interest in the combine they had been deliberately left in ignorance. When they agreed, it was on the supposition that the majority interest was to be exercised by Harland & Wolff. In fact purchase and control were split three ways between J. P. Morgan & Co. and the two German lines.[30] One is left to imagine the chagrin of the Dutch at discovering the triumph of their arch-competitors in Bremen and Hamburg.

Publication of the terms of the Germano-American treaty was delayed, at the Americans' request. Throughout the early weeks of 1902, in a series of meetings held mostly at the Morgan offices at 23 Wall Street, they had been completing detailed arrangements for the entire amalgamating operation. The provisional agreement which emerged, dated 4th February 1902 though not published until 9th May,[31] was entered into between five vendors – Messrs Ismay Imrie & Co. (for White Star), Messrs Richards Mills & Co. (for Dominion), Messrs Peter A. B. Widener and Bernard N. Baker (for the Atlantic Transport Co.) – of the one part, and Messrs J. P. Morgan Co. (the bankers) of the other. Its explicit purpose was the acquisition before 31st December 1902 of certain maritime properties and businesses by a corporation organised under the direction of the vendors and to the satisfaction of the bankers. The trust when formed was to be under the voting control of a board consisting of five members, three Americans (Morgan, Steele and Widener) and two Englishmen (Ismay and Pirrie). Of its thirteen-man directorate, eight were Americans and five British. Its president was Griscom and its vice-president Pirrie: its executive and finance committee were all-American. Initially the promoters used the chartered incorporation (at Trenton, New Jersey) and the Philadelphia headquarters of Griscom's International Navigation Co., but in October the title was changed to the International Mercantile Marine Co. (IMM), by which we shall hereafter refer to it.

Since the IMM's structure was compound rather than complex, it may be best simply to itemise at this point the maritime properties and businesses it was to take over:

1. 750 shares of £1,000 each fully paid of the Oceanic Steam Navigation Co. Ltd, including all rights in the name and flag of the White Star Line.
2. The business, goodwill, assets and property of White Star's managing partnership of Ismay Imrie & Co., excluding certain properties and rights reserved.

3. All the shares of the British & North Atlantic Steam Navigation Co. Ltd (Dominion Line), and of Mississippi & Dominion Steam Ship Co. Ltd with all rights in the name and flag of the Dominion Line.
4. The business, goodwill and assets of the Dominion Line's managing partnership of Richards Mills & Co., excluding certain properties and rights reserved.
5. 118,463 ordinary shares and 58,703 preference shares of the capital stock of Frederick Leyland & Co. (1900) Ltd – equivalent to a controlling interest in the Leyland Line – at the price ($11 million) at which J. P. Morgan Co. had acquired them in April 1901 plus 6% interest.
6. The capital, stock, properties and assets of the International Navigation Co. (American and Red Star lines), holders of whose 8% preferred stock were to get a share-for-share exchange for 6% cumulative preferred in the new combine, and common stock holders one half-share of the new common for each old share. (The enhanced cash requirements of the merger, however, definitely precluded the paying off of the bonded debt of Griscom's company.)
7. The capital, stock, properties and assets of the Atlantic Transport Co. of West Virginia (Atlantic Transport Line). The better performance of Baker's company was recongised in terms whereby its stockholders were to receive cash for declared but unpaid dividends, plus three shares of new preferred and one of common stock for each common share held in the old company.

The first four of these enumerated properties and businesses were under the agreement to be taken over at a price equal to ten times their net profits for the year 1900. Net profits of items 1 and 3 (the two shipping companies) werre to be ascertained after deductions of 6% to cover depreciation, and of $3\frac{1}{2}$% to cover the cost of insurance, from the amounts at which their properties stood in their respective companies' books on 1st January 1900. Payment for items 1, 2 and 3 was to be made by 25% in cash, 75% in preference stock at par, plus a bonus equivalent to $37\frac{1}{2}$% in common. Items 6 and 7 were to be taken over, subject as to the American Line to $19,686,000 of 5% bonds, at the price of $34,158,000.

Small bonus payments in the new combine's preferred and common stocks were to be made to Griscom, Baker, Widener and certain senior managers of the White Star and Dominion lines, in recognition of services rendered by these vendors in promoting the merger. The J. P. Morgan partners received as managers' fee over $2 million worth of new stock. Legal fees were remarkably low, amounting to little more than $109,000.[32]

Pirrie's reward took the form of a clause of the agreement, operative for ten years, providing that all orders for new vessels and major repairs in the United Kingdom were to be placed with Harland & Wolff, though the combine might also place orders in the United States. His Belfast firm was to be paid at cost plus 5% on new building, plus 10% on new machinery installed in old vessels, or plus 15% on repairs. Reciprocally, Harland & Wolff agreed not to build for any client other than the combine and its German associates so long as the latter's orders kept them fully employed.

White Star, Dominion and Leyland lines all had orders outstanding for new tonnage; so too had Baker's Atlantic Transport, for which purpose (it will be recalled) J. P. Morgan Co. had already advanced a loan. These total commitments represented nearly $17 million and brought the initial cash demands on the new trust up to some $50 million. This figure was about twice the original estimate of cost, and in excess of what could readily be raised by sale of preferred stock. The promoters therefore decided to reduce the issue of preferred, and additionally to issue $50 million of 4½% collateral trust bonds, thus reducing the priority (and therefore the expected market price) of the preferred stock. The total capital of the new corporation was to consist of $60 million preferred stock, carrying a cumulative dividend at 6% p.a.; and $60 million common stock, limited to dividends of 10% p.a.; together with the additional $50 million collateral trust debentures.

On paper the sum of these figures looked enormous. It greatly surpassed the aggregated capital stock of the combine's component companies. Was it therefore exorbitant? Critics, as we shall see, were quick to speak of overcapitalisation. Looking at it for the moment from Morgan's point of view, we must note, however, that the figure for their aggregate stock would take no account of the companies' surplus and reserve funds, which in some cases – we have particularly noted that of White Star – were substantial. The auditors' estimate of the total valuation of the trust's physical assets and working capital as of December 1902 was around $75 million.[33] When this is compared with the cost of the acquisitions in cash paid (to be estimated in detail later), plus the anticipated opening market values of the securities issued in payment – an estimated total $83·7 million – the discrepancy does not appear quite so alarming. Much would depend on the earning power of the lines acquired. This in the year 1900, considered by itself, was reassuringly large. Averaged over the four years immediately preceding the amalgamation, on the other hand, it would look little more than $6 million p.a. net. And this figure, as the *Economist* pointed out, after fixed charges had been met, would certainly not suffice to pay the full dividend on the combine's cumulative preferred stock. Great reliance, however, was placed on the economies to be expected from centralised administration and concentration of management.[34] If this faith were justified, the estimated gap of less than $10 million (between $83·7 million and $75 million) would not have seemed impossible to bridge once the new tonnage came into service. Morgan himself may well have appraised the risk as not unjustifiable.

For several reasons, however, it cannot have been an easy one for him to take. By the agreement the vendors gave his House, as bankers, until 30th April to organise a syndicate for the purchase of the stock and underwriting of the bond issue. Failure would mean the calling-off of the merger. At any time during the interim the bankers could withdraw from the provisional agreement but the vendors could not. Several factors ensured that Morgan's responsibility during this waiting period would not sit lightly upon him.

First among these factors was the fate of the Frye subsidy Bill,[35] which (as we may remember) at the time the provisional agreement was struck still hung in the balance. Though the legislative session of 1901 had failed to act, the Fifty-seventh Congress had reassembled under strong pressure for action on the measure, which now lay before the Senate. On 17th March the Senate indeed sent it to the House, but only after several last-minute amendments, the most serious of which had struck out the subsidy provision for ships built abroad. On the 20th Morgan lunched in Washington with Hanna. As the senator was – it will be recalled – one of the Bill's chief supporters, we need not doubt that one item of their conversation was its prospects. Whatever Hanna's predictions, the Bill was in fact sleeping its last sleep. It was never to be reported out of the House committee. Failure was total: neither shipbuilders nor shipowners would get a penny.

How grievous a setback was this for the combine's promoter's? Evidence suggests that none of them had admitted pinning his faith in success absolutely on the Frye Bill's passage. Pirrie afterwards wrote to the London *Times* to deny that the one enterprise was contingent upon the other. Baker had earlier said that even if the Bill were lost, the ships his line was building would be amply employed in the coastwise trade. Yet there can have been little comfort in the reflection that no American substitute was now available should British subsidies be withdrawn when the White Star fleet changed hands. Moreover, the probability of the Frye measure's success had been used by the combine's promoters to whet the appetite of investors. Reciprocally, the trust's proximate formation was offered by them to Congress as a good reason why subsidies should be enacted. Both ploys were now in vain. All that could be hoped for was a revival of the Bill after the forthcoming mid-term elections, and rumours of such a resuscitation were to gather once more after Theodore Roosevelt's message of January 1903 had again pressed for subsidies.

Meanwhile Morgan's dilemma was unenviable. Step by step, each one costlier than foreseen, he had been led by the protagonists of the scheme – first Griscom, then Pirrie – into a sphere, the world of shipping, with which he was totally unfamiliar. His house's loans were financing a substantial proportion of the new building programme of the American lines due to enter the combine. A number of these vessels had furthermore been ordered from domestic yards, at high American prices, in the expectation of a federal subsidy for at least home-built ships. That the Bill had totally failed meant that even for these no subsidy was assured; and the outlook for the American component of the combine would be as black as the situation Griscom had faced a decade earlier, when the profits from the

European element in his company had been devoured by the losses on his American operations.

Nor could Morgan have derived any consolation from the latest trend in the general economic climate. After the boom year of 1900 the North Atlantic carrying trade had declined steadily throughout 1901 and, more ominously, was still failing to pick up. Though the aggregate quantity of seaborne foreign commerce remained undiminished, the wartime shortage which had over-stimulated shipping at the turn of the century was notably easing, and vessels were no longer tied up in the east. Government demands slackening, a dearth of shipping capacity had been transformed into a glut, which by the beginning of 1902 had become so marked as to amount to a recession. (Significantly, the Frye Bill, when reintroduced in December 1901, had omitted that part of its preamble expressing the need to stimulate building). Late in March 1901 Cunard, which in the year preceding had nearly doubled its dividend, halved it again; and even so its disbursements continued to exceed its earnings.[36] The attraction of the new combine to investors, on whom it so largely relied, was brought, for the time being at least, seriously into doubt. Yet Morgan's options on completion of the purchase of Leyland and White Star were fast running out: and once agreement had been reached with the Germans over the terms of their association, formal arrangements for consummation of the trust could be no longer delayed.

One other factor enjoined caution. Morgan seems to have been genuinely surprised by the strength of the alarm and hostility his plans, or rumoured plans, were arousing in Britain and Germany, both in press and government circles. These reactions were already manifesting themselves even before the official announcement of his combine's formation. During his deferred European trip of April 1902, and on subsequent visits that summer, he strove to allay them, and to ensure that the profit-sharing arrangements with the German lines were allowed to stand. Morgan's opportunities for pacification included dining with Edward VII and his consort at the American embassy (he was later to attend, in court costume, the coronation in Westminster Abbey), and conversations with the Kaiser at Berlin and during Kiel Week, when his New York hospitality of February was returned.

It must have been mid-April when Morgan decided to go ahead. Ballin was then permitted to send a summary of the Germano-American treaty to the German embassy in London. On the 19th the British press made the first semi-official announcement of that document. On 9th May it published the main lines of the entire merger agreement: on the 28th an extraordinary general meeting of Hapag shareholders was given the details.[37] By the end of the month White Star and Dominion stockholders had, almost to a man, ratified the proposal of sale. In June stockholders of Baker's Atlantic Transport and Griscom's International Navigation began turning in their shares in exchange for stock in the new trust. In October the IMM was formally incorporated, share exchanges and payments being completed by early in 1903.

Loss of the subsidy Bill, however, did impose two limiting conditions on Morgan's course of action and that of his fellow promoters. One was that no further financial resources could be put at risk for the purpose of acquiring Cunard. The agreement contained no provision for adding any further lines to the combine. By a statement designed for public consumption, Morgan indeed seemed to encourage the inference that his interest in Cunard had not lapsed, and that acquisition might be considered once organisation of the parent trust had been completed.[38] But in reality such a course was at that juncture practically precluded. This circumstance was not, of course, immediately apprehended in Britain, where the belief still prevailed that special measures were necessary to defend Cunard against American capture or control.

The second exigency imposed on Morgan by Congress's refusal to help was the need to negotiate for the continuance of British subsidy to those vessels which had been receiving it prior to their purchase by the Americans. Griscom's original plan, as we have seen, for an all-American shipping combination stemmed from his desire to free United States commerce in the North Atlantic from its heavy dependence on British-operated lines flying the red ensign. Now, however, it had become economically vital to leave the newly acquired British tonnage under the British flag if the new combination were to entertain any hope of reaping the sorely needed benefit of continued British subsidy and lower operating costs. Morgan and his colleagues therefore restructured their amalgam of shipping so as to group all its British-flag lines under a single head – Griscom's British subsidiary, the International Navigation Co. And Morgan himself opened negotiations with British Ministers, in a manner to be studied in the succeeding chapter, with the proffered concession that all these vessels should remain British-registered, British-manned and,where existing agreements so provided, at the disposal of the British government.

By comparison with these problems, the bankers' difficulties in actually forming the syndicate were minute. The name of Morgan, already magnetic, had been lately enhanced by the immediate profitability of those transactions which gave birth to US Steel. Potential underwriters of the International Mercantile Marine Co. abounded, and the only problem was the merely procedural one of how best to allocate participation between them. According to one biographer, Morgan here followed his usual practice of first offering the opportunity to subscribe *pro rata* to those who had come into his last underwriting syndicate.[38] At any rate, most of the IMM's underwriters were large trust or insurance companies, who assimilated the new bonds to their other investments. A few others, such as Rockefeller himself, were wealthy individuals who did likewise. But there were also many individual underwriters, down to a few whose participation did not exceed a single $1,000 bond, who probably desired only to participate in the risk function, using the house of Morgan as their marketing agents. The compensation on this risk per $1,000 bond was 1·4 share of preferred stock and four shares of common, totalling $440 at par. The return at anticipated market values was not expected to fall below a normal rate for underwriting participation at that period – about 15% on the amount risked. That those who put up the cash for the merger would represent a substantial ownership in it was evident from the arrangement by which nearly half the common stock issued was to be distributed to underwriters in bonus shares. Nearly 30% of the underwriting, we may note in passing, was allotted through the London subsidiary, J. S. Morgan & Co., many of the bonds so placed going ultimately to Dutch investors.[40]

The promotional difficulties of the House of Morgan, whether real or hypothetical, did not enter directly into the calculations of British Ministers. Throughout these anxious months the government saw its task as fourfold. It must soothe public anxiety when confronting the new transatlantic titan. It must seek to agree with the latter some *modus vivendi* which would best serve the ends of national security, present and prospective: here the government's strongest card was its subsidy to the reserved White Star vessels. It must strive to deny the new and formidable rival any fresh accession of strength that would involve further British shipping losses. And it must encourage the remaining British lines in the North Atlantic to reorganise in the most efficient way to face the severe competition to be anticipated there. It is time to consider the means chosen, and the incidental problems faced, in pursuit of these ends by a government ostensibly committed to preserving the doctrine of free trade.

NOTES

1 This and the immediately following paragraphs draw principally upon F. B. Herschel: *Entwicklung und Bedeutung der Hamburg-Amerika Linie* (Berlin, 1912); O. Mathies: *Hamburgs Rederei 1814-1914* (Hamburg, 1924); P. Neubar: *Der Norddeutscher Linie, 50 Jahre der Entwicklung 1857-1907* (2 vols., Leipzig, 1907); and anon.: *Seventy Years of the North German Lloyd, Bremen 1857-1927* (n.d.)

2 *Times*, 12 Dec. 1902; more generally, see extract from a report submitted to the Foreign Office through our commercial attaché at the Berlin embassy, William S. H. Gastrell, and the British ambassador there, Sir Frederick Lascelles, in Foreign Office papers at AF 50295.

3 Select Committee on Steam Ship Subsidies, *Report*, H. of C. 385 (1902), App. 36; *Times*, 2 May 1902.

4 S. Pollard: 'British and world shipbuilding, 1890-1914: a study in comparative costs', *Journal of Economic History* 17:3 (1957), 429–34; Royal Meeker: *A History of Shipping Subsidies* (New York, 1905), p. 94; G. Jaensch: *Die deutsche Postdampfersubventionen, ihre Entsehung, Begründung, und ihre volkwirtschaftlichen Wirkungen* (Berlin, 1907), pp. 111–12.

5 Cited in J. Ross Hoffman: *Great Britian and the German Trade Rivalry, 1875–1914* (Philadelphia, 1933), p. 156 n.

6 H. O. von Borcke and Hugo Heeckt: *Entwicklung und Aussichten der deutschen Passagierschiffahrt auf dem Nordatlantik* (Kiel, 1956), pp. 3 and 31; *Shipping World*, 1 Apr. 1891, p. 372; B. Huldermann: *Albert Ballin* (1922), p. 53; J. Clapham: *An Economic History of France and Germany*, 4th edit. (1961), p. 359.

7 Testimony of Sir Robert Giffen to Select Committee on Steam Ship Subsidies, see n. 3 above; *Times*, 31 Aug. 1901, letter of Ballin, and 13 June 1902. For specimens of British press alarmism see Hoffman: *op. cit.*, pp. 214–15.

8 E. Cecil to J. L. Garvin, 23 Oct. 1920, Joseph Chamberlain papers 17/5/7 (University of Birmingham).

9 *Times*, 22 May 1902, leader; also in the same strain its issues of 3 Feb. and 16 Aug. 1902 and 28 Jan. and 18 Sept. 1903. The Kaiser's telegram is quoted in E. L. Woodward: *Great Britain and the German Navy* (1935), p. 49.

10 *Times*, 28 May 1902; *Morning Post*, 3 Feb. 1902; 'Ignotis' in *National Review* 39:559–563 (1902).

11 Huldermann: *op. cit.*, pp. 60–1, 21–3; P. F. Stubman: *Albert Ballin, ein deutscher Reeder auf internationalen Feld* (Hamburg, 1957), p. 12.

12 Erich Murken: *Die Grossen transatlantischen Linienrederei, Verbände, Pools und Interessentengemeinschaften bis zum Ausbruch des Weltkriegs* (Berlin, 1922) contains a fairly full treatment of North Atlantic conferences; much varied testimony as to the value of such devices was later to be elicited by the Royal Commission on Shipping Rings and Deferred Rebates, *Report*, P.P. 1909, xlvii and xlviii.

13 Huldermann: *op. cit.*, pp. 41, 43–5, 60.

14 *Ibid.*,pp. 47–50. No date is given for the memorandum.

15 *Ibid.*, pp. 50–3, Ballin's notes.

16 Selborne to Chamberlain, 19 May 1902, JC 11/32/20; to G. W. Balfour, 21 May 1902. The latter communication, together with the documents it refers to, are in the Board of Trade records in the Public Record Office at 30/60/48. This collection is generally headed Gerald Balfour papers, but is not indexed in detail.

17 *Loc. cit.*, Plate to Wiegand, 6 Nov. 1901.

18 See page 37 above.

19 Huldermann: *op. cit.*, pp. 54–5.

20 GB 30/60/48, Wiegand to Plate, 15 Feb. 1902.

21 *Loc. cit.*

22 Huldermann: *op. cit.*, p. 56.

23 GB 30/60/48,*loc. cit.*

24 GB 30/60/48, Wiegand to Plate, 23 Feb. 1902.

25 *Loc. cit.*

26 Huldermann: *op. cit.*, p. 57.

27 GB 30/60/48.

28 Huldermann: *op. cit.*, p. 55.

29 GB 30/60/48, Wiegand to Plate, 15 Feb. 1902.

30 Murken: *op. cit.*, p. 206

31 In (e.g.) the *Liverpool Daily Echo* of that date.

32 Records of Price Waterhouse & Co., auditors to the J. P. Morgan Co., cited by T. R. Navin and M. V. Sears: 'A study in merger', *Business History Review* xxxviii: 4, 1954 pp. 311–14.

33 *Op. cit.*, p. 313.
34 *Economist*, 16 Jan. 1904, pp. 83–4, citing *Commercial and Financial Chronicle* for its detailed information; see also *Wall Street Journal*, 2 Dec. 1902, reporting an interview with one of the combine's promoters.
35 S. 1348, H. R. 4564, 57 Cong., 2 sess.
36 *Wall Street Journal*, 1 Apr. 1902.
37 Huldermann: *op. cit.*, pp. 58–9.
38 *New York Times*, 22 Apr. 1902, p. 8.
39 Carl Hovey:*The Life Story of J. Pierpont Morgan* (London, 1912), p. 257.
40 Navin and Sears, *op. cit.*, pp. 315–16. For particulars of the initial distribution of the IMM's cash and stock see Appendix II (b).

CHAPTER 4

British response

It is hard in retrospect to conceive the pitch of excitment to which news of the American shipping combine temporarily roused public opinion on both shores of the Atlantic. 'The Press,' exclaimed an MP, 'has made it the question of the hour.' 'Bewilderment, alarm, indignation,' wrote another,

> such has been the prevailing mood of the public mind since the news ... burst upon it a few weeks ago. That something was wrong somewhere – that someone had stolen a march upon us – that something ought to be done – such was the comment of the man in the street and in the newpapers.

'The reorganisation of the Leyland fleet,' said *Fairplay* in May 1901, 'is undeniably the sensation of the new century.' Already its man in Washington was reporting that 'the principal topic here at present' was Morgan's purchase of it, 'which it is said is but the beginning of his investments in vessel property'; and soon the *Times*'s Washington correspondent was referring to 'cabled dispatches which give a lurid picture of the distress caused in England' thereby. 'London Hysterical over Morgan Coup', proclaimed the New York *Herald*, since 'the Combination practically places the American merchant marine in first position in the tonnage of the world'. 'Atlantic to be an American Lake,' rejoiced the New York *Journal*.[1]

In Britain voice cried to voice in a chorus of woe. One periodical blamed the government for not preventing 'an intolerable national humiliation' which would make her 'a mere annex of the United States'. 'The supremacy of the merchant marine,' echoed another, 'had slipped from us while we slept.' The shipping trust, said a third, 'must mark, unless speedily neutralized, the turning-point in our commercial fortunes of three centuries.' To the American shipbuilder, Charles H. Cramp, it seemed clear that the prospective merger had roused the British from their lethargy 'into an almost feverish realisation of the actual conditions which confront them'. 'Our brokenhearted cousins,' commented a *New York Times* leader, had been 'frightened to a degree which discredits their Anglo-Saxon phlegm.'[2]

'One cannot escape,' commented the *Nineteenth Century*'s shipping expert, 'a feeling of humiliation at the outcry which has been raised in this country over the transaction.' That reactions of such alarm could seem for one moment plausible must indeed, in the circumstances, defy credibility. For this was Britain's heroic age on the five oceans. There needs no labouring the obvious, that the growth of a nation's mercantile marine is directly related to the expansion of its seaborne trade; and when the nineteenth century ended British ships were carrying about half the seaborne trade of the world. 'Looking,' as did the *Times* in 1895, 'at the place which our mercantile marine holds in comparison with the merchant service of other countries, there is solid ground for satisfaction'.[3] Indeed, the ubiquity of the British flag in this era was compared to that of the Phoenicians of old. The empire it patrolled, moreover, was a free-trade empire. True, Britain's command of the seas rested on a unique combination of various factors, geographic and economic. But no protectionism handicapped her builders by raising the cost of materials, or by restricting imports made her owners' home cargo difficult to find. The British merchant marine of the steam age was the corollary, indeed the creature, of free trade.

Practically all the causes of decline in the United States' foreign trade marine were absent from the United Kingdom. In protectionist America, as we have seen, the slowness of conversion to steam and steel gravely handicapped oceanic development. In Britain, on the contrary, sail had been rapidly rendered obsolete by the sheer growth rate of overseas and imperial commerce. Here were great and peculiar advantages: large iron and coalfields at home and well distributed coaling stations abroad; ample capital at low interest rates, which made her shipping independent of State aid; and a population, doubling between 1850 and 1900, to provide an increasing demand for food and an abundant supply of labour. The transition had been short and sharp. In 1870 the United Kingdom possessed a steam fleet of some 1·1 million tons, still largely wooden. In 1900 it was over 12 million tons, mainly of steel, and represented nearly half the world's steam fleet.[4] In 1902 three-fifths of the world's shipping was being built in British yards. Correspondingly, over the last six years of the old century the value of British exports had risen by 25% to £354 million in 1900, by when new shipping was being launched at the rate of over a million tons annually. What stimulated growth stimulated technical advance also. The reciprocating engine was giving place to Sir Charles Parsons's steam turbine, progressively refined until in 1905 Britain prepared to launch the first two turbine-driven liners upon the Atlantic. Possessing so clear a commercial supremacy, why should Britain worry if a mere 300,000 tons of her shipping passed to American control? Why resent the progress of a German marine whose total steam tonnage was barely one-sixth of her own?

To take the latter question first; so far as Germany was concerned, one must recognise a distinct mutual animus. British uneasiness over the combine was noted with a certain *Schadenfreude* by German newspapers. The *National-Zeitung* was quoted as jubilant that 'British trade, shipping and wealth have suffered a severe blow ... all the greater in as much as the German lines have been able to keep out of the Trust and maintain their independence'.[5] The imperial press, inferred the *Times*, had been officially directed

> to depict in glowing terms the preferential position which the German lines had secured for themselves ... and to contrast with the patriotism of the German shipowners, who have subordinated their financial interests to the national interests of the Fatherland, the selfishness and supineness of the British shipowners, who have thought only of making a good bargain for themselves.

Be that as it may, Ballin certainly confided to his diary for 5th June 1902 the reflection that 'what makes people in England feel most uncomfortable is not the passing of the various shipping companies into American hands, but the fact that the German companies have done so well over the deal'. To some English minds, however, occurred a more subtle apprehension. Supposing Germany's aims here were, as always, the poisoning of Anglo-American amity, by official encouragement of her press 'to strengthen the impression that the Americans are really aiming at the destruction of British shipping supremacy?' If this ploy, ruminated the *Times*, succeeded in breaching 'the very stronghold of Anglo-American friendship, namely the world of business', Britain might be tempted into a war of reprisals on the North Atlantic.

In such a struggle all the old feeling and jealousy between America and England ... would very soon be revived, and Germany would not merely be able to play her favourite role of *tertius gaudens*, but would be the first to reap direct political and commercial benefits from this estrangement.[6]

But such speculation does not go far towards explaining British alarm at the combine as a whole. It may be better to ask whether, in the new century, some general feeling of insecurity was not besetting (in ways our first chapter illustrated) the age's sole claimant to world power. Had that power reached, and passed, its apogee? One cannot help sensing an official consciousness that in shipping particularly – so basic to her prosperity, security and status – Britain now faced growing competition, above all in the North Atlantic. From the Board of Trade's tables, for instance, it now appeared that since 1890 the proportion of domestic steam tonnage employed in the carrying trade between the United Kingdom and foreign countries had for the first time slightly fallen. This the Board, in its evidence to the Steamship Subsidies Committee of 1902, made light of by pointing to the much lower levels from which the tonnage of foreign competitors was, however rapidly, rising.[7] Yet four nations, Germany among them, had managed at any rate to dislodge British shipping from first place in their own ports. Moreover, the increase in Britain's exports was now at last failing to keep pace with the rise of her imports. True, the enterprise of her shipowners and insurance brokers was still yielding a rich harvest of invisible exports: but in 1900 the external trade deficit these had to make good was of the unprecedented order of £160 million. Pressure of competition was beginning at length to make publicly articulate the concern of Britain's politicians for her overseas trade. At the very least, the year 1900 may be taken as marking the point when competition between British and foreign shipping as a whole began to engross more public attention than rivalries within Britain's own.

To dwell exclusively on public expressions of alarm, however, would be to distort the image of the nation's total response to overseas challenge at this juncture. There were buoyant reactions also, though some of them were simply cocky and unreflecting. 'All a storm in a teacup,' pronounced one MP robustly. 'We can lick the Morgan syndicate easily' and run it or any other body 'off the face of the water'. There were 'only three or four good ships' among its acquisitions, and 'British shipowners need not be lugubrious over what is being done'. Another saw the whole transatlantic consolidation as simply

> a tribute to, and an acknowledgement of, the soundness of British policy with regard to the carrying trade. What has happened is a confession and acknowledgement that the Americans cannot build in their own yards ships to compete with you, and practically they have bought from you for half as much again as they are worth a lot of English ships in order to carry on competition with Great Britain in the carrying of their own products from their own ports. That is what the scare is about. (Cries of 'No'.) I think it is very largely so, and I think it will be found out when dividend day comes.

Confidence, however, was more usually either reasoned or based on a calm faith in the benefits expected to accrue from the free play of economic forces. Most regular shipping commentators were ready to welcome the American scheme as a healthy and necessary adjustment to the logic of the commercial situation. Increasingly public demand for ever more rapid and luxurious travelling to and from the United States had resulted in a great many expensive steamers which, since the North Atlantic passenger demand was seasonal, could not be remuneratively employed all year round. To rationalise the service, as Morgan proposed, might serve to iron out cyclic fluctuations in the British shipbuilding industry, so as to avoid the overbuilding which allegedly contributed to the 'coal famine' of 1900 and might if unchecked lead to a glut of tonnage when the British steamers recently taken up for Boer War service were released to their normal functions.

So the *Times* invited its readers 'to regard this combination calmly as a movement determined by the free play of commercial forces'. 'Competition nowadays is the preliminary to combination'; and one must rejoice 'that the ruinous competition for the North Atlantic carrying trade is to give place to regulated co-operation'. We must welcome this evidence that, instead of a shipping war, certain British shipowners were substituting 'a community of interests'. The *Economist* agreed in viewing this latest American trust as 'just a sort of elaboration of the 'conference' system familiar to British shipowners, along with a system of freight pools, which is also not unknown'. The syndicate, while allowing its component lines to continue to manage their their own sailings and other arrangements, would supply a central board to direct the distribution of services so as to avoid wasteful competition. 'No one', said the *Times*, 'can seriously imagine that they would have done better for the country had they frittered away a large amount of British capital in a losing fight against American capital backed by the United States Government.' Rather, Britons should recognise and accept an inevitable shift in the world's centre of economic gravity as a growing United States inevitably sought a greater share of international shipping. As the President of the Board of Trade, Gerald Balfour, was later publicly to express it when stressing the 'community of interest' between the two countries,

> It is impossible that we should expect that the Americans should be permanently content to remain without a considerable share in the Atlantic trade nor is it, in my opinion, desirable that they should remain without a considerable share in that trade. But it is desirable that this inevitable development should take place with the least possible friction between the two peoples.

That both the Ministry and the chief national newspaper were at one in preaching a 'least possible friction' attitude does not necessarily imply collusive adoption of some official line. Yet a degree of mutual pre-consultation there was, and of a kind interesting enough to deserve detailed notice. On 20th May 1902 Sir Thomas Sanderson, Under-Secretary of State for Foreign Affairs, wrote to Joseph Chamberlain's private secretary, Lord Monk Bretton, about his recent interview with Valentine Chirol, now head of the *Times*'s foreign department but formerly its Berlin correspondent. Chirol, wrote Sanderson, appeared 'very earnest and particularly uneasy' as to what Chamberlain's reaction to Morgan's plan would be. He

> had apparently heard that the German Emperor was doing his best to work up the King into acute antagonism to the plan, and to represent that German companies (who according to Chirol's information had got much the worst terms) had managed to maintain an independent attitude with great advantage

Chirol's own view, and I conceive that of the *Times*, was that we ought to be very careful about taking an antagonistic attitude – that it was quite reasonable that the United States should wish to have a larger interest in the trans-Atlantic traffic, that it was moreover to our advantage that this should be the case, as in case of a war between us and a Continental Maritime Power our supplies would be less interfered with, and that to interfere unduly with the use of British ships by the combination would merely result in some exceptional measures for temporarily transferring them to the United States flag, and if vessels were purchased from the Companies for the purpose of a rival (i.e. British) combination the money would be spent on building steamers to replace them in the United States.[10]

Though Chamberlain did not think it worthwhile talking to Buckle, its editor, he made a marginal note that 'the *Times* will not attack H. M. Government for doing nothing in the matter'.

But suppose the Americans demanded more than their share and attempted to establish hegemony or monopoly on the North Atlantic? Then we might still confidently reply on the irresistible force of self-corrective economic circumstances. 'There is no need for the country to take panic,' the shipowning Liverpool MP David MacIver assured his colleagues. 'By the operations of natural laws these combinations were ultimately bound to decay.' 'Every principle of Free Trade,' affirmed the *Fortnightly Review's* regular contributor on shipping affairs,

cries aloud against the assumption that Mr Pierpont Morgan, no matter what combination he may have at his back, can permanently override economic laws and defeat British shipowners in an enterprise that is peculiarly their own.

American producers might find they could still negotiate better shipment terms with independent British shipowners than with the new combine. Even American railroad companies, observed another authority, Benjamin Taylor, could not run continuously at a deficit. Losses from deliberately low freight charges on American goods to Britain could not be recouped by inordinately high charges on carriage of British goods to America: for such a practice would *pro tanto* automatically handicap American importers competitively on the return voyage. Alternatively excessive freight charges on the outward voyage could rebound to the high dissatisfaction of the western states of the USA, her main food producers, who possessed a controlling influence in Congress.

While, therefore, it would be foolish to ignore possibilities in the Combine for which our shipowners and railway companies ought to be prepared, it would be still more foolish to lose heart at what are only possibilities which economic law must ultimately counteract, and which energetic action on the part of Great Britain can altogether prevent.

But, Taylor went on to imply, neutral and inexorable economic law must be given a helping hand.

There is no room for doubt that action prompt, energetic, continuous and cooperative is emphatically called for ... If British shipowners and railway companies wake up smartly to the new conditions of international competition and brace themselves for the struggle ... we have the game in our own hands, and, Cobden Club or no, the people of these isles are not going to submit quietly to having their greatest industry appropriated by others.

But had not the trust already achieved some measure of monopoly, by compelling Harland & Wolff to the role of a tied house? That first-class shipyard had now become, in one critic's view,

the Trojan horse of the attack upon our mercantile supremacy. The Belfast building agreement is simply meant to make as difficult as possible any effort on the part of English capitalists to fight the Trust.

Was that legal, demanded Admiral Sir Edmund Fremantle, if the yard were thereby prohibited from building in future for the Admiralty? In a public and spirited reply Pirrie, for Harland & Wolff, rejected the aspersion, 'as absurd as it is malicious', that his firm had connived at monopoly solely for profit. In preserving their peculiarly exclusive relationship with White Star they were simply adhering to their time-honoured principle 'that we should not build for those whose interests clashed with each other'. For himself, he felt that one salutary effect of the combine would be to make Cunard and other rivals wake up and put their house in order. These assurances the *Times*, for one, was prepared to accept, regarding objections to the combine's tie with Harland & Wolff as 'principally sentimental': for 'men like Mr Ismay, of the White Star Line, to say nothing of others, would not be likely for any consideration whatever to enter into a transaction that would be dangerous for this country'.[12] (We might add that, in any case, the Belfast firm had never built for the Admiralty save two small vessels in 1886.)

Many British commentators, however, were struck less by the patriotism of the vendors than by the economic foolhardiness of the buyers. One cannot fail to note the incredulity with which the terms of the American purchase were greeted at the time. Why, wondered *Fairplay*,

> should a ring of American millionaires want to buy a lot of second hand ships – many of them practically obsolete – at an extravagant price?... The British companies joining the Combine have got rid of steamers – some out of date, some which will be outclassed in a year or two, and most of which are unsuited for any other than the Atlantic trade – at many times their value, and at enormously more than any sane shipowner on this side of the Atlantic would give for them'.

They had chosen to do so in a falling market where freights were rapidly tumbling from the abnormal demand figure of 1900. 'Clearly, then, there is something behind.' Capitalisation of the new combine, as the *Economist* pointed out, enormously exceeded that of the aggregate of the undertakings it had absorbed. Morgan's offer of his trust's 4½% bonds, it prophesied, would not be taken up in a hurry. Having tied up too much capital with insufficient allocation to reserves, he was less well prepared, thought the *Fortnightly*'s shipping expert, 'to pass through years of unprofitable trade and ruinous competition' than his independent British rivals. However,

> it is difficult to resist the conclusion that Mr Morgan can buy any British shipping line he pleases, if only he be willing to make a sufficiently tempting offer, and it would pay him better to buy at a high price, and British shipowners to sell at a high price, than to enter upon, it might be, years of ruinous rate-cutting.

'Let them buy up the lot', was the terser reaction of the shipowner MP for Gateshead, William Allan. 'We can build others'.[13] And how much more fortunate were the British companies thus bought outright by the combine than their German confrères, tied by an arrangement which obliged them to contribute to its prospective profits all the net earnings on a quarter of their capital:

> The British companies, so long as their interest in the combine remains, will obtain a share of the German profits, after comfortably disposing of their own expensive and otherwise unsaleable ships... The German companies are bound hand and foot to the Combine,

with whom they must pool their passengers freights and share their profits. But they keep their boats, and will have to keep them until they are broken up for old iron ... Is there a single individual shareholder of the Hamburg-American Line who would not gladly exchange places with a shareholder in the White Star Line? And does anybody know how many shares are already held by Mr Morgan and his friends in the Hamburg-America Line, whose manager has been congratulated by the Kaiser for preserving the German 'national interest'?[14]

Turning now to those parties whose reactions in face of the combine did not betray the same unruffled confidence, it must be said at once that British unease was not simply at having to meet increased competition of a direct and familiar kind. Rather it was a complex of many distinct fears, most of which were sooner or later to be voiced in Parliament. The developments across the Atlantic were first alluded to at Westminster in a question of 3rd March 1902 as to what action should be taken to safeguard British trade if (as then seemed likely) the federal shipping subsidy Bill passed Congress. One important consequence was the carrying on 26th March of a motion of Sir William Walrond for re-establishment of the Select Committee on Steamship Subsidies, which had been appointed in the previous session under the chairmanship of Evelyn Cecil but allowed to languish since. The Chancellor of the Exchequer promised to refer to its papers concerning the Frye Bill.

Though the Frye Bill perished, MPs from the first day of April onward began seriously to probe the implications of the Morgan combine for British security. First, T. Gibson Bowles, the well informed and highly articulate member for King's Lynn, asked the President of the Board of Trade whether British vessels sold to 'a company with capital of £34 million' and with its principal place of business in the United States would retain their British registry? Balfour replied that hypothetically they would not, but that at present he had no information that such a sale had actually taken place. A few days later he added that he had no official information on the subject of the American combine,

though a good deal of unofficial information has reached me. The effect of the combination on British shipping generally will receive the careful attention of the Board, but any formal inquiry would appear to me to be premature.

The arrangement for White Star to join it had not previously been referred to him, and his department had no legal authority to compel from British shipowners the submission of any proposal of transference of their vessels to foreigners. For this reason he could not tell the House officially even whether the British companies concerned were to enter the combine on precisely the same terms as the German and American lines. He assured members that the possible effect of the combine – 'this tremendous event', as Gibson Bowles described it – was 'engaging the serious attention of His Majesty's Government': but he could not promise the House an early opportunity to debate it.[15]

An early opportunity was nevertheless found a very few days later, when Sir James Woodhouse moved for and secured a debate on the adjournment of 1st May, to be devoted exclusively to the American threat. In this, evidently rather heated, confrontation the various strands of previous questioning converged, only to be deflected by Ministers evidently temporising in some anxiety and uncertainty. As to the Steamship Subsidies committee, Gerald Balfour refused either to promise a debate on its reappointment or to enlarge its terms of reference so as specifically to comprehend the American shipping trust. Nor could the government accept a proposal to legislate so as to prevent transference thereto of the White Star vessels on the Admiralty's reserve.

As to the effect of American developments on our maritime position generally, his brother A. J. Balfour, leader of the Conservative majority in the Commons, allowed that

> We are evidently opening a subject of far greater difficulty and complexity than that which is touched upon by the mere question of naval cruisers, and are brought face to face with problems not only novel in their character but of very great difficulty and complexity.

The government, he repeated, still lacked any official knowledge of the aims and objects of the combine, and their unofficial sources of information they must protect against disclosure. No official communications (the Under-Secretary for Foregin Affairs was later to add) had passed between His Majesty's government and that in Washington.[16]

Publication in Britain on 9th May of the details of the New York agreement of 4th February set off another spate of ministerial interrogation. Assurances were exacted from H. O.

Arnold-Forster, Secretary to the Admiralty, that the navy was secure against cruiser transference and from Gerald Balfour that the Americans had no option or contract concerning the shares or fleet of Cunard. On the 15th the House wrung from a reluctant Conservative leader the promise of a debate when the Steamship Subsidies committee was formally reappointed. Thereafter in the same month the Commons seized three opportunities to discuss the transatlantic threat – on 16th May, on the adjournment, when the scope of merchant shipping legislation was closely scrutinised; on the 18th, in the promised debate on reappointing the Evelyn committee; and on the 29th, over the navy estimates.

Meanwhile, and for months to come, the same anxieties were being aired *in extenso* by the press. First among these was the fear – ill founded though it might appear to those more familiar with American politics – that change of ownership of the British companies joining the combine would prove to be but the preliminary change of flag for their ships, once another subsidy Bill got through Congress. Of the International Mercantile Marine's fleet 85% was of British registry (compared with 12% of American and 3% of Belgian). But how long would that remain the case? Despite the recent failure of the Frye Bill, the *Times*'s Washington correspondent in late April 1902 still read the situation there as indicating that application for American registry for those British vessels, on the Inman precedent, was 'extremely probable'. Managers of other British lines – Harrison's of Liverpool, for one – were warning their United States agents what to expect. Pirrie, for White Star, in a letter to the *Times* of 13th May 1902 and in his evidence before the Steamship Subsidies committee, denied that the formation of the combine had ever hinged on subsidies, whose enactment 'mattered little one way or the other. It certainly had not the slightest effect on Mr Morgan'. But it was Griscom's evidence to the Frye committee that was quoted in the House of Commons:

> If the President and Congress will meet the indisputable economic facts by legislation, it is not too late to hope that a fair proportion of the steamers hereafter required by the new Company will be built in the United States, manned and officered by Americans, and become part of the National Naval Reserve.

Change of flag, it was widely believed in Britain, would entail a shift of business away from British yards to those of the USA, displacement of British naval reservists by American, and other incalculable consequences of federal subsidy.[17]

What substantive loss to British shipping did this transfer of ownership really entail? A just appraisal was made the more difficult because the tonnage figures so freely bandied about in excited debate did not always distinguish clearly between ownership, control or mere registry. For instance, the figure of 'over half-a-million tons' quoted with alarm by the *Fortnightly Review* as passing from British into American hands during 1902 – a shift, said that journal, representing one-fifteenth of our steam tonnage – relates to change of *control*: whereas the Registrar General's return for the same year gives the quantity passing into American *ownership* as only 11,142 g.r.t. Again, the figures proffered by Sir Robert Giffen, when testifying for the Board of Trade before the Select Committee on Steamship Subsidies in 1902 – 136 vessels comprising 672,000 g.r.t. and representing about 5% of British-registered steam tonnage – refers to the *aggregate* of all American-owned ships steaming under the red ensign at that time. More subjective ground for alarm may have lain in the quality of the ships being lost to the IMM. If Cunard were also to be swallowed up, the *Financial Times* reckoned that 'four-fifths of the finest steamers in the country' would have passed under American management.[18]

Yet other commentators preferred to look at our shipping losses to the combine in the broader context of our total shipping sales to all foreign purchasers. Newspapers gave some prominence to Professor E. A. Beazeley's warning to the Liverpool Steamship Association of a growing trend by which more than 2,000 British steamers, with a tonnage of 1,836,000 g.r.t., had passed into foreign hands since 1890. Beazeley was probably drawing upon the official return of British vessels sold since 1865 to ply under foreign flags, published as an appendix to the report of the Steamship Subsidies committee. But in the first place, the greater part of that tonnage comprised obsolete vessels which British companies customarily shed in the normal process of fleet renewal. Every recent year, it was reckoned, about 5½% of British steam tonnage was thus disposed of, two-thirds of which passed into foreign hands. Of steamers bought by foreigners from Britain in the year 1901, calculated the Board of Trade's Marine Department, 48·8% had been built before 1885 and 57·7% before 1890. Secondly, these official figures, though rising over the whole period *pari passu* with the country's total steam tonnage, did in fact reveal a sharp falling off during the last two years.[19]

But even if their vessels remained on the British register, would not the terms under which the principal British companies joined the IMM ensure that effective control would accrue to the Americans through their stockholding predominance? As the *Economist* saw it,

> the arrangement between the American combination and the British shipping companies affords one more object lesson in the unwisdom of parting with securities in undertakings in which British investors can exercise a certain amount of supervision, in exchange for the shares and bonds of an American enterprise whose management and conduct they are powerless to control.

When the President of the Board of Trade had stated that policy control of the British component would remain on this side of the ocean he had been immediately contradicted from New York. The IMM's British board of directors would be entirely subordinate to the American central management. Real power would reside overseas. How would it be used in time of war? Some argued that it would then be advantageous to have our foodstuffs brought across the Atlantic in neutral bottoms. But was it wise to depend for our lifeline upon a power which, without being actively hostile, might take the opportunity inordinately to step up its freight rates? Even in peace, as the *Financial Times* pointed out, American capture of the Leyland, White Star and Dominion lines left no independent British line to compete over the routes Liverpool–New York, London–New York or London–Boston.[20]

The prospective loss to Britain, moreover, was not of so many discrete units of shipping, but of entire lines with all the business connections they had built up. 'The combination has brought the trade as well as the ships'. As Ellerman, their chairman, warned Leyland shareholders assembled to consider the Morgan bid, 'the eventual outcome may be the transfer of a considerable trade from the British to the American flag'. Trade, as some MPs reminded their colleagues, follows not only the flag but capital; and capital is instinctively migratory. The North Atlantic bulk trade was peculiar in being predominantly an eastbound one, profit for British operators lying almost wholly in their return cargoes. 'American capital', warned Ellerman, 'is coming into the Atlantic trade to stay'. Its influence – so British observers feared – would be enormously extended by the shipping trust's supposed link with the railroads, whose eastern 'dictators', owners already of piers, wharves, warehouses and considerable shipping stock, would use the combine to get oceanic traffic under their own control. By offering attractive transit rates direct from supplier to consumer, the American industrial barons would soon be in a position to flood Europe – even as far as Austria, which the Morgan combine was alleged already to be penetrating – with the entire output of their huge empires. 'The shipping lines in the Ocean Syndicate are the tentacles of the Trusts'.

> Remembering what American railway dictators have done, or attempted, in rivalry with each other, one hesitates to predict what they would not attempt in efforts to secure such dominion in the Atlantic trade as would amount to an extension of their rails across the ocean ... Millionaires operating with the unnumbered millions of vast railway corporations have no financial conscience ... The combination may be sufficient to drive both British and Continental competition off the Atlantic.

'It will become practically impossible for any single capitalist or shipowner to compete with such an immense corporation', which therefore 'cannot fail to have the most disastrous effect on the maritime interests of Great Britain'. British competitors for cargo in New York and other eastern ports, whither the railroads would drain the produce of the entire United States hinterland, would get it only at the price fixed by the IMM.[21] Indeed, an additional twist was given the screw by envisaging the victorious American financiers using their hegemony to get Congress to swallow a subsidy Bill, 'making one hand wash the other':

> Let it not be overlooked that the railway and steamer alliances could not purchase, by means of low preferential through rates, the support of the Western States, and the Western States have been hitherto the chief opponents of subsidies. Perhaps we shall not be far wrong in regarding this as the first move in a game to be played with

Congress by the group of millionaires interested in railways, oil, steel and sugar ... The Morgan Syndicate ... may have ... resolved upon a sensational stroke in order to influence Congress and the people for future action.[22]

In view of the deeply ingrained mistrust of the American west and south for eastern financiers, this last speculation may strike us as too clever by half. Nevertheless some commercial circles in Britian did not find it beyond belief.

It was those parties, naturally, that felt concern, not confidence, about Britain's capacity to withstand the transatlantic threat who were most insistent in demanding government action. Of all such representations the common postulate was that the American trusts were entirely new phenomena in the world economic scene, and that new conditions required special remedies. The kinds of government action they proposed covered a wide spectrum, ranging from revival of the Navigation Laws to heavy subsidisation of native steamship lines, new or existing, in their building programmes as well as operating schedules. At the core of all such proposals lies the great free trade/protection controversy, which therefore deserves analysis in a separate and later chapter. For the moment we may simply distinguish the varieties of protective State action clamoured for as either negative and prohibitory or positive and promotional.

Into the former category fall demands that the government re-enact the Navigation Laws, wholly or in part; or at least close the ports of the United Kingdom, and possibly of the Empire too, to shipping of these nations which excluded British ships from their own coastal trade. Alternatively, let it limit this denial of access to vessels receiving subsidy from a foreign government, or else impose either a duty – on the analogy of the countervailing duties on sugar – equal in amount to that subsidy; or some sort of tonnage toll. Critics who feared a flood of American goods in consequence of a supposed consortium between US railways and steamship lines called for a protective tariff.

Among demands for promotional responses by the government to the Morgan trust appears the proposal for an overhaul of Board of Trade regulations in a sense less exigent to native, and more so to foreign, shippers. Most programmes for positive State action, however, advanced in one guise or another the principle of subvention. Sometimes the request is for simple bounties to equalise trading conditions by counteracting the bounties or concessions from which French or German shipping allegedly profited. At other times the desired objective is to improve trade and communications within the Empire, as by establishing fast competing services to Canada. The State should give independent lines, notably Cunard, special incentives to rival, or at least refrain from joining, the combine and to build faster vessels. Particularly the Admiralty's need for more cruisers should be recognised and met.

What we may call the battle over subsidies was to be joined, not mainly in the press or the Commons, but in that incomparable forum the Select Committee on Steamship Subsidies. The pros and cons of the debate waged there we must leave for later consideration. But it is important to understand at this juncture what precisely is entailed in speaking of shipping subvention in the year 1902.

'Subsidy' in the British context then denoted simply payment for services rendered: though, as the select committee noted, the word 'subvention' was sometimes preferred, because 'thought to be more euphemistic and to create less prejudice'. Another select committee of fifty years earlier had distinguished the possible uses of subsidisation as being to provide more rapid, frequent and punctual mail carriage on principal British overseas routes, to promote the construction and growth of modern steamships and lines, and to provide a number of vessels suitable for the national defence in time of war. [23] It was true, indeed obvious, that services in the first of these three categories would tend naturally to follow the lines of heaviest commercial traffic; equally that it would be the clear duty of warships to protect these main arteries of trade. Yet it was typical of the doctrine of *laissez faire* that in practice the second of these three objectives was only very indirectly, if at all, pursued by means of subsidy. Unlike France or Germany, Britain had not by the end of the century employed subsidies in the sense of bounties to encourage shipping as a branch or concomitant of national industry. A small exception was the £40,000 paid annually for some years to Elder Dempster & Co. for their service to the West Indies and Jamaica in furtherance of the fruit trade. But the government did not use this means customarily and deliberately in order either to rival the shipping of other nations or to swell the tonnage of its own. Subventions, even for purposes of communication or defence, had remained limited to a small group of passenger lines. The cargo liners and tramps which composed the bulk of the merchant fleet received not a penny. Still less had the government ever contemplated constructional bounties to shipbuilders.

In fact the American challenge of the early twentieth century had least impact upon what had been the principal form of government aid to British shipping in the nineteenth. This was the subvention for mail carriage. Susidised postal services, as a Post Office witness told the Evelyn committee, were and should be coexistent and coextensive with a great commercial traffic, and follow its lines as a matter of course. The decision taken in 1837 to end HM government's own, alarmingly inefficient, packet service and for the Admiralty to go out to private contract for mail carriage was to give the infant industry of oceanic steam shipping tremendous help towards bridging the gap between high operating costs and assured commercial revenue. That from the start the government's purpose transcended postal communication alone is evident from the language in which these early contracts were expressed:

> to afford a rapid, frequent, and punctual communication with those distant ports which feed the main arteries of British Commerce, and with the most important of our foreign possessions; to foster maritime enterprise, and to encourage the production of a superior class of vessels which would promote the convenience and wealth of the country in time of peace, and assist in defending its shores against hostile agression.[24]

It was frequently stipulated that (e.g.) subsidised ships should be strong enough to be used as troop carriers in time of war.

By the 1840's the service of the Cunard, Peninsular & Oriental, Royal Mail and Pacific Steam Navigation companies were linking Britain with all corners of the world. In particular, and for several decades thereafter, she was the only European country in a position to forward her mail direct to the United States by steamer. Despite occasional parliamentary objections about cost, followed by the Post Office's overhauling of its North American contracts, in 1902 between one-sixth and one-seventh (£113,640) of the government's aggregate annual mail subvention was for the New York service. On the North Atlantic, however, this money was hard-earned. On that route by the 1880's high speed was demanded, and a stand-by ship to maintain the schedule. Taking into account moreover the seasonal nature of its trade pattern, the general experience of steamship companies was that on the North Atlantic one had to earn annually a sum equivalent to 25% of one's capital before any sign of profit began to appear. The government for its part had no safeguard against overcharging or inefficiency. Nevertheless, and despite some criticism from either side, little short of £1 million was being laid out on mail subsidies within the Empire when the select committee came to look at the subject in 1902.[25]

By then, State subvention of shipping had assumed a new and additional form. In 1887 there had appeared for the first time in the navy estimates the charge of £10,000 'for the right of preemption or hire of merchant vessels as armed cruisers or transports'. This was the class of subsidy which the great events in the United States shipping world of 1901–02 were obliging the government and its critics to reconsider. Its *raison d'être* was at the time well understood. In the grand design of nineteenth-century Britain, navy and merchant marine had come to fill related and complementary roles. 'The importance', enunciated the Admiralty to the Colonial Conference of 1902, 'which attaches to the command of the sea lies in the control which it gives over sea communications'. 'Keeping the sea routes inviolate', through destruction of the enemy's power to break them, had become received doctrine. But the routes to be protected were the arteries of commerce through which flowed a trade of £1,000 million annually – living proof of Mahan's principle that the need for a navy stemmed from the existence of overseas trade and the shipping necessary to drive it. 'A navy', wrote Fremantle, 'is a useless exotic unless there is a trade to protect'.[26]

To the navy the merchant marine looked not only for protection but for employment. Naval construction, small and technically conservative though it had been under Victoria, was an important factor in the continued prosperity of British yards. Reciprocally, the navy looked to the merchant marine, or its faster element, as both a nursery of seamen and a reserve arm of national defence. Historically, said Mahan, no navy ever had cruisers enough. By the arrangement of 1887 the Admiralty was assured in war, and relatively cheaply, of the use of vessels peculiarly suitable by reason of speed and other features of design as auxiliaries, scouts or messengers – 'the eyes of the fleet'. By 1902 the country was paying £77,813 p.a. for the services of eighteen liners belonging to seven steamship lines or companies – of which the White Star, Cunard and Peninsular & Oriental were the most important – in return for which the recipients undertook also to hold a further thirty-one vessels 'at the disposition of the Admiralty, without further subsidy'. These two categories were together denoted as 'reserve merchant cruisers'; and contracts usually laid down that the Admiralty's approval was requisite for plans or specifications – often to a very minute degree – of any vessels designed to qualify for subsidy. A further condition was that in case of war they should be partially or entirely officered and manned by men of the Royal Naval Reserve, the number carried varying with the amount of subvention, which ranged up to $20 per gross ton annually according to speed. The total payment made under this head from 1887–88 to 1900–01 was shown as nearly £573,594. In this latter year the RNR comprised 1,900 officers and 25,880 men, about 4,000 of whom were in service on foreign-going ships.[27]

The American challenge of 1902 accentuated, though it did not primarily cause, certain deficiencies in this policy of cruiser subvention. It had always been subject to criticism in a Parliament allegedly unsympathetic to, or out of touch with, the navy's needs. Some MP's (notably T. Gibson Bowles) frankly advocated its abandonment and a return to the pre–1887 practice of commissioning vessels *ad hoc*, as followed in France and Germany and envisaged by the Frye Bill before Congress. To Sir John Colomb (MP for Great Yarmouth) the present policy had simply represented a waste of £38 million over fifty years, which recent First Lords had acquiesced in rather than strongly defended. No skill of designers, not even of the official expert Professor (later Sir) John Biles, could ensure that all subsidised cruisers had their engines below the waterline and plating invulnerable to the three-pounder gun. Several vessels still reserved, moreover, had fallen below the minimum acceptable speed. Nevertheless, the arrangement could be shown to have been a good bargain for the Admiralty. The cost of itself building a first-class cruiser, Arnold-Forster told the Commons in 1902, would represent more than a hundred years' subsidy of any one merchant ship at present on the reserve list.[28]

A second cause of doubt about existing cruiser subsidy policy, however, looked anxiously to the future. Subvention was accorded suitable vessels in consideration of their upkeep only, and in no way towards their construction. The best of this kind were capable of a continuous eighteen knots at sea, outsailing any man-of-war and burning up a thousand tons of coal a day. A critical point, however, was now being reached beyond which ships of higher speed were becoming commercially unprofitable for private companies either to build or to operate. Even disregarding the potentialities of new designs for turbine propulsion, the German lines now owned cruisers capable of more than twenty knots, designed with wartime use avowedly in view. What rise in the navy vote would be required if the Admiralty were to induce private British companies to turn out still faster vessels?

Thirdly, the system was no longer yielding a sufficient naval reserve of men. Alarmed by the persistent annual decline in British reservists, the Board of Trade in 1902 appointed a committee to inquire into (among other matters)

> the causes that have led to the employment of a large and increasing proportion of Lascars and Foreigners in the British Merchant Service and the effect of such employment upon the reserve of seamen of British nationality available for naval purposes in time of peace and war.

Its researches showed the number of Britons (including apprentices) serving in the RNR to have fallen from 96,914 in 1857 to 44,290 in 1902 – a drop of more than 50%. This Naval Reserves Committee pointed out that numerically the chief reservoir of skilled officers and men was now our yachts, fishing boats and coastal vessels. Though the number of mariners on reserve 'may and should be increased', the mercantile marine itself could not be relied on to meet all the navy's needs unless it became (what was quite inconceivable) practically a State-subsidised and State-regulated service. If transfer of its present subsidised vessels to foreign control continues, inferred the *Daily Mail*, it would sound 'the knell of the RNR'.[29]

As recently as 24th February 1902 Arnold-Forster had been

confidently informing Parliament how the Admiralty had lately extended its reserved cruiser policy to cover forty-nine vessels of seven shipping companies. At this juncture, subsidised cruiser tonnage of the White Star Line comprised eight vessels totalling 79,485 g.r.t. Three of these – including the *Oceanic*, fastest British ship afloat – attracted Admiralty subsidies at the rate of £21,000 p.a. and five others were contractually in the reserved though unsubsidised class. On the same terms Cunard was receiving £21,000 p.a. for seven fast vessels of its fleet, aggregating 77,182 g.r.t.[30] With the latter company seemingly as vulnerable to American capture as the former, it is time to look at the problem through the Admiralty's eyes.

The first concrete information the British government received of the state of maturity of the Americans' plans was from a private source. From what Dr D. C. M. Platt has demonstrated about the level of the State's commercial intelligence at that period, this circumstance need not surprise us. On 8th March the chairman of Cunard, the second Lord Inverclyde, communicated urgently to Selborne, through Arnold-Forster, what he had just learned from his company's New York agent about the agreement of 4th February concluded there between the parties to the combine and Morgan.[31] It was now clear that the White Star Line would follow Leyland into American control, and at least possible that Cunard would go the same way. When in the past subsidised vessels were, like the Inman steamers, transferred out of British ownership their Admiralty subvention was automatically forfeit. No contractual provision, however, absolutely forbade such a transfer: Arnold-Forster had to tell the Commons that, beyond its option to preempt, his department could not control the disposal of the White Star ships in any way.

To the Admiralty it was perfectly clear that two steps must urgently be taken. First, it must clarify the position with regard to those White Star vessels on its reserve list. Second, it must swiftly set up machinery to review its whole cruiser subsidy policy in the light of American developments. On 22nd March, therefore, the First Lord wrote to Pirrie, and four days later held a meeting with him and Bruce Ismay in consequence of which the latter on 4th April sent Selborne an offer to give an undertaking, in the form of an addition to the contract between the Admiralty and the White Star Line, to the effect that for the unexpired portion of the present agreement, that is to say until the 31st March 1905, none of the eight subsidised or retained steamers named in this agreement will be transferred to a foreign flag without the consent of the Admiralty having previously been obtained.[32]

It is probable that at their meeting of 26th March Ismay also handed the First Lord copies of the documentation relevant to the combine, including the main agreement of 4th February between Messrs Ismay Imrie & Co., and others, and Messrs J. P. Morgan Co.

This instrument the Cabinet certainly had before it when on 7th April it first took official cognisance of the American challenge, together with the comments of the Board of Trade's solicitor, R. Ellis Cunliffe. Cunliffe's opinion, submitted through the Permanent Secretary to the Board of Trade, Sir Francis Hopwood, was that 'by entering into negotiations which contemplate a sale' of their business White Star's managing company (the Oceanic Steamship Navigation Co.) had at least broken the spirit of Clause 8 of their agreement with Admiralty. Yet two difficulties stood in the way of peremptorily enforcing the latter. First, the contemplated sale would technically be of the company's shares only. Although 'in effect, . . . by selling the shares a transfer of the ships can be called for at any moment', and so Ismay Imrie & Co. practically 'are no longer able to give the notice to the Admiralty required by that clause', yet 'it is difficult to advise that because the shares are sold there is a breach of Clause 8'. Secondly, until the new trust were called into existence (which would not necessarily be before the end of the year) the American agreement of 4th February remained unrealised and ineffectual to secure performance of White Star's obligations to it.[33]

The immediate position thus secured, when Parliament began from 24th April onward to resume its inquisition of Ministers about the combine, Arnold-Forster and Gerald Balfour were able truthfully to assure the Commons that the Admiralty had made an arrangement with White Star whereby the reserved merchant cruisers would remain British for another three years, during which 'the control of the Admiralty over them will be as complete as if the combination had never taken place'. Admittedly the line's managing company had not given the government notice of its intention to sell. Nevertheless its negligence did not appear to have contravened the 1887 agreement, a copy of which Balfour agreed to lay on the table.[34]

By 28th April both Houses had also received particulars about a committee being appointed by the Admiralty

> to ascertain in what way, and at what cost, steamers of greater speed than those now employed, and of greater efficiency for war purposes, may be obtained in return for subsidies paid, and also to ascertain and report as to what modification of the existing form of agreement, and what addition to the present rate of subsidy, may be necessary in order to prevent the transfer to a foreign flag without permission of the Admiralty of any ship which receives or has received a subsidy.

Its six named members were to be presided over by Lord Camperdown. The policy of paying subsidies, Arnold-Forster, however, stressed, was not itself open to review. In making a similar communication to the Lords, Selborne was at pains to avoid any semblance of agitation. The idea of such a committee had been canvassed 'weeks before I heard of the possibility of the Morgan combination'. His department's attitude to the combination, he later added, 'is in no sense one of hostility, but it is one of anxiety'.[35]

That it was Balfour who assumed, jointly with the Admiralty's spokesmen, responsibility for explaining and defending the government's marine policy to Parliament is significant of the extent to which his department was inevitably drawn into the eye of the controversy. True, at this period and for some time hereafter, the Board of Trade exercised no great influence in the determination of major commercial policy, falling in this respect somewhat uncomfortably between Treasury and Foreign Office. Administratively it functioned rather as a federation of departments, each exercising separate technical responsibilities. As an entity the Board was still far from becoming what Lloyd-George was to make it, one of the great organs of state.

In one sphere, however, the reception of free-trade doctrine had made the Board the chief agent of government – that of merchant shipping. The old Navigation Acts had, along with tariff protection and colonial preference, formed part of a comprehensive and coherent policy for safeguarding national power. Their repeal (so far as overseas voyages were concerned) in 1849 had left a regulatory vacuum which Parliament was prompt to fill by means of the Mercantile Marine Act of 1850, 'for improving the condition of Masters, Mates and Seamen and maintaining discipline in the Merchant Service'.[36] This statute, foundation for a huge edifice of supervisory legislation regulating ultimately the pressure in a ship's boilers and the number of biscuits in her stores, for the first time designated the Board of Trade the authority to 'undertake general superintendence of matters relating to the British Merchant Marine' through a newly created section which, absorbing many powers from the Admiralty, came to be known as the Mercantile Marine Department. Its first head was that very determined man, destined to serve the Board continuously for forty-three years, T. H. (later Lord) Farrer, whose views were known from his work on *The State in its Relation to Trade* (now in 1902 appearing in a second and revised edition).

Besides its manifold duties of technical supervision, some of the functions of Farrer's new sub-department carried international implications which a later Permanent Secretary of the Board of Trade has conveniently summarised as follows:

> Political and commercial relations, including the fixing and enforcement of the conditions under which a vessel is entitled to fly the British flag and to claim the privileges of a British ship; the conditions and limits subject to which foreign vessels may be permitted to trade to and from British ports; and the protection of the interests of British shipping in foreign ports both as regards trading rights and facilities and the rates of dues and charges.[37]

Some supplementary regulation followed almost immediately. A Customs Consolidation Act of 1853 enunciated a right of retaliation (never actually to be invoked) upon countries which might practise flag discrimination against British ships; and, subject to this implied reciprocity, foreign vessels were in the following year admitted to the British coastal trade. Thus the last scrap of the Naviagation Laws was swept away. Another Act of the same year (1854) consolidated these and other provisions; and for the next half-century parliamentarians – and not merely agitators like the member for Derby, Samuel Plimsoll –

were continuously concerned with improving conditions in the merchant service. Scarcely a session passed which did not see either a commission sitting or a Bill preparing: so that the next consolidation, by the great Mercantile Marine Act of 1894, digested a whole mass of merchant shipping law in a single 300 page code.[38] In 1900, under pressure from the Manchester Chamber of Commerce, the President of the Board of Trade had furthermore appointed an Advisory Committee on Commercial Intelligence.

This corpus of regulation, if it eliminated some of the less efficient or more casual elements of the shipping industry, had in its early years been regarded by that industry itself with some suspicion, even hostility. It was accused of weighing the shipowner down with numerous standards and obligations (of manning, operation, etc.) to which he was inclined to attribute the onus of blame when commercial success fell short of expectations. At Westminster he was represented by a vocal minority who owed their seats to a party advocating the free-trade doctrine, sometimes in its purest form. With the rise of economic nationalism in 1890's, however, whereby the most pressing mercantile problems had become less insular and more international in character, this somewhat resentful reaction was coming to be balanced, though not effaced, by the growing tendency to look to the Board of Trade as the industry's champion against the gathering host of foreign competitors. Relations between its Mercantile Marine Department and the shipowners had meanwhile been improving as numerous opportunities for co-operation presented themselves.

One effect of the new threat from America on the North Atlantic, however, was to disturb this balance again with revived criticism of Board of Trade regulations as onerous and disabling. In his address to Leyland shareholders on 7th May 1901, and in a letter to the *Daily Mail* the following day, Ellerman complained of the aggregate effect of restrictions – many from the age of sail imposed on British ships as to the number of compartments, boats carried, load line, provisioning, crew space, deck cargo, manning, repatriation of seamen, etc. In the Commons sweeping statements were again heard, such as the declaration of Gibson Bowles during the debate on the adjournment of 1st May 1902, that 'the government has rarely interfered with the Merchant Marine of this country except to its disadvantage'. More reasoned demands were revived in the press to change 'a system which seems based on a theory that the British shipowner is the natural enemy of mankind, and treat him as a deserving and desirable member of the State'. In its own defence the Board of Trade's Marine Department, preparing to rebut such charges before the Select Committee on Steamship Subsidies, averred that

> The cry of 'harassing regulations' is repeated so often that many shipowners have come to believe it. When any particular case is examined the grievance is generally found to be minute or nonexistent.

Some regulations were admittedly antiquated in form, but did not hamper in practice, for the Board exercised its discretion to waive them. Unwaived, however, riposted *Fairplay*, they imposed a cost handicap of at least 10% on our shipping as against foreign. The demand that these restrictions be enforced on all vessels, foreign equally with native, using British ports the Board rightly regarded as quite unpractical. It may be conceded that some individual proposals for change appeared reasonable enough – that light dues be abolished, for instance, and the coastline lit and harbours improved at public expense. Collectively, however, the effect of all such regulations was deemed by some authorities to be comparatively insignificant, and it may be doubted whether their total repeal would have made much competitive difference to British trade.[39]

A much more crucial problem, however, faced the Board over the matter of ownership and control of the British vessels entering or about to enter the American combine. Confronted with this probability, Gerald Balfour consulted his Board's solicitor. When the Cabinet in early May 1902 first discussed the business, he had then bluntly to tell them that, the Admiralty's pre-emption rights apart, there was 'nothing in our law which stands in the way of a transfer' of ownership of the main body of the White Star fleet. Moreover, these vessels, even when effectively possessed and controlled by non-Britons, might not be prevented from continuing to ply under the British flag. 'The present law', he explained to his colleagues, 'allows a British ship to be under the complete financial control of foreigners'.[40]

How could this quandary have arisen? Public policy as expressed in the Merchant Shipping Act of 1894 was designed to make clear that ownership carried with it certain obligations. This it sought to do by laying down conditions for the registry of a vessel which made establishment of ownership the vital point. Under the Act a ship was not to be deemed British unless wholly owned by qualified persons, which category Section 1 very elaborately defined. Under Sections 25 and 71 a vessel might not, upon pain of forfeiture, continue on the British register and fly the British flag if its ownership (technically divisible into sixty-four parts) were transferred, in whole or in part, to non-British hands. The statute's clear intent was that vessels registered at Customs House as British should be really, not nominally, owned by British nationals.

The loophole, however, was a clause allowing ownership in a vessel to be acquired by 'corporate bodies established under and subject to the laws of some part of Her Majesty's dominions'. In this respect the 1894 Merchant Shipping Act merely repeated that of 1854, which had been framed in the days well before the machinery of incorporation had come to be freely used – as in the now prevalent American style – for purposes of trading. British trading corporations had tended chiefly to proceed by development of the laws of partnership rather than by the common law of corporations. Meanwhile, however, the Companies Acts had come to accord great freedom of action to incorporators. Under that of 1862, for instance, it had been held by the courts that 'there is nothing to prevent an alien not an enemy from holding shares in a British company'. Something of a *contretemps* was therefore seen to have arisen, in that the considerable liberty conceded to aliens by the Act of 1862 was now difficult to reconcile with avowed policy of excluding them from ownership of a British ship. The Companies Act, in short, permitted the violation of the Merchant Shipping Acts. And the Morgan combination could absorb as many British vessels as it chose (including – the implication was obvious – Cunard's) simply by acquiring shares in corporate bodies nominally registered as British. Balfour had to tell the Commons that vessels so absorbed might continue to fly the red ensign so long as the corporate body to which they belonged was established under British law and had its principal place of business on British soil.[41]

Knowledgable critics, in Parliament and outside, were quick to draw attention to this contradiction between legal intent and content. If an American concern bought 742 out of 750 shares in the Oceanic Steamship Co. the latter's vessels would *de facto* have ceased to be British in any effective sense just as much as if they, and not merely the shares, had passed outright to a foreigner. Yet so long as the company's domicile remained British, the White Star Line was entitled *de jure* to continue flying the British flag. Thus the 1894 Act, said Gibson Bowles, 'became mere waste paper and idle verbiage'. Change of shareholding was effectively a change of ownership. 'The government ought to step in.'[42]

But how? By striking the American-bought vessels off the register, said some: in not immediately doing so the government had let Morgan's out of a very tight corner and simply connived at a statutory breach. We must not allow the red ensign to be used as a cover by foreign fleets competing for our trade. When Gerald Balfour assured the Commons that the particular British companies now entering the combine would remain not only nominally but really British, the *Financial Times* raised the bogey that, if the Morgan syndicate later desired to move them on to the American register, 'all they have to do ... is to pass the necessary resolutions for the liquidation of the English companies to arrange a sale direct to the Trust'. But this threat was academic so long as the registration laws of the United States remained as stringent as we have seen them to be.[43]

To his Cabinet colleagues Balfour had extended as cold comfort the 'question whether our legislation on this important subject is suitable to the requirements of the present day', himself being 'disposed to think that careful consideration must be given to the propriety of making some amendment'. It would be possible, of course, so to amend the 1894 Act as to make the shipping register at Customs House more clearly distinct from the companies register at Somerset House. On the other side of the argument it was, however, observed that far more British capital was invested in American companies (particularly in railroads) than *vice versa*. For this freedom, so commercially beneficial to us, did not reciprocity require equal liberty for Americans to buy shares in our shipping concerns? Other critics again were for speedily bringing a test case under the 1894 Act.

When such an action did eventually come before the Chancery Division of the High Court, late in 1903, it was to be after the nature and composition of the International Mercantile Marine Co. had become clearly apparent; and Mr Justice Byrne was then to distinguish between English and non-English public companies, and to classify the IMM in the latter category.[44]

Not until mid-June 1902 was a British Minister to be in direct contact with a representative of Morgan. The situation meanwhile prevailing throughout April and May of that year was that the government were slowly taking the measure of events in the United States, about which their information was still unreliable and imperfect. In the press, rumours abounded that Cunard were soon to be added to the transatlantic consortium. At Westminster the Ministry confronted representatives of interests greatly alarmed by what they apprehended. In Whitehall it was digesting the advice of its legal officers and awaiting the report of the hastily appointed Admiralty committee and, at a further remove, of the reappointed Committee on Steamship Subsidies. Until they had before them the advice of these various specialists, Ministers could only temporise in plain uncertainty, holding off parliamentary critics with ministerial concessions and largely negative reassurances. One course the government early and explicitly rejected. Balfour refused to contemplate bringing in a Bill to prevent transfer to another flag by a British owner of any ship which might be suitable in wartime as cruiser or transport. Such a degree of legislative intervention would be 'startling'.[45]

Positively, however, two complementary policy objectives were beginning to emerge. For one, the government must seek to prevent further British losses to the combine by acting to encourage some consolidation of independent British shipping resources on the North Atlantic round the one British company there, Cunard, which was still uncontrolled by the Americans. By what means this end was pursued the following chapter will show. At the same time the government recognised the parallel need to reach some accommodation with the Morgan trust, on the 'least possible friction' basis, which we must now consider directly. These objectives are the guiding threads through the maze of subsequent negotiations.

It was early May before the Cabinet first considered the

American challenge in its fullest implications. They did so on the basis of a memorandum from the President of the Board of Trade, dated 30th April, analysing the respective relationships to the combine in which the British and German lines would be standing. The latter, he noted, would face 'not absorption, but alliance on equal terms between organisations which maintain their separate identity'. Any closer relationship was 'held to be inconsistent with political requirements' in Germany. 'The scrupulous care,' added Balfour, 'shown in the German Agreement to safeguard national interests contrasts unpleasantly with the apparent indifference of our own ship-owners to this aspect of the matter.' British companies entering the combine would indeed continue to exist and to be nominal owners of their respective fleets. But in contrast to the German,

> whether they sail under the American or the British flag, it is evident that they will, in fact, if not in name, become the property of the American Corporation and the general result of the arrangement will be a practical absorption of the British companies by that Corporation.

As to policy and methods, the corporation presumably expected its profits to accrue not so much from the raising of freight charges on the North Atlantic as from limiting the number of vessels employed there

> to those strictly necessary for the traffic. The idea is that they will be able to do this, and yet defy competition, by reason of the control exercised by Mr J. P. Morgan over railways on the other side. As the remainder of their fleets will then be free for employment elsewhere, it is evident that the proposed plan of campaign may have a far-reaching effect upon competition in the shipping industry, and especially upon the interests of British ship-owners in every part of the world.

On the whole Balfour was inclined to think that the combine 'does not carry with it any immediate consequences of a grave character'. The Admiralty's interests in White Star were for the present safeguarded by the agreement with Ismay, and 'this gives us time to look round and take stock of the position'. But it must be admitted that foreign control of three important British lines threatened more than some loss of maritime prestige. The trust might absorb others. Congress might, against the probabilities, agree to admit those British vessels to American registry. Even without such a transfer, foreign control might be used to injure British commerce. And the combine was likely to build more of its new ships in American yards than in British.[46]

Of these possibilities the Cabinet did not at this juncture do more than take note. Doubtless it was also apprised of the negotiations (which our next chapter will study) currently proceeding with the chairman of Cunard. But Morgan, as we have seen, had been touring Europe in an endeavour to allay British and German fears, and the next approach was to come from his side, through the agency of a Briton who had recently resigned from the civil service at the age of forty-one in order to accept a partnership in Morgan's London subsidiary, J. S. Morgan & Co. Son of a Foreign Office official, brother of two distinguished soldiers, and himself formerly private secretary to Goschen at the Exchequer, Clinton Edward Dawkins had in the preceding year been chairing the Committee on War Office Reorganisation, which service had earned him a knighthood. Morgan now appointed him chairman of the combine's British committee.

On 11th June 1902 Sir Clinton Dawkins sent Balfour a memorandum volunteering certain assurances on Morgan's behalf, which the latter professed to regard as a matter of course but in return for which he looked for some token of goodwill from the British government. This memorandum[47] proffered a contractual assurance for fifty years that any British ship in the combine, built or to be built, would not be transferred to a foreign register without the written consent of the President of the Board of Trade, and would carry as many British sailors of all ranks as other similarly subsidised vessels were required to do. During those fifty years British ships in the combine would be at the Admiralty's disposal for hire or purchase, or for chartering at thirty hours' notice, 'provided that the terms are similar to those offered to other lines'. A fixed percentage, to be agreed, of all ships hereafter built for the combine should be constructed in British yards; provided that, if it ultimately became cheaper to build ships on the other side, the difference in cost should be made up to the combine.

In tendering these assurances, which he did not at this stage insist on being cast into formal agreement, Morgan's objective was twofold. He wanted to ensure that the government would not discontinue its existing subsidies to those vessels entering the combine, and would not discriminate thereafter against their operating companies, in favour of British lines remaining outside, as regards future tenders for ships, naval and mail subsidies, etc. The former objective – Selborne having already received Ismay's assurance of 4th April on behalf of White Star – was not difficult of achievement. By the end of June the Admiralty had clearly made up its mind not to exercise its option to purchase the eight vessels concerned, but to leave them on its reserve list for the remainder of the contract. Morgan's second objective, of parity of treatment for British lines inside the combine with those outside, was not so easy to express. That he and the government were treating, however, became an open secret which was twice during July the subject of anxious parliamentary probing.

On 5th and 7th August government spokesmen had to tell the Commons that, while any financial settlement would naturally be subject to Parliament's approval, no agreement was expected to be ready to lay before the House that session. The new Prime Minister, A. J. Balfour, did, however, disclose that negotiations were being conducted by a 'Committee of the Cabinet'.[48] Its members were his brother for the Board of Trade, Selborne for the Admiralty, and Joseph Chamberlain at the Colonial Office. Chamberlain, one may infer, was probably included not only in consideration of his previous experience at the Board of Trade and his close family connections in the United States, but in recognition of the fact that his present department would be interested in any new steamer services to Canada which might evolve from reorganisation in the North Atlantic. Be that as it may, the return of peace to South Africa had now released his not inconsiderable energies.

The key date was the Cabinet's meeting of 7th August, when the agenda before it included not only a number of alternative proposals for the future of Cunard but Dawkins's proposals of 11th June on behalf of Morgan.[49] The three-man committee on this occasion stated one of the 'main objects which it is desired to keep in view' as being to

> avoid unnecessary friction with the Morgan Combination, and in particular to abstain from action likely to stir up national animosities or provoke a war of subsidies with the United States ... Once we had to come to terms with the Cunard Company, it would be open to

us to enter into negotiations with Mr Pierpont Morgan, and endeavour to arrive at a friendly understanding with him on the lines of Sir Clinton Dawkins' Memorandum.

The Cabinet having thereupon taken the decision to approve an arrangement with Cunard involving (on terms we shall later examine) the building of two new and very fast steamers, Balfour on the following day met Morgan and Dawkins to explain what had been resolved. Morgan at once asked to be allowed to tender for the two new flyers. Balfour explained that it was of the essence of the Cunard contract that the latter company should be responsible. Morgan then suggested that the combine should be allowed to tender for a further two: but Balfour insisted that only one pair were at present required. 'For a moment,' recorded Balfour,

> Mr Morgan appeared to think that the action of the Government was unfriendly to the Combination, but he was satisfied when I pointed out that the fast ships were not built to create trade competition, but merely for purposes of naval defence.

– a point which Dawkins agreed was necessary, to put British security ahead of German. Morgan intimated 'in strong terms' his intention to maintain the British nationality of the ships in the combine, and generally to adhere to the undertakings of Dawkins's memorandum, but also his expectation that the British government would show its goodwill in extending equal treatment to the component British companies in respect of 'all services which His Majesty's Government desire to have rendered by the mercantile marine'. This matter Balfour promised to refer to his ministerial colleagues. But how best to give effect to these mutual understandings – by formal treaty, exchange of letters, or mere verbal assurances? 'It was clear that both Mr Morgan and Sir C. Dawkins favoured a more or less formal agreement,' in view of the particular arrangement pending with Cunard and of the circumstance that Morgan's informal protestations of goodwill could not bind his successors. Accordingly, when the Cabinet returned to the matter in the following week, it accepted its committee's recommendation that 'it would be well to obtain a more precise statement of the nature of the assurances of goodwill and fair treatment which the Trust would expect to receive in the event of a formal Agreement being entered into'. Such a statement Dawkins duly supplied on 19th August. Being due to sail for New York at the end of the first week in September, he offered to get any consequent agreement ratified by his fellow directors or by the voting trustees of the International Mercantile Marine Co. and executed as a binding contract.[50]

With the Cabinet's blessing, Balfour occupied the next ten days in consulting his colleagues about the acceptable terms of such an instrument. Chamberlain, not at first enthusiastic for a formal declaration of reciprocity, wanted to ensure that it would not bind the government, when requiring the fast new ships, to invite tenders from *all* British companies in the combine and to accept the lowest. If, on the contrary, what Morgan wanted was no more than an assurance that these companies would receive the same consideration from Post Office and Admiralty as before, he would not demur – though recommending that the agreement make this explicit. Sir Francis Hopwood on the other hand, as Permanent Secretary to the Board of Trade, saw much to be said for formalising Morgan's proposals. The new ships to be looked for from Cunard might stir the combine competitively into offering the government better terms for fast cruisers in future: for 'a great and wealthy Combination such as this must in self-defence "turn out" the best material', thus giving Britain the full benefit of their enterprise. A written treaty 'will also draw the sting which has penetrated the popular mind' by providing tangible evidence of the retention for a considerable period of British registration by the ships bought. Selborne concurred, with the proviso that the agreement require unequivocally that at least half the ships to be built for the combine were British-registered. By early September Balfour was ready to present the redrafted instrument, together with the concomitant correspondence, as a minute for the Cabinet in the express hope of settling the whole business before Parliament reassembled in October. In practice, however, tidying up the last minutiae of the draft was to occupy Treasury and Board of Trade solicitors into 1903.[51]

In its final form the agreement comprised twelve articles, of which nos. 2 and 6 represented the government's reworking of Morgan's undertakings into a form agreeable to all parties. Article 2 provided that the British companies in the IMM, and a majority of their directors, should remain British. Article 3 laid down that no British ship in the combine, or thereafter to be acquired by or built for any of its component British companies, should be transferred to a foreign registry without the written consent of the President of the Board of Trade, 'which shall not be unreasonably withheld'. The inclusion of this latter phrase, at Dawkins's request,[52] merely recognised the common practice of companies to sell off their obsolete vessels. Nothing should otherwise be done, the article continued, whereby any such ship might forfeit its right to fly the British flag.

If this article reassured those who feared the loss by transfer of British shipping, Article 4 placated those who lamented the decline of British sailors. It stipulated that British ships of the combine, now or to be added later, should be officered by British subjects and carry the same proportion of British nationals in its crew 'as His Majesty's Government may prescribe or arrange for in the case of any other British lines engaged in the same trades'. Article 5 entrenched the Admiralty's right to take up, by hire or purchase and upon current terms, any British ship in the combine or later to be built for or acquired by any of its British components. By Article 6 it was agreed that at least half the tonnage built for or acquired by the IMM in each successive three-year period – including 'a reasonable proportion of the faster classes of vessels' but excluding any abnormally fast ship built by special arrangement with either the British or United Stated governments – should accrue to its British companies and be registered as British. Those who, like Hopwood, relied on the inherent efficiency of British shipbuilding to ensure lowest prices, and on the good sense of the British directors in the IMM, would have preferred to regard this article as dispensable, but were conscious of the need to allay public anxiety.[53]

Article 1 was the government's *quid pro quo* for Morgan, and as such required the most circumspect drafting. In its final form it promised British companies within the combine treatment 'on the same footing of general equality with other British companies in respect of any services naval military or postal which His Majesty's Government may desire to have rendered by the British Mercantile Marine'. It was not acceptable that the government should engage itself to approach *all* relevant companies for competitive tenders for such purposes: that had never been the Admiralty's practice and rarely the Post Office's. The contingency could be met, Balfour and Chamberlain agreed, by insertion of a phrase specifying that such equality of consideration should be 'as heretofore'. The crux, as they well saw, was the novel problem of vessels of abnormally high speed requirements. With these in mind, a proviso was added 'that nothing in this Agreement contained shall extend to vessels of uncommercial speed which His Majesty's Government may specially require to be constructed and what are primarily designed for service in time of war'. It was informally assumed that, the current negotiations with Cunard apart, in future Cunard and White Star should be allowed to bid against each other, being the only two British lines in a position to compete in that class. At no time was it proposed to open such tendering to foreign builders; and had Morgan held out against this exclusiveness, Chamberlain for one would have favoured the Admiralty's taking up the fast White Star vessels.[54]

The duration of the whole agreement was set by Article 10 at twenty years, thereafter to be renewable for five-year periods by mutual consent: but power was reserved to the British government at any time to terminate it unilaterally if the combine pursued 'a policy injurious to the interests of the British Merchant Marine or of British trade' – an interpolation to which Morgan did not object. The government also added the provision, finally embodied as Article 12, that in the event of conflicting interpretations of the instrument, final arbitration should rest with the Lord Chancellor. It was observed, however, that since no penalties were provided for breach of any part of the agreement, the only effect of this would be to declare when a breach had occurred.

'Really a very good arrangement for us,' opined Chamberlain at last. 'Taken together with Cunard proposal, I think it is a sufficient "repartee" to the American combine.'[55] When it came with the committee's endorsement to the Cabinet on 12th September, however, four more articles were felt to be needful. Of these, Article 7 was purely explicatory, making clear that the phrase 'the British Companies included in the Association' covered also all such as were hereafter admitted to or brought under control of the IMM: of which accretions Article 8 now required the combine to give the government notice. Article 9 provided for the legal execution of the agreement on the former's part; while Article 11 established the legality of the instrument under British law and of the agencies appointed by the combine in Britian. The document in its final form[56] was signed almost twelve months after Balfour's first draft, on 1st August 1903, by two commissioners for the Admiralty, Balfour for the Board of Trade, Dawkins and an Assistant Secretary for the IMM, and by principal officers of the latter's respective component companies.

In thus bringing to a conclusion its negotiations with Morgan the government had reached one of its four principal goals (as we distinguished then at the close of the preceding chapter) – a *modus vivendi* with the new Atlantic power. Thereby it had gone far towards attaining another objective, the relief of popular anxiety over national security at sea. At the same time, and through a second set of negotiations, it had been painfully pursuing its two further goals – to preserve Britain's remaining shipping lines on the North Atlantic, and by some means to fortify their resistance to the severe competition expected from their new American rivals there. The Morgan agreement represented, therefore, only one of the two pillars from which the arch of twentieth-century maritime policy was designed to spring. For its twin the Cunard company would have to serve as the core. Around this last major British line to survive in independence in the disputed ocean the Ministry's parallel negotiations revolved.

Not one but a pair of contracts were therefore necessary. They were, as the Prime Minister pointed out, 'very closely bound together'.[57] A treaty with the Americans, for the enforcement of which no teeth had been provided, could be credible only if complemented by a reconcentration of British strength on the North Atlantic. Before signing with Morgan the government must be sure of Cunard. How best to strengthen the latter's competitive position, however, was to remain in doubt until pressure of circumstances compelled a hesitant Cabinet to make up its collective mind.

NOTES

1 *P. Debs.*, 4 series, 107:477 Edmund Robertson, 'The shipping combination and the British flag', *Nineteenth Century* 51:873 (1902); *Fairplay* 36:757 (4 May 1901) and 820 (16 May 1901); *Times*, 27 April 1902; quotations from American press in *Fairplay* 38:744 (5 May 1902).

2 *National Review* 39:592 (1902); *Annual Register for 1901*, p. 250; 'Calchas' (J. L. Garvin) in *Fortnightly Review* 71:948 (1902); C. H. Cramp, 'The steamship merger and American shipbuilding', *North Atlantic Review* 175:12 (1902); *New York Times*, 26 May 1902, leader.

3 Benjamin Taylor, 'British and American shipping', *Nineteenth Century* 52:19–33 (1902); *Times*, 28 Aug. 1895, leader.

4 Board of Trade returns, Marine Dept., in PRO at MT9 730/M9283/02, in preparation for the Board's evidence to Select Committee on Steam Ship Subsidies.

5 Quoted in *Times*, 14 May 1902, p. 7.

6 *Ibid.*, 22 and 27 May 1902; Huldermann: *op. cit.*, p. 61.

7 Select Committee on Steam Ship Subsidies, *Report*, H. of C. 385 (1902), ix, para. 32.

8 *P. Debs.*, 4 series, 108:862–3.

9 *Times*, 16 and 19 Apr. 2 and 22 May 1902; *Economist* 60:645 (1902).

10 T. H. Sanderson to Lord Monk Bretton, 20 May 1902, Joseph Chamberlain papers 11/39/134.

11 *P. Debs.*, 4 series, 107:494; *Fortnightly Review, loc. cit.*; B. Taylor, 'The threat of the combine', *Nineteenth Century* 52:32–3 (1902).

12 *Fortnightly Review, loc. cit.*, p. 943; *National Review* 39:592 (1902); *Times*, 26 Apr., p. 13, and 13 May, p. 9 (Pirrie's letter), 1902.

13 *Fairplay* 36:757, 38:904; *Economist* 60:1599 (18 Oct. 1902); W. Wetherell in *Fortnightly Review* 71:515–p 575 ff. (1902); *P. Debs.*, 4 series, 107:489.

14 *Fairplay, loc. cit.*

15 *P. Debs.*, 4 series, 106:183, 1324, 107:30, 31, 427.

16 *Ibid.*: 107:427, 429, 1081.

17 *Times*, 28 Apr. and 13 May 1902; John W. Hughes to A. le Blanc, New Orleans representative, Harrison MSS, 1 May 1901, quoted in Hyde: *op. cit.*, p. 32; *P. Debs.*, 4 series, 112–1132.

18 *Fortnightly Review* 71:942–56; Select Committee on Steam Ship Subsidies, *loc. cit.*, Minutes, p. 9; *Financial Times*, 5 June 1902, p. 3.

19 Board of Trade, Marine Dept's figures, in MT9 730/M9283/02; *National Review* 39:592.

20 *Economist* 60:732–3, 1527; *Financial Times, loc. cit.*

21 *Times*, 16 and 20 May (letters) and 22 May (Vienna dispatch) 1902; *Fairplay* 36: 757 and 782, 38:700; *P. Debs.*, 4 series, 107:459, 484; 108:863: 127:361; *Fortnightly Review, loc. cit.; Economist* 60:646.

22 B. Taylor in *Nineteenth Century* 52:32.
23 Select Committee on Steam Ship Subsidies, *Report, loc. cit.,* p. 3, para. 2; Select Committee on Contract Packets, *Report,* Cd. 1660 (1853), xcv, pp. 2 and 3.
24 Quoted in Sir Evelyn Murray: *The Post Office* (1927, p. 57; Select Committee on Steam Ship Subsidies, *loc. cit.,* evidence of H. Buxton Forman.
25 Memorandum of Arnold-Forster, 13 June 1902, App. D, p. 16 (Selborne papers, Ministry of Defence); Select Committee on Steam Ship Subsidies, *loc. cit.,* Apps. 12 and 29.
26 Admiralty memorandum, quoted in A. B. Keith (ed.): *Select Speeches and Documents on British Colonial Policy, 1763–1917* (1933), ii.230; Fremantle in *National Review* 39:595 (1902).
27 *P. Debs.,* 4 series, 108:1208; see (e.g.) the six volumes of Admiralty instructions for fitting merchant cruisers for war purposes and the very elaborate designs for the *Campania* and *Lucania* in Adm. 116/907, case 971(PRO); Select Committee on Steam Ship Subsidies, *loc. cit.,* p. xi, App. 24, and Minutes of Evidence, pp. 132–3. The navy regulations of the time did not forbid RN reservists from sailing in vessels under a foreign flag for short periods, but did allow special leave of absence for that purpose. The forty-nine vessels held at the Admiralty's disposal at this time were listed, for Parliament's information, in a *Return* of Merchant Liners under Contract with His Majesty's Government for use as Armed Cruisers in War, PP 1902 (218), xcii, 327 (17 June 1902).
28 *P. Debs.,* 4 series, 107:29 and 108:963–5.
29 Parliamentary return, Cd. 1491, and *Report,*Cd. 1607, of 1903, paras. 16–18; see also Hopwood's memorandum of the preceding year in GB 30/60/45. On the low state of the RNR see W. L. Clowes, 'The condition of the Naval Reserve', *Nineteenth* Century li (1902), pp. 550–61.
30 *P. Debs.,* 4 series, 103:976; Committee on Merchant Cruisers, *Report,* Cd. 1379 (1902).
31 D. C. St M. Platt: *Finance, Trade and Politics in British Foreign Policy, 1815–1914* (1968); for Inverclyde's warning to Selborne see chapter 5 below, n 7.
32 Ismay to Selborne, 4 Apr. 1902 Arnold-Forster papers 50295 P. 66 (British Library).
33 Memoranda dated 7 Apr. 1902, Paper No. 1, Austen Chamberlain papers 16/6/1 (University of Birmingham); draft in GB 30/60/48.
34 *P. Debs.,* 4 series, 106:1181–2, 1321–3; 107:30, 431, 473, 1350–2; and 112:698.
35 *Ibid.,* 106:1145–6; 107:28; and 110:1061.
36 13 and 14 Vict. c. 24.
37 H. Llewellyn Smith: *The Board of Trade* (1928), p. 90.
38 Respectively 17 and 18 Vict. c. 21 and 18; 57 and 58 Vict. c. 60.
39 *Daily Mail,* 8 May 1901; *P. Debs.,* 4 series, 107:468; B. Taylor in *Nineteenth Century* 52:33; MT9 730/M9283/02; *Fairplay* 36:784

and 838–8, 38:905; *Times*, 4 July and 30 Sept. 1902, letters of Pirrie and G. W. Balfour.

40 AC 16/6/2, memorandum by G. W. Balfour headed 'The Atlantic Combination as affecting British Shipping', printed for the Cabinet 1 May 1902.

41 *P. Debs.*, 4 series, 107:430.

42 *Ibid.*, 107:30; 108:506–7.

43 B. Taylor, 'British shipping and the State', *North Atlantic Review* 179:244 (1904); *Financial Times*, 5 June 1903, p. 5.

44 AC 16/6/2; *Lomonby and Another v. Carter and Another*, 19 Dec. 1903, in respect of shares originally held by a testatrix in the Oceanic Steamship Co. Ltd. See also a discussion of the problems by Charles A. Lightbound: *The Shipping Trade and Fiscal Policy* (Liverpool, 1904).

45 *New York Herald*, 22 Apr. *Standard*, 5 May, and *Daily Chronicle* 6 May 1902; *P. Debs.*, 4 series, 107:429 (1 May 1902).

46 AC 16/6/2.

47 Headed 'The Morgan Shipping Combination' and printed for the Cabinet 6 Aug. 1902, AC 16/6/3. p. 7.

48 *P. Debs.*, 4 series, 110:1074–5, 111:1367–8, 112:651, 696, 698, 972, 1088 and 1120.

49 AC 16/6/3.

50 Memorandum of interview between Balfour, Morgan and Dawkins, printed for the Cabinet 15 Aug. 1902, AC 16/6/4; draft in GB 30/60/48.

51 Chamberlain to Balfour, 26 Aug., and Hopwood to the same, 25 Aug. 1902, GB 30/60/48; Balfour to Chamberlain, 27 Aug., JC 11/6/2; and to Selborne, 28 Aug., GB 30/60/48, enclosing draft dated 28 Aug. 1902; Chamberlain to Selborne and to Balfour, 29 Aug. and 2 Sept. 1902, *ibid.*; Balfour to Chamberlain, 1 and 11 Sept. 1902, JC 11/6/4 and 5, Cunliffe to Hopwood, 6 Oct. 1902 and T. H. Mellor to Cuncliffe, 23 Jan. 1903, GB 30/60/48.

52 Dawkins to Balfour, 9 Sept. 1902, *ibid.*

53 Hopwood to Balfour, 2 Sept. 1902, *ibid.*

54 Chamberlain to Balfour, 2 Sept. 1902 *ibid.*

55 Chamberlain to Balfour, 9 Sept. 1902, *ibid.*

56 Laid before Parliament as Cd. 1704 of 1903.

57 *P. Debs.*, 4 series, 114:602 (11 Nov. 1902).

CHAPTER 5

The Cunard contract

Since the Crown first began, in the 1830's, to make a regular practice of going to private steamship companies for its packet services, many different lines have stood in contract to it. But none has enjoyed so long and continuous a relationship with the government as Cunard. Its earliest agreement – for delivery of mails between Halifax, N.S., and Boston, Mass. – was signed in 1815 and enlarged in 1841 when the service was extended to include Quebec. Cunard's first transatlantic contract, however, dates from 1839, when it agreed with the Admiralty to carry bi-monthly mail from Liverpool to Boston and New York alternately. On the strength of this subsidy – £60,000 p.a. for seven years – the company had Robert Napier build it four side-lever paddle steamers on the Clyde; and the new service was inaugurated on 4th July (auspicious date!) 1840, when the *Britannia* departed on her maiden voyage from the Mersey. Eight years later Cunard won a competitive contract worth £140,000 p.a. for a weekly service direct to New York, henceforth to be its chief American point of call.

That year of 1848 is credibly held to mark the triumph of steam over sail on the North Atlantic, which was soon to become the area *par excellence* where British mail contractors had to face competition from both domestic and foreign tenders. But Samuel Cunard's strength was that he alone could offer all-year-round service with vessels suitable also for wartime employment. (Indeed, it was their usefulness in the Crimean War that earned him his knighthood in 1859.) Reciprocally, the subsidy enabled his company to weather critical periods and so to survive where others failed. True, in 1850 it lost the Canadian mail contract when that colony inaugurated its own Quebec–Liverpool service through the Allan Line. Nevertheless by 1853, when Parliament first showed alarm at the mounting cost of mail subsidies, Cunard were earning about three-quarters of the £850,000 p.a. and more which the government was disbursing for that purpose. In particular this steady subvention helped Cunard beat off the short but sharp rivalry from the Collins Line which in 1850 had threatened to 'sweep the Cunarders off the ocean'. Had not the Americans' reckless speed resulted in two disasters which, together with Congress's withdrawal of subsidies, brought them to ruin, they might have succeeded in their policy of (as Cunard's chairman put it) 'breaking our windows with sovereigns'.

It was competition from the Inman – first line on the Atlantic to carry second-class and steerage passengers – which obliged Cunard belatedly to turn from the paddle-wheel to the screw propeller. Its reluctance to do so earlier had hastened the departure of Samuel's partner, George Burns. After Samuel's own retirement in 1863 the senior partnership passed to George's son, the less able Sir Edward Burns; and thereafter for a decade the company went slowly downhill. In 1869, year of Sir Edward's death, the Post Office overhauled and reduced its North American contracts. Cunard received only the New York and Boston assignments, at a much reduced payment of £70,000 p.a., while the Halifax contract went to Inman at half that figure. In 1876 the Atlantic mail subvention was again divided, this time three ways between Cunard, Inman and White Star.

For size, speed and modernity Cunard had now been surpassed by both the White Star and Guion lines, remaining content with vessels which were, by the rising North Atlantic standards, of second grade. Its Mediterranean service, however, had always been profitable. In February 1878 this was amalgamated with the line's Atlantic fleet under the title of the Cunard Steamship Co., wherein the Burns, MacIver and Cunard families in triple harness for a while continued each to own one-third of the stock. All three families were raised in the shipping business and approached their vocation in a conservative and unspeculative spirit. While inexperienced newcomers burned themselves out or fell victims to marine disaster, such men did more to raise the reliability of maritime service than any speculator or agitator. In a year when Plimsoll was wildly denouncing the risks of seafaring, Cunard could justly claim that during thirty-four years of North Atlantic crossings they had not lost a life or a letter. But private management was becoming increasingly impracticable. In 1880 Cunard registered as a limited company, with a capital of £2 million whose

100,000 £20 shares – 60,000 fully paid up and 40,000 half paid –
became for the first time available to the investing public. When
early in 1883 David MacIver & Co. withdrew from the management, control was vested in a board of directors.

So long as the company had remained supreme on the
Atlantic – up to the late 1860's – its operations there had not
escaped criticism for lack of enterprise. As a public company,
however, it rapidly ceased to merit such reproach. In 1881 it
acquired its first all-steel vessel, the *Servia* (lit throughout by
electricity). In 1883–84 followed the *Aurania, Umbria* and
Etruria, from John Elder's Fairfield yard. The last two of these,
over 7,000 tons and the most powerful single-screw vessels ever
built for the line, signified Cunard's revived interest in speed,
and gave it the fastest and best balanced fleet in the Atlantic.
The 1890's, as we have remarked, were a period of unprecedented competition, when the Blue Riband passed with great
rapidity from country to country. In 1893 Cunard recaptured it
with the *Campania* and *Lucania* – its first twin-screw fliers, also
from Elder, of 13,000 tons, whose big, raked-back funnels symbolised a sensational advance in design (the first liners, incidentally, to cross the Atlantic carrying refrigeration plant and
no sail). Costing between £600,000 and £700,000 apiece, their
capability of twenty-two knots soon became the normal requisite for the best North Atlantic mail and passenger service.
More significantly for this study, they mark the point beyond
which extra speed would become prohibitively expensive to the
operator.

In return for its subsidy, ever more essential as construction
and operating costs rose (for expresses burned up fuel inordinately), the Admiralty expected to be consulted about the design
of any vessel admitted to its reserve list as potential auxiliary
cruiser or troop carrier. It had had a big say, for example, in the
shape of the *Gallia*, a 4,800 tonner laid down in 1879, insisting
that designs be modified so as to carry her bunkers right up to
the main deck for protection. Subvention of the *Ivernia* and
Saxonia was in recognition of their capacity, unique in their
day, for transporting men and horses. Again, only the prospect
of subsidy could relieve Cunard's doubt, when the cost of the
Etruria was estimated at £400,000, as to whether any single
ship was worth so much. But payment was conditional upon

satisfying the Admiralty that she could carry 4·7 in. and Nordenfeldt guns, and steam for sixteen days at eighteen knots. Admitted to the reserve list, she and her sister the *Umbria* were in 1902 together earning their owners a subsidy of £8,000 p.a., while another £10,000 was paid by the Admiralty in respect of the more recent *Campania* and *Lucania*. A sore point with Cunard, however, and one to which we shall return, was the circumstance that from these figures the Admiralty deducted 25% in consideration of the fact that these vessels also earned a mail subsidy from the Post Office. Cunard all along contended that the mail contract was scarcely remunerative *per se*, and that the deduction had no basis either in reason or equity.

After the Blue Riband had been in 1897 recovered by Germany, where it was to remain for the next ten years, charges of timid management began again to be levelled at the staid and venerable British line. True, the size of its Atlantic operations did not markedly exceed that of Baker's Atlantic Transport, its profits were somewhat smaller, and a large proportion of these the directors husbanded with great care for insurance and to swell reserves for depreciation. Analysis of the twenty years 1883–1902 shows that out of £4,650,000 earned in profits, the management allocated only 18·8% to the owners and ploughed back every penny of the remainder. 'Only by the most careful economy,' wrote one analyst in 1904, 'by the utmost prudence and conservatism in distribution of profits, could the Cunard Company over a twenty-year period average 2·6% to its stockholders and, during the last ten years, earn 3·1% on a capital which at no time exceeded the book value of its ships.'[1] In two years of the 1890's the company had passed its dividends completely. Although in 1900, with the shipping boom, it declared a dividend of 8% this was a peak not to be scaled again until 1908. For the four years immediately preceding 1902 the average was 5%.

Internal dissatisfaction with this state of affairs was, though not widespread, occasionally sharp in expression. In 1901 the company had felt obliged by circular among its shareholders to answer the published complaints of a few of their number that the chairman's most recent annual report 'fails to convince anyone that the business of the Company ... is making any headway at all'.[2] Such grumbling was probably in Steele's mind when he reportedly spoke, as a Morgan partner, of the need 'to elect a sensible Board and establish a capable manager of the Line' (pp. 85–6 above). This period of greatly fluctuating net earnings, moreover, coincided with a change at the top. In February 1901 died the chairman of its board of directors, George's son John Burns, since 1897 first Baron Inverclyde but less formally styled 'the mighty I' or 'the most kenspeckle man on Clydeside'. After a stopgap interregnum of the next senior partner, David Jardine, the succession fell in January 1902 upon John's eldest son and heir to the title, the forty-year-old Sir George Arbuthnot Burns.

His first year of chairmanship the second Lord Inverclyde was to find one of great responsibility, anxiety and excitement. The boom of the late 1890's in world shipping trade was turning many eyes towards Cunard as a desirable property. Though its shares were by now too widely dispersed to be acquired at one swift stroke, a number of overtures with a view to purchase or amalgamation were made to its directors from late 1897 onward. Collectively they demonstrate the liveliness of the shipping market, and some at least of them are noteworthy because of their bearing upon those major transactions that concern us here. In November that year, for example, Cunard's chairman received the first of a series of approaches from a former secretary of his Line, one T. A. Bellew, now secretary of the Liverpool Underwriters' Association. At first, it appears, Bellew was acting on his own account, as an independent broker in search of commission, to endeavour to interest Ellerman and Inverclyde in a purchase by Leyland either of Cunard's assets on an out-and-out basis or of two-thirds of its shares. These advances Cunard repeatedly rebuffed. They led, however, to direct proposals from Ellerman, by correspondence with the first Lord Inverclyde between July 1898 and August 1899, for some form of amalgamation involving the purchase of about 20,000 of Cunard's preference shares. This, too, the company declined, as it did a further offer by Bellew in March 1900, purporting to be on behalf of another Leyland director, Walter Glyn, of £1·4 million for the stock: Cunard's assets at that juncture were evaluable at about £2 million.[3]

It was in a confidential letter from Ellerman to Inverclyde on 22nd March 1900, however, that the shadow of things to come was most sharply cast. As Leyland's biggest shareholder Ellerman adverted to its possible acquisition of Cunard as a transaction which 'could not be done with better advantage than at present, as we have acquired the Atlantic Transport Line, with all their new steamers building; and are on the point of closing terms with another business', and would be coming out to the public with a preference share issue to consolidate these acquisitions with Leyland. Ellerman's revised offer was for either the whole or at least 51% of Cunard, which in the latter alternative would remain a separate undertaking but would give Leyland a proportionate voice and vote on its board. Inverclyde's rejection of this latest proposal was endorsed by his fellow directors:[4] in any case, Ellerman's plans to buy Baker's new line were, as we have seen, destined not to materialise.

When Bellew again enters the picture – between May and October 1901 – it is as claiming to represent a leading but unnamed firm of London solicitors with 'influential clients willing and eager to purchase' the Cunard business and property on an out-and-out basis, on whose behalf he seemingly wished, by correspondence or interview, to probe Jardine as to his company's willingness to sell.[5] Were Bellew's principals at this juncture, whether so known to him or not, American? We can only note that he referred *obiter* to a prospective Morgan–Ellerman deal: at one point (31st August 1901) proffering the information that Pirrie and Ismay were on their way to New York to learn how the land lay for preserving Harland & Wolff's link with any American combination; and at another passing on the rumour that a big change was pending for White Star. It would appear that Hamburg-America, too, were showing some interest at this stage.

By the following spring of 1902, with world shipping markets in an excitable condition, the various approaches to Cunard became correspondingly more numerous and hard for the historian to disentangle. They came from at least five different directions. In the first place, Bellew during March and April renewed his suit on behalf of his still anonymous clients. Secondly, the stockbrokers acting for the trustees of the first, now late, Lord Inverclyde's estate were approached on 18th March by a firm of Glasgow stockbrokers (Messrs Watson & Smith), also on behalf of unnamed principals, with an offer to take up an unlimited quantity of Cunard shares at the highest price paid during the previous ten years, i.e. £20 a share. Thirdly, the London financier O'Hagan has recorded that he arranged for an offer of purchase to be made to Cunard on behalf of the framers of the American shipping combination, and this must have been at about this juncture. Fourthly, on 14th March, hearing of the possibility of an unknown but probably American bidder, the engineers and shipbuilders Vickers Son & Maxim intimated their interest in taking up a large number of the company's shares which execution of its late chairman's estate had brought on to the market.[6] Fifthly, and in the same month, an interview was sought with its new chairman by a prospective British buyer who already possessed considerable Cunard stockholdings. The shipowner Sir Christopher Furness, head of Furness Withy & Co. and of the Furness Line of steamers, and Liberal MP for Hartlepool, sharply revived an interest he had earlier evinced in obtaining control of the company. The extent of his plans for its future was shortly to become evident.

It was in the midst of this ferment of maritime diplomacy that Inverclyde heard on 8th March 1902 from Cunard's New York agent, Vernon H. Brown, the gist of the agreement signed on 4th February between the parties to the American combine, and was thereby apprised for the first time of the degree of maturity their design had reached. What Inverclyde learned he immediately (as we have seen) communicated to Selborne at the Admiralty. By letter and in person he gave the First Lord further to understand, in general terms, the pressure Cunard were currently under from these numerous inquirers seeking at least a controlling interest in the company. He warned him that, while he would try his best to delay such negotiations, the trustees' first concern must be the interests of their share-holders, the majority of whom he thought likely to jump at any such offers as Leyland had lately had. Inverclyde here represented himself as having kept conclusions in abeyance hitherto but, lacking even a bare majority of his company's shares, as powerless to prevent it passing out of control.[7]

At 'so vast' a project as the American, Selborne naturally expressed himself as 'disturbed and uneasy'. After consulting ministerial colleagues, on 17th March he asked Inverclyde, as a first step, to consider adding to Cunard's contract with the

Admiralty a pre-emptive clause to prevent the transfer of any of their reserved steamers to a foreign owner without the government's consent for the unexpired term of the contract (i.e. to repeal the provision for twelve months' notice of intention to terminate). He also asked Inverclyde to weigh the desirability of adding faster vessels to its fleet.

Inverclyde at once objected to the former request as trebly onerous, for it would prevent the company from getting the most advantageous terms of sale, and might reduce its freedom to compete with the increased American competition which must now be expected. The company liked no more than did the Admiralty to see British ships surpassed in power and speed. But to build faster vessels was for them impossibly uneconomic without adequate government support. He offered instead to hold thirteen named vessels at the Admiralty's disposal until the end of the year in consideration of an increased subvention; and in the meantime the building of new ships could be discussed. This offer Selborne in turn declined, questioning Inverclyde's contention that to give the Admiralty an increased lien on their vessels would diminish their saleability or the company's share value.[8]

These early exchanges can be seen in retrospect as marking the opening of the first stage of negotiations between Cunard and the government – negotiations which were to prove complex, arduous and protracted beyond anything that either side envisaged at the start. They led immediately to the two parties defining their respective positions. Surveying the course of discussion over the following few weeks, we may from the surviving correspondence summarise those positions as follows.

The Admiralty, through Selborne, adhered to the view that the matter of existing steamship subsidies (currently under consideration by the revived parliamentary committee) must be kept quite separate from the question of any future governmental subvention for cruiser building. His policy was 'that the whole attitude of the government shall be reconsidered. I must first thrash the matter out by means of a committee. Till I have its report I cannot know what its conclusions will be.' He would then consult his colleagues and Parliament. Until the government had thus worked out its long-term policy – over about a year, Selborne estimated, – his first duty was to seek to safeguard the Admiralty's interest *pro tempore* by revision of its existing pre-emptive rights over merchant vessels: and any additional subvention meanwhile must be considered strictly *ad hoc.*[9]

On the other side Inverclyde, supported by his fellow directors, naturally saw his duty as being to insist that the affair be treated in relation to his company's position as a whole, including its future policy. For them it was not possible to separate the matter of existing subsidies from that of building new ships. For the question of the number, type and design of the latter would determine the number of existing ships that Cunard would find it profitable to retain while itself being determined by whether these new vessels were required for commercial use only, or must suit the Admiralty's purposes also. This standpoint Inverclyde reinforced with figures to show the relative costs of building and working large, very fast, ships on the North Atlantic run. He pointed out that the United States government paid the American Line for a weekly service of only three ships a mail subsidy £156,000 p.a., much larger than any subvention-plus-subsidy that Cunard were now suggesting, and that the subsidy Bill pending before Congress would very greatly increase this. His company could not bind itself more tightly to the Admiralty until it knew what the government was prepared to offer in return.[10]

By the second week of April 1902 the situation remained inconclusive, if not deadlocked. A number of events, however, were combining to give the government a nudge. First, at Cunard's annual general meeting on 11th April, some shareholders displayed the keenest interest in rumours of generous offers having been made for the company's property. Secondly, a sixth suitor for Cunard appeared – this time a direct American inquiry: Morgan was performing his promise to Ballin. On the same day, 12th April, that Furness obtained his long-sought interview with Cunard's chairman, Inverclyde met also Henry Wilding, bearing instructions from Griscom to ask whether either Cunard would enter the combine or the latter could obtain control of the company by purchase at par value of £18 per share. The first alternative, it was quickly conceded, was not feasible. And while Inverclyde agreed that the Cunard directors might consider an offer to purchase, it would have to be on the basis of a distinctly higher valuation (Messrs Watson & Smith's client, it will be recalled, offered £20 a share). Wilding appeared surprised at the price asked, and withdrew to consult Griscom by cable.[11]

No doubt sensing his hand strengthened, Inverclyde forthwith wrote again to the First Lord on a slightly sharper note. The two sides, he said, must agree to differ. The best thing would be for Selborne to send him a scheme whereby the Admiralty would offer a material *quid pro quo* in return for extended control over the Cunard ships in question. His shareholders could not be expected quixotically to place the national interest above their own pockets. What – for he must tell them – was the concrete value of that which the government was asking them to give up?[12]

At a further meeting with Inverclyde on 19th April Wilding submitted a revised offer from the combine of £18 per share for 55% of Cunard. It was declined, and no further direct communications appear to have passed. By the 24th the Morgan syndicate was known to have closed its subscription list. Some mystery or misunderstanding seems to have survived this breaking off of negotiations between Morgan and Cunard, at least in Ballin's mind. Nevertheless the inference is inescapable that, when it came to the point, the American combine were not seriously disposed to purchase Cunard's total assets but only a sufficiency of shares to give them control, and that they had abandoned even this intention by the end of April 1902.

On business considerations alone Inverclyde was undoubtedly right to stand out for a better offer. Had Cunard entered the combine on terms comparable to those offered White Star, the purchase price might have been expected to be considerably higher than Wilding's or any other offer yet received. Its net profits for the year 1900, upon which the relevant sum would presumably have been calculated, were recorded as over £356,000. Multiplying this (as in the case of White Star) by the factor of ten would yield a figure in respect of which Cunard would have expected to receive – aggregating cash, preferred and common stock – not far short of £5 million.

The third prod to the government was administered publicly, at Westminster and in the national press. Shortly after he had first broken the news of the American combination to Selborne, Inverclyde had, with the latter's acquiescence, seen Sir Edward Grey and Lord Rosebery with a view to having questions asked in both Houses. But in neither had the matter been raised, and Selborne had decided against the advisability of himself making a parliamentary statement. From 24th March onward, however, searching questions were put in the Commons respecting the subsidised vessels about to enter the American combine which involved both Admiralty and Board of Trade in replies. Arnold-Forster announced the appointment of the Mercantile Cruisers Committee (p. 125 above). On the 26th newspapers in London and Liverpool began to call for energetic action by the government. On the same day Inverclyde received notice from Messrs Watson & Smith that their clients were withdrawing their offer of purchase, on the grounds that 'the events of last week' had 'completely changed the situation' in that regard. Whether this referred to the failure of Wilding's approach or to manifestations of public alarm, it signalised an informed judgement that Cunard would not, after all, be for sale.

Certainly the communications between Cunard and the Admiralty, when renewed in the closing days of the month, betray a new urgency. Inverclyde bluntly reiterated that his primary object must be the interest of the shareholders, who would part with their holdings to whoever offered the best terms, irrespective of what might be conceived to be the national interest. The prospect that control of the North Atlantic shipping trade would practically be henceforth entirely in American hands made the position, he feared, far more serious than the government showed signs of recognising. Selborne, agreeing that 'vast issues' were at stake with the probability that supremacy would pass to the Americans, again begged him not to commit he company without giving the government further time to consider. It was highly regrettable that White Star and the other British companies who had entered the combine had failed to consult him: consequently it had at no juncture been within the government's power to stop the American combination, whose agreements were already signed and sealed before he first got wind of them from Inverclyde.[14]

Nevertheless, as oversight of the situation passed at this point to the three-man 'committee of the Cabinet' (see p. 134 above), the government on 2nd May took a fresh initiative. Selborne again saw Cunard's chairman and invited him to submit his company's proposals in greater detail. This Inverclyde did in a memorandum which on the 5th he handed to Selborne, Balfour and Chamberlain at the Colonial Office.[15]. Its proposals – entirely consistent, incidentally, with the evidence Inverclyde was to give the Mercantile Cruisers Committee on 7th May and 9th June – were in outline that the government should enter into a twenty-year agreement with Cunard by which it would provide the latter with a £5·2 million loan at 5% interest for the building of nine very fast steamers, of which the government would be mortgagee, and should increase the present Admiralty subvention, as these flyers became available in the North Atlantic trade, in such a way as to ensure the shareholders a guaranteed 5% annual dividend (the average declared by Cunard over the previous four years). In return the government would be getting the benefit of the fastest vessels afloat, the finest reserve fleet in the world, secured against alienation by transfer to a foreign power. The details of these proposals we may return to when the government did, which was not until August.

For this point, early May, marks the end of the first and the beginning of the second phase of its negotiations with Cunard. These now cease to be purely bilateral; and for the next three months Inverclyde's scheme lies in abeyance while the initiative and main focus of attention pass to Cunard's would-be purchaser, Sir Christopher Furness.

Furness was in the south of France when in March 1902 popular rumours about the American combine became fairly circumstantial. Though he had been visiting American shipyards and steelworks as recently as the previous October, there is no evidence that he had any inkling of this development. During the latter half of 1901, however, his interest in Cunard had been perceptibly quickening. Since June that year he had been buying in his own name 120 of its fully paid, and 658 of its £10 paid, shares and was to continue augmenting his holdings of both until by October 1902 they were to amount to 1,978 and 3,198 respectively. In January 1902 he had approached

Inverclyde about the possibility of buying a controlling interest in the company, and now on 22nd March requested an interview with him. Without wishing, he said, to interfere with the general policy of 'the oldest Atlantic company' – a directorship of which he claimed to have been offered during the first Lord Inverclyde's time but to have declined – Furness expressed his satisfaction that American bids for 'this practically national concern' had been rejected; and he again offered to buy the interests of any colleagues who wished to sell. When he met Inverclyde on 12th April, and again on 7th May, Sir Christopher made it clear that what he sought was control of the company on the cheapest terms possible. He claimed to know that Morgan's people could not afford to improve their offer and would not bid again. He showed Inverclyde a list of the White Star steamers under contract to the Admiralty and asked him what his position would be if the latter exercised its option to purchase and resell them to Cunard.[16] His own intentions he did not at either interview fully disclose to its chairman.

He did, however, reveal them – probably between 5th and 8th May – to the government. They amounted to nothing less than the proposal that he should himself purchase not only Cunard but the Elder Dempster Line and the eight White Star vessels on which the Admiralty had a lien. The latter part of this proposed operation was obviously contingent upon the Admiralty's willingness to exercise its option of purchase, forbid their sale to the Americans, and resell them to Furness instead. As to buying Elder Dempster, this promised to fit very well. Its president, Sir Alfred L. Jones, already possessed a considerable interest in Cunard: when his holdings were added to Furness's the aggregate would probably reach 5,000 of fully paid and nearly 7,000 of £10 paid shares.[17] Parenthetically, some inspired leakage of these plans to the national press may be suspected from the fact that on 23rd April London and Liverpool newspapers had simultaneously mooted a proposal that Cunard might form the nucleus of a new British combination to fight off the American.

The attraction of Furness's scheme for the government was obvious. It promised to provide on the North Atlantic a strong British mercantile force whose efficiency would not depend upon increased State bounties to a single company or the quite unprecedented circumstance of a Treasury loan. With Furness's alternative proposition in hand, Selborne wrote to Inverclyde on 8th May that he and his colleagues, after giving the latter's memorandum of the 5th careful attention, had concluded that the objections against it were too serious to warrant their proposing it to the Cabinet. Assuming that Furness had already taken the Cunard chairman fully into confidence, Selborne expressed to Inverclyde the view that such a British amalgamation as Furness proposed, with Cunard as its principal component, would be preferable to the latter company's opposing the Americans single-handed with increased government assistance, because such a larger anti-combine would be more strongly based, would be easier for the government to deal with, and because a proposal for a wider-spread subsidy, as against one concentrated in a single company, would probably be more congenial to the Commons.

Promptly and somewhat indignantly, Inverclyde denied knowledge of any plans for his company to enter such a combination, voicing dissatisfaction at the government's sudden change of course after two inconclusive months of negotiating, and some resentment at this attempt to propel Cunard into an arrangement to the discussion of which it had not been a party. Faced with this response the First Lord felt bound to try and justify the Ministers' *volte face* by pointing out, as he saw them, the limited number of courses open to Cunard. They might join the Americans, a step to which the government would 'strenuously object', and would do all it could to help the chairman justify himself to his shareholders for refraining from. Alternatively the company could remain as it was and try to fight the Americans single-handed with some unspecified increase in government aid. Or, thirdly, it could enter some form of 'anti-combine' with other British shipowners; which course, if feasible, the government 'should distinctly prefer'.[18]

But it was not until 14th May – by when the main lines of the American combination had been expounded in the British press and further questions asked in the House – that Inverclyde met Selborne in Chamberlain's office at West-minster to clear up the 'misunderstanding'. On the following day Furness unveiled his plans for the first time to Cunard at their London headquarters. In essence they were as follows. A combination should be formed of the Cunard (114,000 g.r.t.) with the Elder Dempster and Beaver lines (133,000 g.r.t.), whose assets should be taken over at agreed values. The government should exercise its right to buy the eight White Star ships (80,000 g.r.t.) and should resell them to the combination. The latter should then itself build three 25 knot vessels for its New York service, two 20 knot vessels for its Canadian and three 16 knot for its Vancouver service, with the ultimate goal of conflating and improving all British communications with the east coast of the United States and Canada. To this end the government should give the combination an immediate subvention of £350,000 p.a., rising to £850,000 p.a. when all the newly built ships had come into service.

To round out the shape of this projected counter-combine Furness immersed himself from the second week of May onward in collecting data from all relevant sources and transmitting detailed proposals to Chamberlain and to Cunard in a series of memoranda and meetings. That serious negotiations were now in progress, as a basis for a full and formal approach to the government, Cunard shareholders learned on the last day of the month in a circular from their chairman.

By then, on 29th May, Furness had submitted his complete scheme in its final form.[20] His new amalgamation would be called the Cunard Imperial Steam Navigation Co., with headquarters in London, and would have a capital of £20 million divided half-and-half between preference and ordinary shares of the low denomination of £1. 'I feel,' explained Sir Christopher, 'that the undertaking being placed on so substantial a basis, I want to give an opportunity to the smallest investor in the land to participate.' The capital valuation was to represent real assets, with no water in the form of allowances for goodwill, etc. The new company would undertake to build three of the largest passenger steamers afloat to provide a weekly express service of twenty-five knots to New York. Their dimensions would be 50 ft longer, 6 ft broader and 3 ft deeper than the largest of the German ships, the *Deutschland*, their displacement being 30,900 tons as compared with the latter's 23,000, their horsepower 55,000 as against her 33,000. Each new vessel could carry eight guns in wartime. It would also build three express steamers of twenty-two and a half knots to provide a weekly service to east Canada, and another three of nineteen knots for a similar service to Vancouver. The total cost of all this new tonnage Furness estimated at £6,675,000.

The new company, to whose board the government should have power to appoint three directors, would look to receive from the Treasury a subsidy comprising all subsidies at present paid to Cunard (i.e. amounting to about £120,000 p.a. for mail carriage and about £40,000 as Admiralty subvention), to the Royal Mail and Imperial West Indies companies, as well as what was currently paid by the Canadian government to the Allan Line and the Australian Company, plus a sum to be agreed with Ottawa for the weekly express service to and from the United Kingdom. The aggregate annual sum to be paid by the British and Canadian governments was proposed as £1 million sterling. The contract would run for twenty years, during which period those vessels earning subsidy would not be transferred or sold to anyone without prior governmental consent. A double weekly mail express service was proposed between New York and the United Kingdom. The ships from part of this service, Furness added,[21] together with such other vessels as might be selected by his new company, would be at the government's disposal for hire or purchase, as well as those at present plying between Britain and Boston, Montreal, the Gulf ports and the Mediterranean.

This grand, not to say grandiose, project was decidedly more considerable than Balfour and most of his colleagues felt able immediately to entertain. Their first reaction therefore was to ask the projector for a reduced scheme, less costly to public funds both in loan and subsidy. As to this latter, Inverclyde was ready to expound and defend the grounds on which the heavily increased subvention was sought for the New York service to be supplied by Cunard and the eight White Star vessels. This service if regarded on its own – for the Canadian component of the scheme was not his province, being separately negotiated between Furness and Sir Alfred Jones – he calculated as requiring a subsidy of £350,000 p.a., rising by stages to £1½ million p.a. as the new ships came into use.[22] Inverclyde stuck to his point that such vessels could not possibly be run in the highly seasonal North Atlantic passenger trade on ordinary commercial lines. And his estimate, taking into account the costs of building, insuring and operating the proposed new tonnage, plus depreciation, was supported as reasonable by a colleague, Sir Thomas Sutherland, chairman of Peninsular & Oriental.

There ensued a series of meetings between Furness (with his accountants) and the directors of the lines principally involved, where from 3rd June onward the government was unofficially and informally represented by a highly placed confidant, the international financier Sir Ernest Cassel. Of German paternity, Cassel was perhaps the nearest thing to a J. P. Morgan that Britain could boast. His German and American business connections, too, were doubtless felt to be appropriate to the parallel set of negotiations the government were pursuing with the American financier. Believed to have been brought into the matter as a consultative intermediary by none other than King Edward VII[23] (to whom he stood in intimate relation as banker, financial adviser and bridge partner), Cassel, though possessing an interest in Vickers Maxim & Co., had none so far as is known in any of the shipping lines involved. Throughout the next two months he rendered valuable service in the Cunard discussions, some of which took place at his town house, 48 Grosvenor Square (Furness's was No. 21).[24]

These discussions were by mid-June revolving round a second set of proposals from Furness (formally submitted on 19th June) wherein the element of new shipbuilding, and *pro tanto* the total subvention sought, was at Balfour's request markedly reduced. At even this diminished scheme, however, the depth of ministerial misgiving was becoming apparent before the month was out. It had earlier been Inverclyde's belief that the Americans' plans would prove abortive because the Admiralty would refuse to release the White Star vessels. But now he felt the balance beginning to tip the other way, and sensed the government's response to Morgan to be wavering. The critical point, if there was one, seems to have been at a meeting at the House of Commons on the 25th between the leading protagonists, at which the Ministers, fortified with Ismay's written undertaking (p. 124 above), made it clear at least that they must decline either to recommend the scheme as it stood or to exercise the governmental option to take up the reserved White Star ships.

Chamberlain asked for yet another exercise, further reduced in scope and omitting those eight vessels. Inverclyde, while continuing to press for their inclusion on grounds not only of prestige but of operational economy, tried again with a still more shrunken plan. The government, still awaiting the Mercantile Cruisers committee's report, meanwhile sought an independent valuation of Cunard's assets from a third party, the shipowner C. H. Wilson, MP for Hull, who incidentally had himself earlier received an inquiry from the Morgan trust asking his price for his New York pier. Wilson's valuation corroborated former ones, being in the region of £2 million.[25]

The government, lamented Furness, 'want too much and give too little'. But it was the Canadian component of his huge project that was to prove the most vulnerable. The Allan Line had stood in uniquely close, though at times rather insecure, relationship with the Canadian government ever since its first mail contract of 1856. Despite opening a New York service from Glasgow (its home port) in 1891, its fleet lay in the doldrums, having had for some years to share its mail contract with the Dominion Line. Recently it had undertaken an extensive rebuilding programme in order to stave off competition from White Star and Cunard. Now a new rival was appearing. In 1901 the Canadian Pacific Railway had opened a branch line from Montreal to St John's, Newfoundland, thus giving access to an ice-free eastern port from which it henceforth had the advantage – the 1900's were the decade of the great Canadian immigrant boom – of being able to book passengers and goods through to any point in the dominion. Canada, like other Commonwealth countries, possessed the constitutional right to legislate for its own merchant shipping; and to Furness it seemed as though the CPR were going to put up a stiff fight in Ottawa with their competitive bid for government contracts, both express mail and cargo.

In the event the CPR were in 1902 to buy the Canada–Liverpool business of the Beaver Line from Elder Dempster (who in 1898 had bought it from D. MacIver & Co.) and by this means bring pressure on the Allan Line to the point where, in 1915, it could absorb it. In 1902, however, the Ottawa situation was so unclear that Furness agreed with Chamberlain that it would be best to defer discussion about including Allan and

Beaver until the Canadian Prime Minister, Sir Wilfred Laurier, and his delegation to the forthcoming Commonwealth Conference could be personally consulted in London. After an encounter with them there on 1st July, however, Furness had to accept the conclusion of Sir Alfred Jones and Messrs Allan that any Canadian arrangement must be kept separate from his main project. This disappointment effectively marks the collapse of Sir Christopher's design in its grandest form, though a diminished version of it was kept before the government until August and he himself continued to negotiate with the Canadian government for provision of a fast service.[26] It marks also the end of the second phase of the Cunard negotiations. The third is the return *faute de mieux* to bilateral discussions between Ministers and Cunard on the basis of a revised plan to enlarge the latter's resources with Treasury subvention – what Selborne had seen in mid-May as the second of the three alternative contingencies. This swing back from Furness and towards Inverclyde gained decisive impetus from the report of the Mercantile Cruisers committee, signed on 9th July though not made public until December.[27] The government was now armed with an official and professional appraisal of what was required to be done, and an estimate of the cost of doing it.

The five-man committee, under Lord Camperdown's chairmanship, contained representatives of Admiralty, Treasury and Post Office, together with Professor J. H. Biles of the Institute of Naval Architects. It had held a dozen meetings, taking evidence from many directors of shipping lines and yards as well as from the Board of Trade, in order to investigate the initial cost of vessels of between twenty and twenty-six knots' speed and the size of annual subsidy a commercial company would need to make good its loss in running them on the Atlantic. Such costs, the committee felt, might be met by any of three ways. The Admiralty might contribute outright a lump sum towards the first cost of each ship. Or it might guarantee a sum representing the first cost, so as to enable the owners to raise the necessary capital at 3% instead of the normal 5%. Or the owners might be given an annual payment extending over an agreed period. The committee plumped for the third of these possibilities. If adopted it would entail (they reckoned) a subsidy, guaranteed for ten years, of £110,500 p.a. for a 24 knot vessel or of £149,000 p.a. for a twenty-five knot one. To achieve an increase in speed from twenty to twenty-four knots, the committee incidentally noted, would require a doubling of engine power and more than double a vessel's initial cost.[28] Professor Biles offered detailed proposals for structural modification of reserve cruisers so as to carry modern armament, involving a loss of cargo space for which, in trades where deadweight was of importance, a further subvention of the operators would be necessary. The committee then went on to recommend steps for keeping such vessels under the British flag, and to advocate interdepartmental consultation before future subsidies were awarded. Thus was expert backing provided for Inverclyde's contention, expressed repeatedly in correspondence and in evidence before the committee, that to build and run vessels of this speed would be for his company a commercially unfeasible venture. The committee's views, moreover, were to receive the prompt and unequivocal endorsement of the First Lord himself, in the form of a special communication of 1st July which the Cabinet as a whole were to consider when, five weeks later, they came to take their crucial decision over Cunard. It is headed 'Memorandum of the Situation created by the building of four German Steamships for the Atlantic Trade of twenty-three knots and upwards', and marked 'concurred in unanimously by the Board of Admiralty'.[29] These new German expresses, Selborne pointed out, were not only faster than anything built or projected in Britain, but carried much more coal. While the Cabinet must be judge of the likelihood of war,

> personally, I do not think the possibility can be omitted from our calculations ... No experience of the past can give a guide to the impression on the public mind and the effect on British trade if it were known that we possessed absolutely no ship which could by any possibility except that of a sheer fluke catch these German ships. The result might be disastrous and upset all our calculations based on previous experience as to the course of trade during war. Something like a panic might be produced.

But he could not recommend that the Admiralty itself construct the faster vessels needed, for

> the cost would be as great or greater than that of a battleship, and yet the ships would be weak in fighting power compared with a

battleship. They would be too cumbrous in size for general naval use, and would make a great drain on the manning resources of the Navy. The most effective and economical method of making provision against this danger would be by subsidising merchant cruisers to be specially built.

Nevertheless the government still hung back. A. J. Balfour succeeded his uncle in the premiership. The king's illness, requiring preparations for the coronation to be deferred, upset Ministers' timetables. On 7th July Chamberlain met with his serious cab accident. On the 30th, still convalescent, he told Inverclyde that it would not be possible to come to any conclusion about the government's Cunard policy before October, after the summer recess.

To a major commercial enterprise whose policy-making had been frozen since March, the prospect of another ten weeks' moratorium was intolerable. On 1st August Inverclyde protested to Chamberlain in the strongest terms about the serious position in which the government's vacillation had already placed his company, both as to current restraints on shareholders and threatened paralysis of its future policy. There was the grave possibility that at the end it might, in the face of heightened American competition, confront the stark alternatives of 'absorption or annihilation'. He pointed out that for more than twenty weeks, ever since he first put himself into communication with Selborne with information the government did not then have, discussions with Ministers had practically inhibited him from negotiating in other directions. Selborne had then said that the government 'strenuously objected' to Cunard's joining the Morgan combine, and had promised all the help they could in justifying him to his shareholders for temporising. But Cunard could not afford to wait until the autumn session of Parliament. They had the right to look to the government for very substantial help in maintaining their position on the North Atlantic, where henceforth they would in effect be the only truly British steamship company remaining.[30]

On the same day Inverclyde sent Cassel 'the very best proposal that the Cunard Company can make', and with it he coupled the blunt warning that unless Cunard received some concrete evidence of the government's interest and support 'the directors may be compelled to make the best terms possible for the transfer of the business'. Cassel at once forwarded the proposals to Chamberlain with brief but favourable comment.[31] Events moved thereafter with gratifying swiftness. On the 4th Chamberlain replied to Inverclyde in sympathetic manner, expressing appreciation of his difficulties and assuring him that he would arrange to meet Selborne and Balfour the very next day, when they would decide on some recommendation to put before the Cabinet at its Thursday meeting on the 7th. When the three met, they agreed to place the government's further conduct of the negotiations with Cunard solely in Balfour's hands.

The Cabinet session of 7th August was lengthy but decisive. Members had before them, as well as Dawkins's proposals of 11th June (p. 133 above) and Selborne's letter of 1st July, a digest of five alternative courses of action all of which variously affected Cunard, together with the commentary and recommendations of its 'committee' of Chamberlain, Selborne and Gerald Balfour.[32] In the opinion of these latter, the 'main objects which it is desirable to keep in view' were four: to save the remaining British lines, and especially Cunard, from American absorption; to provide for the Admiralty's benefit at least two new steamships of twenty-four to twenty-five knots; 'to secure these results at the least possible expense'; and in so doing 'to avoid unnecessary friction' with the Americans.

Of these alternative courses the first – Inverclyde's earliest proposal of 5th May – was ruled out as 'financially inadmissible'. The second was Furness's original grand design of 29th May, and the third the reduced form of this scheme, submitted on 19th June as agreed between himself, Inverclyde and Cassel. These two versions of 'the proposed rival Combine', involving (as they both would) very heavy subvention, the Cabinet committee would prefer not to consider 'until we have seen whether it is possible to come to an amicable arrangement with Mr Morgan'. The remaining two alternative courses were, confessed the committee,

> somewhat novel in their character, and objection might be taken to them on the ground that they seem to bring the State into a kind of partnership with a Shipping Company. This is, however, a matter of degree, and even the simplest form of subsidy payment is in some measure open to the same objection.

Of these, alternative 4 was one which had not yet appeared on paper, having been submitted orally by Cassel. It proposed simply that the two twenty-four–twenty-five knot vessels desired should be constructed wholly at the government's expense and leased to the Cunard company on terms to be fixed, in the first instance, for two years only. The fifth and last proposal was that embodied in Inverclyde's letter of 1st August; and in the strong light of the Mercantile Cruisers committee's report the three Ministers came down unanimously in its favour. 'We are of the opinion that this proposal affords a basis for a satisfactory agreement with the Company, and that the subsidy demanded is not excessive in view of the services to be rendered.' Establishment of a fast service to Canada (they added), towards which 'this country is practically pledged to give some assistance', would have to be the subject of a separate arrangement. But once the government had come to terms with Cunard, as proposed, it could then proceed to an understanding with Morgan along the lines of Dawkins's appended memorandum.

After long debate the Cabinet determined to follow its committee's recommendations and opt for the fifth course. Immediately after the meeting Balfour had an interview with Inverclyde to confirm that the heads of agreement proposed by the latter on 1st August were, with some small amendment, satisfactory to the government. These heads, as embodied in a memorandum of the interview,[33] are important because they form the basis of the final, if unexpectedly protracted, phase of negotiations for the contract. Cunard were to build two steamships capable of twenty-four–twenty-five knots. For this the government would lend them £2·4 million, at 2½% interest over twenty years, repayable at 5% p.a. As soon as they came into service the company would receive an annual Treasury subvention of £150,000: strong feelings were, however, expressed in the Cabinet against raising the existing subsidy meanwhile. Payment for mail carriage was to continue at 'not less than' the present rates, and Cunard would undertake to employ its fastest ships in the North Atlantic all year round. It was insisted as a *sine qua non* that the government's security for repayment of the loan should be the general assets of the company, in addition to its new vessels. Special provision was to be made to preclude sale of its shares to foreigners.

So the die was cast. And during the days that followed Cunard's chairman received the private congratulations of his colleagues. Their shareholders, who had remained in the dark since the company's circular of 31st May, must be told as soon as possible, for their co-operation was required. Inverclyde's strategy was to call them to a meeting before the new agreement was sealed by the company's officers and laid before Parliament: not in order to submit its terms to them – for premature disclosure might give opponents, within and without the company, grounds for exception – but to obtain their consent to certain amendments in the articles of association necessary to make the new contract effectual. Then a second shareholders' meeting could be called to confirm the agreement *after* it had been approved by Parliament.

Accordingly, the terms of a draft letter to shareholders were submitted by Inverclyde to Balfour, who obtained the concurrence of Selborne and Chamberlain with its contents. But, Chamberlain wondered, should they not have the consent of the Cabinet 'or at least that of a majority'? – a reminder that it had been Salisbury's wont in his later years as Prime Minister to let domestic matters be decided there by voting. Consent was secured on 22nd September and the letter went to the shareholders on the 30th. That was, by collusion, the day preceding that on which Balfour first publicly announced the principles of both agreements now concluded – with Cunard and with Morgan – to the annual feast of Master Cutlers at Sheffield. The toast was 'Our kindred beyond the seas', and the American ambassador replied. On the same day, too, Balfour showed Cunard's solicitors for the first time some portions of the Morgan agreement in draft.

The solicitors, Messrs Hill & Dickinson, had already been instructed to prepare a document giving effect to the heads of 7th August. This was drawn up in conditions of some secrecy, the type being broken up as soon as printed, and submitted to Balfour on 10th September. He judged it on the whole acceptable and put the Board of Trade's solicitor, Ellis Cunliffe, in touch with Norman Hill, senior partner of Cunard's representatives. Balfour also agreed that the form of alterations in Cunard's articles necessary to ensure permanent British control of the company, as well as the form of trust deed to secure the government loan, should be arbitrated between the parties by reference to a well known authority on company law and practice, F. B. Palmer, although this gentleman was not one of the Crown's standing legal advisors.

If the final phase of discussions occupied an unexpectedly long time – as a restless House of Commons had repeatedly to be told – there were various good reasons for it. Firstly, as we have seen, the Cunard agreement was running in harness with the complementary arrangement with Morgan, the Prime Minister having decided that both should be laid before Parliament simultaneously. Secondly, its subject matter – a government loan to a modern commercial shipping company – was hitherto unique. There was no existing procedural pattern to follow in negotiating it, and all concerned were feeling their way with the aid of their lawyers. Thirdly, this subject matter was such as necessarily to involve no fewer than four different departments of state (and the head of a fifth) all of whom had to be satisfied. When in February 1903 Inverclyde complained to him about the unconscionable delay over the contract, Bonar Law, then Parliamentary Secretary to the Board of Trade, expressed himself unsurprised:

> It has been going back and forwards between the four Departments which are concerned, each of these Departments looks at everything entirely from its own point of view, and under such circumstances the Board of Trade Solicitor who is trying to get it through has not an easy time of it.[35]

Repeatedly Inverclyde found himself compelled to emphasise that the agreement must be viewed as a many-faceted whole, not as a congeries of bilateral deals between Cunard and each respective departmental head. Treasury, Admiralty and Post Office each considered itself entitled to reopen questions of principle which Inverclyde and Gerald Balfour believed to have been settled; while the legal advisers felt at liberty to criticise and amend the wording of any clause touching the interests of their respective departments, even where such wording had been agreed on as between the solicitors of the Board of Trade (co-ordinating department for the government's side) and Cunard. The consequent delays and retracing of steps were all highly frustrating. Nevertheless, to the historian of public administration some account of these protracted last stages will not seem tedious.

After their first meeting with Cunliffe the company submitted on 30th September a redraft of the agreement. By then it had been decided to drop the proposal to raise the present annual subvention: instead the government would relieve the company from paying interest on the loan until both new Cunarders were running. Against such repayment the government's security would be the general assets of the company, in addition to its new vessels. Inverclyde did not object to the insertion of a clause forbidding undue raising of freight charges or undue preference to foreigners. Balfour for his part accepted Cunard's freedom to sell old or obsolete ships. One other highly gratifying concession was held out. At a further Cabinet meeting of 15th August Balfour had fulfilled his promise to Inverclyde to recommend that the government waive the provision in its existing contract with Cunard whereby the Admiralty subvention of £20,000 p.a. was subject to a 25% reduction in consideration of the company's mail subsidy from the Post Office. It had been partly by undertaking to press this point upon the Cabinet that Balfour had succeeded in inducing Inverclyde to abandon 'the objectionable proposal' to increase the Cunard subsidy from £20,000 to £66,000 p.a. pending completion of the new ships.[36] Inverclyde's suggestion that the government might be represented on the Cunard board of directors, which Balfour and his colleagues had recommended the Cabinet not to follow, was reserved for later reconsideration. On one very important matter, however, the British public's mind, and that of Parliament, was set at rest. The third of the points in Cunard's circular of 30th September to shareholders ran:

> The Cunard Company pledges itself until the expiry of the agreement to remain a purely British undertaking, and that in no circumstances shall the management of the Company be in the hands of, or the vessels of the Company held by, other than British subjects.

On 10th October Cunard's solicitors met Cunliffe and counsels to the Treasury and Admiralty, with Palmer in attendance, to decide how the company's articles must be amended. The proposed alterations were subsumed in a further redraft of the agreement printed on the 23rd. From that date until 2nd December runs the first round of negotiations with the individual departments concerned, during which the alterations made were mostly on points of detail, though a few matters of principle did arise. A reprint of 2nd December showed the position reached at the end of this phase, and was accompanied by a summary, prepared by Hill, showing the points still in question. A second round of negotiations with departments then occupied the parties until the end of February 1903. Towards the end of it, when delay was the most exasperating, Bonar Law recommended Inverclyde to press for a meeting of all departmental representatives simultaneously around the contract, and promised, 'I shall speak to House of Commons representatives of all Departments today and ask them to hasten it.[37] On 28th February, after all departmental views were believed to have been conflated and reconciled, the Board of Trade returned the draft to Hill, showing the revisions proposed, some of which now departed from the arrangements settled on 2nd December. Cunard's observations on these changes were then discussed between its chairman and Balfour on 10th and 11th March. The further revised agreement and trust deed were returned by the company to the Board of Trade solicitors on 25th March. The third and final round of discussions lasted from this latter date until the document in its final form was accepted by the Cabinet on 14th July 1903.

Since the main causes of delay were departmental misgivings, it is as well to give a little space to understanding what these were about.

In a way, matters were simplest with the Board of Trade, for they had one main concern only, which was to ensure that Cunard remained a purely British undertaking. Both the Mercantile Cruisers and the Steamship Subsidies committees emphasised the absolute necessity of placing subsidised vessels under such obligation as would preclude their transfer, direct or indirect, to foreign control. This reservation, which signifies the prime impact of the Morgan affair upon these committees and upon the Cunard negotiation itself, went far beyond an insistence (by clause 5.13 of the agreement) that the company's head office should remain in the United Kingdom and that the company register and keep registered all its fleet under the British flag. The government had the paramount objective of trying to ensure that ownership and control remained truly British too.

The legal difficulties besetting any attempt to entrench such a provision we have already noticed when considering the American combine. Cunard were easily able to satisfy the government that foreigners held for the time being les than 1% of its shares, having compiled a list of thirty-five names and addresses of the only shareholders thought to be foreign, twenty-five of whom had private or holding addresses in Britain. The shareholders ratified an all-British amendment of its articles of association, in terms we have already quoted, in order (as their chairman put it to them) to 'place beyond possibility of doubt the cardinal principle upon which the government is treating with us, ... that the Company is to be and is to remain British'. Yet, as the *Economist* objected,

> This is a pleasing form of words, but words only ... There is nothing to prevent Mr Morgan from buying up if he likes the majority of the shares in the Cunard Company, and enjoying the benefits of an arrangement supposed to be made to counteract his own expansive devices.

And the *Times* called the amendment futile: could not the shareholders at any time reverse this provision, and so would it not be better to stipulate simply that the *board* of Cunard be always British?[38] (In this connection it may be observed that in May 1902 the two great German lines had modified their charters so as to restrict membership of their directorates and boards of management to German subjects residing in German territory.)

To meet such contingencies several new entrenching devices were considered. Hill at first drafted a clause whereby the company would have purported to undertake not to alter the all-British clauses of the agreement during its life. But Palmer advised that the company could not in law enter into such an undertaking, as under the Companies Act the shareholders possessed an inherent right by a three-quarters majority to amend its articles of association whenever they pleased. The Mercantile Cruiser committee had suggested

> that the desired security might be obtained by a scheme by which, during the term of the subsidy, the Admiralty would be

the registered owners of not less than 33/64ths of the vessel; the management and profits being left wholly to the Company, and legal security being taken that all owners' obligations should appertain exclusively to the Company.[39]

In the upshot two precautions were built into the second schedule of the agreement, following the Cunard shareholders' meeting of 29th July 1903. This ratified an amendment of the articles of association so as to ensure that no foreigner might hold office as a director or be employed as a principal officer of the company, and that no share should be held, directly or indirectly, to the benefit of a foreigner (present foreign holders excepted) or of a corporation under foreign control – the terms 'principal officer' and 'corporation under foreign control' being defined in the second schedule.

At the government's request the shareholders then empowered the directors to enforce compliance with this condition by drafting a special declaration of British nationality or registration, to be administered to all transferees of the company's shares, whether individuals or companies. They could thus call upon any shareholder to prove his nationality and title, and complete the surrender of his shares if proof of British nationality were not forthcoming, meanwhile suspending his voting rights. The *Economist*, which had earlier criticised the lack of such security, now called these 'unprecedentedly hard terms'.[40] But nothing less stringent was likely to satisfy Parliament. And to this day they have remained effectual in preventing attempts of foreigners to take over the company.

Secondly, under clause 11 of the agreement, as ratified by its shareholders, the company would issue one £20 share to each of two nominees of His Majesty's government. In all questions relating to the management and general policy of the company this share gave the holder no more than ordinary voting power. But if ever the entrenched all-British stipulations were brought into question, the two nominees were empowered to demand a poll in which they were to be free to exercise an additional voting weight equivalent to one quarter of the shareholders' total voting strength. The legal stipulation of a three-quarters majority was thus not contravened, but got round. Again, the *Economist* complained that this 'government share' device was 'a large come-down from the 33/64ths registered ownership suggested by the Admiralty Committee'. Yet it went as far as was practicable toward making shares in the company analogous to shares in a British ship. (And the *Economist* was incidentally wrong in adding that the voting power of the government share was undefined and wholly at the directors' discretion.)

To the same end Cunliffe under Balfour's instructions had at one point proposed that Cunard act to limit the holdings of a single company to one-tenth, and of any aggregate of companies to one-half, of its issued share capital. But this was objected to by Inverclyde as seriously prejudicial to the negotiability of its shares. He pointed out that the ultimate weapon for use against any possible capture of his company by another was the government's right under the third schedule of the agreement at any time to purchase the whole Cunard fleet at cost price. Cunard did not demur, however, when the Board of Trade refused it freedom to repay the loan before expiry of the twenty years, on the ground that in so doing it would prematurely free itself from observance of the all-British conditions.

The stipulation of Cunard's existing Admiralty contract, that men of the Royal Naval Reserve should make up not less than half the complement of the *Campania*, *Lucania* and *Umbria*, was temporarily re-enacted with slight variation (Clause 5.9). But furtherto, and by the same section of the new contract, the company undertook that on *all* its vessels the master, officers and engineers in charge of a watch should always be British subjects, and so should three-quarters at least of the crew. This protection is interesting as marking the first departure from the law of 1854 which opened British ships to the seamen of all nations. The *Economist* stigmatised it as 'unreasonable' and 'just of the character of the restrictive regulations which cripple American shipping'. To the US Commissioner of Navigation it indeed appeared, when taken together with the other all-British provisions, to commit Cunard 'to the ultimate limit of American exclusion'.[41] But Balfour was particularly anxious to secure such an undertaking, because under the Morgan agreement the government could require no more than that British ships of the American combine carry the same proportion. Like the Morgan combine, too, Cunard was not required to pledge itself not to dispose of its unwanted ships to foreigners; for the company could not be expected to cut itself off from the lucrative foreign market for outworn or outclassed vessels. Negotiations with the Treasury involved details slightly more contentious. Not until the agreement had first been drafted did Ritchie (unfortunately moved by the new Premier from the Home Office to the Exchequer) discover casually – for his predecessor as Chancellor, Hicks Beach, had never alluded to the matter – that no reference in principle had ever been made to his department. On being shown the agreement in draft, Ritchie demurred at the rate of interest proposed to be charged Cunard. The Treasury would have to raise the amount of the loan by way of a terminable annuity over the period allowed the company for repayment, by borrowing from the National Debt Commissioners at the standard rate of 3% p.a. – that is, ½% higher than the rate to be charged Cunard.[42] The latter, nevertheless, was allowed to stand as agreed in the contract.

Then, after the government had satisfied itself as to the security for the loan provided in the trust deed, there was the matter of insurance, regarding which it sought the advice of the Joint Permanent Secretaries to the Treasury – Sir Edward Hamilton and Sir Francis Mowatt. For Cunard, Hill pointed out that for years the White Star Line had effected no outside insurance, and that the P & O gave no mortgages and assumed no insurance obligation towards its debenture holders. In his view a large company – and the Cunard fleet with its new acquisitions would be worth upward of £4 million – possessed sufficient security in itself to assume its own insurance risks. This fleet ought not to be run for the underwriters' benefit; the debenture loan would diminish annually; and the company had the right to expect as much freedom in the conduct of its business as was compatible with minimum security for its debenture holders. Hill's view was accepted.

One further point remained. Through its chief solicitor, Lord Desart, the Treasury claimed the liberty to pay for any vessel acquired by the government in cancelled debenture stock. Inverclyde, on the contrary, argued his company's interest in their own solvency as well as the government's in their efficiency. By 2nd July 1903 the matter was settled to mutual satisfaction by the provision that in any event the company were to be paid out of the purchase money such a cash sum as would enable them to replace any vessel the government had bought by another vessel suitable to their own requirements; and that the balance (if any) over and above this sum should be paid, not by cancellation of debentures, but by transfer of such stock at par to the company or its nominees (who would almost certainly be its builders or bankers). Cunard on its part agreed, in the event of a sale of either of its new ships, not to replace the vessel by a similar one unless the government so requested.[43]

With the Admiralty the line's relationship was governed by the current Armed Cruiser contract which had been in force since 1st April 1900, though its last republication[44] was dated 24th October 1902. This laid down the conditions under which the company agreed to hire or sell to the Admiralty on request seven named ships, and gave the latter certain pre-emptive rights over any vessels of seventeen knots or more which the company might later build. In consideration of its keeping three of the named vessels always at the Admiralty's disposal, Cunard received £10,000 p.a. in respect of the *Campania* and *Lucania*, and £8,000 p.a. for the *Umbria*; hitherto subject in each case (as we have noted) to a reduction of 25% – representing a total deduction of £7,000 p.a. from the Admiralty subvention – so long as the line were earning from the Post Office a mail subsidy also.

It was hoped that, in order to minimise discussion, the wording of this existing contract could be followed fairly closely in the new agreement, as was ultimately done in Clauses 3–5, 7 and 8 of the latter. Selborne had expected that the Admiralty's interest could be determined at the first draft stage, 'which I will push confidentially through the mill'. Cunard on its side made no demur to the requirement that the new vessels be built to designs approved by the Admiralty, whether or not – a contradistinction from the equivalent provisions of the Morgan agreement – such designs might prove compatible with the company's business needs. The Admiralty's solicitors, however, advised that particular care should be taken to insure against failure of the two new ships to reach and maintain their twenty-four-twenty-five knot minimum average ocean speed, and to 'put pressure on the Cunard to screw them definitely to this point if possible'. Rather than make technical stipulations about minimal horse-power of engines, etc., it was thought best simply to lay a general onus on the company to secure guarantees from their builders. Accordingly at first the Admiralty through Balfour pressed for the speed of the new Cunarders to be defined as twenty-four and a half knots' average steaming in moderate weather over at least one complete voyage a year, maintained throughout the twenty years' life of the agreement. Shortfalls from this speed would be penalised by proportionate diminution of the £150,000 subsidy – a figure regarded as inclusive of the existing £15,000 Admiralty subvention – £4,000 being deducted for every quarter-knot deficiency down to twenty-three and a half knots. If the average speed fell below twenty-three and a half knots the whole of the subvention would be forfeit. This was unacceptable to Cunard. After consulting the Director of Naval Intelligence, therefore, Balfour decided to recommend that questions of speed deficiency should instead be referred to arbitration; and to this the Admiralty assented on the understanding that it would yield them the security they wanted.[45]

Notwithstanding, the question of penalty was reopened by counsel to the Crown as late as May 1903 with the renewed proposal to make payment of the whole £150,000 conditional upon the two flyers reaching and maintaining the stipulated speed. From mid-June it was thrashed out direct between Inverclyde and Arnold-Forster, as Secretary to the Admiralty, with Balfour holding the ring. The Admiralty, said its Secretary, were paying an 'extraordinary subsidy' for which they expected an 'extraordinary result'. The new ships were not merely to be fast, but assuredly faster than anything the foreigner had. Substantial penalties for fall-off in speed were therefore of the essence. Again Inverclyde protested that the subvention was not to be regarded as purely a cruiser agreement: practically the £150,000 was to enable his company to face the total risk incurred by binding itself as to capital and interest over a long period of years. It could not contemplate finding itself left the bankrupt possessor of two expresses, neither of which had been designed solely with commercial viability in view. Nor could it bind itself against failure by builders. Despite the most careful tests made with the Admiralty's permission at Haslar, no guarantee could be procured from any yard against shortfall of final speed. As his company were virtually staking their all,

Inverclyde could not agree to the Admiralty's proposed penalty scale. In the upshot the government agreed to let the arbitration clause stand (as Clause 7) while Inverclyde consented to its amplification so as to envisage reparation in the event of speed deficiency, either initially or later in the vessels' service life. In such a case, if company and government could not agree as to the amount deductible from the subvention, the sum would be fixed by arbitration.[46]

One last detail remains to be noticed. Balfour had promised Cunard's chairman (as we saw) that his company should have the benefit of the 25% Admiralty rebate on the three vessels named above; and this promise was redeemed by correspondingly increasing by £7,000 Cunard's subvention from the Post Office.

Discussions with this last department were attended with some acrimony. The new Postmaster General, Austen Chamberlain (appointed in July 1902), was dissatisfied on a number of grounds. First, there was the undeniable circumstance that his department had not been consulted about the contract until 8th October, and then at short notice from the Treasury, after the preliminary drafting had been done. They would, he complained, be made to look foolish in the House of Commons if, when so big a thing were concluded by the government with Cunard, the Post Office, the latter's largest customer, appeared to have had no say in the matter at all.[47] Anxious 'to ensure that the arrangements made shall comprehend all Imperial interests', the Mercantile Cruisers committee had specifically recommended that before any future shipping subsidies or contract be entered into, Admiralty and Post Office should invariably consult together. Selborne appeared to have ignored this. And Chamberlain, believing that 'the Post Office requirements and the Admiralty requirements hang so closely together that any bargain affecting the one ought certainly to be made to cover the other',[48] was chagrined at being left to learn what he could from the public press.[49]

Secondly, there was the question of the basis upon which payment for mail carriage should in future rest. Cunard's existing contract with the Post Office (it will be recalled) was that of 31st July 1899, terminable by either side on twelve months' notice; and this provided for payment by weight of mail carried.

The resultant remuneration to Cunard had risen, in round figures, from £58,000 in the first year to £62,000 in 1902. His department were not satisfied with this, Chamberlain declared, 'but the Company have always been too strong for us, and we did the best we could'. Anticipating an even more rapid rise in weight of mails carried, especially if (as confidently expected in 1902) penny postage to the USA were soon introduced, the Post Office saw its own interest to lie in securing the substitution of a fixed annual payment – something Cunard had always resisted. But the first draft of the new agreement provided simply that 'payment for mails shall be continued at not less than the present rates'. 'The Admiralty and the Board of Trade,' commented Murray, 'are to pay Inverclyde £150,000 p.a. in order that he may be able to raise his prices on the Post Office. Such is the way in which this great Empire is run!'[50] In the end Inverclyde was persuaded by Balfour to acquiesce in a fixed payment of £68,000 p.a., arrived at by taking the annual average mail earnings of his company on that route over the years its existing mail contract had been in force (£61,000) and adding thereto a notional £7,000 which (as we have noted) represented the rebate they would otherwise have lost under the Admiralty contract. Inverclyde would have preferred that this arrangement were not made part and parcel of the agreement. Austen Chamberlain on the other hand desired it so, in order that he should not have to defend it in isolation when facing the Commons, with whom the Post Office vote had never been a popular one since, in 1854, that department's expenditure had been entirely separated from its revenue. Balfour sided with Chamberlain; and so the new postal contract was included as Part II of the final document (Clauses 13 to 37).

Thirdly, the Postmaster General was anxious about the quality of service his department would be getting for its money. He strongly objected to being obliged to continue to employ for the whole twenty years' life of the new agreement the existing Cunarders, two of which (the *Campania* and *Lucania*) would be ten, and two others (the *Umbria* and *Etruria*) twenty, years old when the proposed contract came into force. Professor Biles in his remarks appended to the Mercantile Cruisers committee's report had urged that all future government mail contracts should stipulate that a definite proportion of the contractors' ships must fulfil the Admiralty requirements as to speed and other essentials. It had been the Post Office's view that the project of a twenty-knot service to Halifax in conjunction with the Canadian government would, if and when realised, get mail to Chicago and possibly to New York a day earlier than the present Cunard one. If notwithstanding the department were to be compelled to bind itself to Cunard for another twenty years, at least it was entitled to some assurance from the latter about frequency and speed, and better facilities for sorting mail aboard ship without extra payment.[51] Chamberlain wanted exact safeguards as to performance, over and above a general assurance that the company would employ on its normal Saturday service the fastest ships available at any one time. He therefore asked Inverclyde to agree to stipulate a definite time within which each voyage would be completed; to guarantee the normal availability of at least one ship weekly of twenty knots for the New York run; and to give the Post Office the unlimited use, without additional charge, of any fast mid-week service to the United States that the company might put on. These demands Chamberlain justified on the grounds that the Post Office's payments to Cunard, unlike those to foreign lines, had always been at double the Postal Union rates;[52] that any extra charge accruing to his department under the new agreement must either be met out of its current appropriations or incur parliamentary criticism; and that provisions of this kind were common form in all long-term subsidy contracts.

Inverclyde, lamenting to Balfour the Post Office's seeming lack of confidence in his line after all these years of service, refused to bind the company to such onerous particulars. Here he took the same position as when resisting the Admiralty's conditions, namely that the £150,000 subvention must be balanced against the company's undertakings and risks as a whole, and not simply against its services to any one department in particular. Thwarted again, Austen Chamberlain in early November 'practically threw up the discussion and went away', leaving further negotiation to be conducted by his new permanent secretary, Sir Robert Hunter, with the assistance of H. Buxton Forman, who had been the Post Office's spokesman before the Steamship Subsidies committee. When persuaded back to the bargaining table in the following spring, Chamberlain went on to complain to Balfour of the March redraft of the agreement that 'in fact, every provision inserted to procure a better mail service has been struck out by the Company ... I simply cannot face the House of Commons with such a proposal.' Rather, he would prefer to abide by the old subsidy-by-weight arrangement: and he threatened categorically to take immediate steps to free the Post Office from dependence on Cunard.[53]

Who was in the right of it? Over competitive routes – to the West Indies, for example, or South America – Chamberlain would have been correct in holding that a mail contract was not essential to the Post Office, which might fairly expect to get satisfactory service at a lower figure per mile than was represented by the level of the Cunard subvention. But where, as in the North Atlantic, fast boats were required to ply over a route commercially subject to seasonal variation, a regular mail service could be obtained only by means of a specific contract. And in any such contract hitherto Postmasters General had taken the sensible view that any attempt to impose extraneous conditions curtailing the shipowner's freedom to handle his traffic as he thought best must in the long run be reflected in increased cost which would be passed back to the hirer. One is inclined to attribute some of Austen's petulance to his very short experience in that particular office.

All Balfour's pacifying arts were required before he could be induced to make 'one more attempt' to reach agreement. After further conferences between the solicitors of all concerned on 13th May 1903, the Post Office clauses were finally settled on 16th June. Cunard agreed to give that department the benefit of its improved Wednesday service to Boston and (for up to 10% of the department's normal Saturday mail) of its occasional Tuesday service to New York. But if the latter were to become a regular fast mid-week service, extra subvention would be looked for. The company were, however, to carry without additional payment up to 100 tons of parcels weekly in each direction. The consent of the Post Office, as well as of the Admiralty, was required before it might sell, lay up or permanently substitute vessels. For the rest, Inverclyde persuaded the negotiators that the department's interests could be adequately secured by the government under the agreement's general arbitration clause.[54]

Concord with the Post Office removed the last obstacle to satisfactory drafting. In its final form the contract obtained the Cabinet's approval on 14th July 1903. On the 29th a general meeting of Cunard shareholders unanimously approved the necessary amendments to their articles of association. Sealed by the company, the agreement was at long last laid on the table of the House of Commons on 3rd August, together with the agreement with Morgan.[55] We must, wrote Hill to Cunliffe, see 'our friends among the newspaper people' and 'our friends in the House'; and he asked for access to one of the government whips[56] Early press comment was favourable. And on 12th August a thinly attended chamber after debate approved both documents by ninety-two votes to eighteen. The Lords gave their consent the following day. On 20th August, the measure having passed on to the statute book, a further meeting of Cunard shareholders duly ratified the amendments already resolved in the company's articles. The completed transaction was given legal and financial effect by the Cunard Agreement (Money) Act of 15th August 1904.[57]

The significance of the Cunard contract for Britain's merchant shipping as a whole was to be much debated in the months ahead. For the moment we need observe only that its value to the company itself was unquestioned. As we have seen, some details Cunard would have liked to be otherwise. It would have preferred, for instance, not to have been bound to run its new flyers right through the winter or to tie itself to a regular Saturday service. Yet much had been gained which at one time during the negotiations had not appeared feasible. Payment of 5% of the loan annually would, in form, extinguish the indebtedness at the end of twenty years: but the ships would be able to earn a materially higher rate of depreciation and consequently cancel the indebtedness in a shorter period of time. Meanwhile the relief from interest until the new vessels had been built was a substantial set-off. The previous 25% deduction from the Admiralty subsidy had been waived; and the new scale of Post Office subvention under Part II of the agreement would become immediately effective as from 30th July 1903. Pending a satisfactory outcome to its negotiations with the government, the Cunard directors had had in mind the possible need to increase the company's capital: now that would not be necessary.

It had been, as they reminded their shareholders, 'no small matter for the Company to relinquish its right to enter into business combinations with foreigners for the advance of its own business interests as it might find expedient'. In the event it had contrived still to preserve the negotiable value of its shares. Now the self-confidence with which it faced the future in the North Atlantic was implicit in its readiness to back the trust deed by first mortgages upon every vessel in its fleet. 'No other shipping Company than Cunard,' boasted its directors, 'whose fleet was free of all charge, could have offered any such security to the Government.' 'The whole thing has worked out,' commented another colleage to Inverclyde, 'much better than at one time seemed likely.' 'I must say,' echoed his fellow director, E. H. Cunard, 'we ought to consider ourselves lucky in getting such an arrangement,' more especially since 'our position had become so uncertain that we were not in a position to dictate terms'. 'This result,' he added, 'has been brought about entirely by your own efforts, ... and the scheme, as accepted, is entirely your own suggestion.' For the Board of Trade, Cunliffe proffered his congratulations too: 'Your Company should be everlastingly grateful to you.'[58]

NOTES

1 E. H. Meade, in W. Z. Ripley: *Trusts, Pools and Corporations* (New York, 1905), p. 362. The full appraisal of the line over the years is F. E. Hyde: *Cunard and the North Atlantic, 1840–1973* (London, 1975).

2 Circulars of 4 and 6 Apr. 1901, quoted in *Fairplay* 36:589–90.

3 Cunard papers, vol. i, p. 13. In 1905 the company instructed their solicitors, Messrs Hill Dickinson & Co. of Liverpool, to assemble all documentation relating to the company's contract of 1903 with the government. Compilation was divided between two volumes, the first comprising the solicitors' report of the negotiations, with the agreement in its successive drafts and the debenture stock trust deed appended; the second volume containing the relevant correspondence. For a list of Cunard's Atlantic fleet at the time see Appendix II(d).

4 *Ibid.*, 1:13–14.

5 *Ibid.*, 1:3–12.

6 *Ibid.*, 1:34–35, 2:19–23; O'Hagan: *op. cit.*, 1:384.

7 Inverclyde to Selborne, 12 Mar., 1902, Cu. 2:14, and interview of same day.

8 Selborne to Inverclyde, 13 and 22 Mar., Inverclyde to Selborne, 18 Mar. 1902, Cu. 2:33–6.
9 Selborne to Inverclyde, 22 Mar., 3 Apr. and 5 May 1902, *ibid.*, 2:36–38.
10 Inverclyde to Selborne, 29 Mar. and 5 Apr. 1902, *ibid.*
11 Cu. 1:29.
12 Inverclyde to Selborne, 12 Apr., 1902, Cu. 2:27.
13 Cu. 1:31 and 42.
14 Selborne to Inverclyde, 24 and 28 Apr., Inverclyde to Selborne, 26 and 30 Apr. 1902, Cu. 2:28–32.
15 Inverclyde to Gerald Balfour, 5 May 1902, GB 30/60/48.
16 Furness to Inverclyde, 22 Mar., 1902, Cu. 1:38 and 49; 2:18 and 94; Balfour to Chamberlain, 9 May 1902, GB 30/60/48.
17 Cu. 1:52.
18 *Ibid.*, 1:50–3; Selborne to Inverclyde, 8 and 10 May, Inverclyde to Selborne, 9 May 1902, Cu. 2:37.
19 Cu. 1:55; Furness to Inverclyde, 18 May 1902, Cu. 2:43.
20 Furness to Chamberlain, 29 May 1902, enclosing his memorandum of the same date, GB 30/60/48.
21 Furness to Chamberlain, 19 June 1902, *loc. cit.*
22 Balfour to Furness, 29 May, and Inverclyde to Chamberlain, memorandum of 3 June 1902, *ibid.*; Furness to Inverclyde, 5 June, and Inverclyde to Furness, 20 June 1902, Cu. 1:63 and 104; Furness to Chamberlain, and to Balfour, 19 June 1902, GB 30/60/48.
23 On this point see Dawkins's conjectures, p. 241 below.
24 Viscount Esher: *Journals and Letters* (1934), 1:332, 336 and 338.
25 Furness to Inverclyde, 1 and 5 July 1902, Cu. 1:68 and 72.
26 Balfour to Chamberlain, 28 Aug. 1902, JC 11/6/3.
27 As Cd. 1379 (1902).
28 See Appendix II(e).
29 AC 16/6/3, Appendix B.
30 Inverclyde to Chamberlain, 1 Aug. 1902, Cu. 1:71.
31 Inverclyde to Cassel, 1 Aug. 1902, GB 30/60/48, containing Balfour's pencilled marginalia.
32 AC 16/6/3, printed for the use of the Cabinet, 6 Aug. 1902.
33 AC 16/6/4, *ditto* 15 Aug. 1902.
34 Inverclyde to Balfour, 23 Aug. and 10 Sept., Balfour to Chamberlain, 13 Sept., Chamberlain to Balfour, 16 Sept. 1902; Cunard circular in draft, printed for Cabinet 19 Sept. 1902, all in GB 30/60/49. The circular was later published in *Fairplay* 39:534 on 2 Oct. following.
35 Bonar Law to Inverclyde, 24 Feb. 1903, Cu. 2:195.
36 Inverclyde to Balfour, 8 Aug. 1902, GB 30/60/48; AC 16/6/4, p. 1.
37 Bonar Law to Inverclyde, 24 Feb. 1903, Cu. 2:195.
38 *Economist* 60:1600, 18 Oct. 1902; *Times*, 3 Oct. 1902, leader.
39 *Report, loc. cit.*, p. iv, para. 12.
40 *Economist* 61:1303, 25 July 1903.

41 *Economist, loc. cit.*; E. T. Chamberlin, 'The new Cunard steamship contract', *North American Review* 177:538 (1903).
42 Ritchie to Balfour, 10 and 16 Sept. and 4 Oct. 1902, GB 30/60/48.
43 Cu. 1:86–7.
44 Cu. 2:271.
45 Selborne to Balfour, 6 Sept. 1902, GB 30/60/48; P. Watts to W. G. Greene, 16 Oct. 1902, *ibid.*; Balfour to Chamberlain, 11 Sept. 1902, JC 11/6/5; Arnold-Forster to R. B. D. Acland, 11 Feb., and to Selborne, 22 May 1903, A-F 50295, ff. 79–81.
46 Arnold-Forster to Selborne, 22 May, 11 June and 1 July, and to Inverclyde, 18 June 1903, Arnold-Forster 50295, ff. 81, 83, 87–90; Inverclyde to Balfour, 10 Dec. 1902, Cu. 1:167.
47 G. H. Murray, by telegram, to A. Chamberlin, 8 Oct. 1902, AC 16/6/13; P. Watts to W. G. Greene, 16 Oct. 1902, GB 30/60/48; Balfour to Inverclyde, 21 Oct. 1902, Cu. 1:80–81; Inverclyde to Hill (of Hill Dickinson & Co.), 10 Nov. 1902, Cu. 2:144.
48 Murray to A. Chamberlain, 9 Oct. 1902, AC 16/6/9.
49 His Permanent Secretary, Sir George Murray, was sympathetic. 'I daresay,' he wrote to his chief, 'you may remember that we hung up a useful little contract of ours with the Royal Mail in order that "all Imperial interests" might be duly safeguarded; and this is all the return we get for it! ... The moral – as I was saying the other day – is – avoid philanthropic impulses in your intercourse with other Departments: you will always be giving and never taking.'
50 A.Chamberlain to Murray, 4 Oct., and Murray to A. Chamberlain, 5 Oct. 1902, AC 16/6/7 and 8.
51 A.Chamberlain to Murray, *loc. cit.*, who agreed. For the Post Office's case for better accommodation see memorandum of H. Buxton Forman, 10 Oct. 1902, headed 'Sea Post Offices on Atlantic Mail Packets', AC 16/6/11.
52 i.e., the uniform scale of charges for carriage of foreign mails, as agreed internationally by the Postal Union Congress (originally at Berne in 1874, and roughly quinquennially thereafter) to which Great Britain was a party. Parenthetically it may be recalled that, although she had recently, and with Commonwealth cooperation, laid a cable under the Pacific, Britain was not to possess an Atlantic cable until the German ones were cut and confiscated on the outbreak of war in 1914.
53 Inverclyde to Hill, 10 Nov. 1902, Cu. 2:144; A. Chamberlain to Balfour, Cu. 2:204.
54 Inverclyde to Balfour, 16 Apr. 1903, Cu. 2:209.
55 As Cd. 1703 and (1903) respectively.
56 Hill to Cunliffe, 29 July, and Cunliffe to Hill, 31 July 1903, Cu. 2:290 and 292.
57 4 Ed. VII c. 22.
58 Cu. 1:365; A. P. Moorhouse to Inverclyde, E. H. Cunard to same, 10 Aug. 1903, Cu. 2:295; Cunliffe to Hill, 6 Aug. 1903, Cu. 2:294.

CHAPTER 6

Peril and protection

That outside the Cunard company rejoicing should be universal was too much to hope for. Neither of the twin treaties ratified by Parliament in August 1903 was likely to lack objectors, for each in its own way was distinctly novel. The agreement with Morgan marked the first occasion on which Britain, the world power, had deemed it necessary to come to a bilateral accommodation over shipping with a challenger. And by its contract with Cunard the government had virtually bound itself in an unprecedented type of relationship with a private company: thereby large and contentious issues were involved, the determining of which was to be influential, not for the current crisis only but for subsequent State policy also. Immediately, then, the agreements elicited a wide spectrum of comment. It ranged from mere grumbles about procedural haste during the closing hours of a busy Parliament ('The way the House was treated,' complained Dilke, 'was really a scandal') to a review of the government's whole attitude toward *laissez-faire* itself.

First, the critics of the Cunard contract. The more jaundiced were those who saw in the deal nothing more than an uncovenanted bonus to a company which had contrived to turn a national threat to very advantageous private use. If Cunard had held out against the Americans, said one MP in the heat of the debate, it had done so 'not from any patriotic motives, but purely as a matter of business. They were like the last voter of a corrupt borough before the Ballot Act, who kept back his vote in order to get the biggest price.' And even in comparative tranquillity two years later the American historian of shipping subsidies believed that in the atmosphere of national alarm 'the Cunard company had shrewdly taken advantage of Britain's pride in the British merchant marine, and coined its "patriotism" into good pounds sterling'. It could now proceed – at public expense and at no commercial risk, for its interest payments to the Treasury could easily be met out of its mail subvention alone – with a programme that would enable it to compete for passengers and mails on those terms considered most important at the time, viz. speed, size and luxury. It was calculable, too, that the government's hiring terms per month per gross registered ton would exceed the corresponding earnings of the company in its most prosperous days. As to this latter, however, defenders pointed out that the favourable terms of hire were no more than a necessary insurance for the company against the disruption of its regular traffic by the abrupt withdrawal of its largest and fastest units. All in all, another MP felt inclined to congratulate Cunard more on their courage in undertaking the contract than on their luck in getting it.[1]

Other critics, without impugning Cunard's patriotism, nevertheless doubted the financial soundness of the contract. 'A thoroughly bad business transaction,' Walter Runciman called it, and he had the support of certain other parliamentarians with shipping interests. The State was making a private company a loan of £2·6 million – a figure well above the latter's nominal, and practically double its real, capital. Working out at about £40 a ton, it must in those days have looked a colossal amount to be investing in two vessels. And the rate of interest Cunard would pay would not merely (as the Mercantile Cruisers committee had recommended) be below the open market rate of borrowing – 5% – but as little as half that figure. Overall, for a net payment of £150,000 p.a. Cunard would become owners of vessels having a capital value of £2·6 million: for which sum, hazarded one opponent rashly, the government might have built at least four complete cruisers which could fight as well as run. What would the country be getting instead? Consuming a thousand tons of coal a day, how effective would the two flyers be in war? In peace, £4,000 per trip would be locked up in each of them in coal that would be filling the cargo space. As despatch vessels they might be too large: as cruisers, too weak and vulnerable, It was worth neither the Admiralty's nor the Empire's while 'to place on the ocean vessels which are not wanted and will never pay'. The government had committed itself for twenty years, regardless of the probability of obsolescence. Yet within five the new boats might themselves be superseded by something faster and more efficient. Under the terms of the advance the government had become *de facto* mortgagees of the Cunard fleet until the £2 million was repaid.

What if, in consequence of technical progress, the company's future shareholders declined to go on with what might by then prove to be a heavily losing bargain and compel the mortgagees to foreclose? In that case the government would find itself the owner of derelict liners running in competition with modern, perhaps oil-fired, ones. 'The fact that the Morgan syndicate have made a bad bargain,' concluded the *Economist* severely, 'will not make the Cunard bargain a better one.'[2]

All these criticisms the government and its supporters were notwithstanding prepared to meet and deflect. Even had no American threat developed, the Cunard agreement (said Sir William Allan, MP for Gateshead and himself head of a well established 'short sea' shipping company) represented the cheapest method of meeting Britain's foreseeable needs. Mails would travel with maximum speed and economy, whereas the Canadian government (observed Sir John Colomb) were encountering great difficulty and expense in getting a mail service inferior to what Cunard would be giving. More important, the agreement was justifiable on grounds of national security. The Mercantile Cruisers committee had advised the government, with statistical evidence, that vessels of sufficient speed for use with the navy could not be constructed or run at a commercial profit. As Lord Brassey had warned the Select Committee on Steam Ship Subsidies. 'If you want that speed in your auxiliaries you have to pay for it.' Indeed, said Allan tartly, the Admiralty had never yet itself built a ship which proved to possess the velocity she was designed for. Now they would be assured – not on the Atlantic alone but on all the seas that divided or united our Empire – of two steamers which for their speed and coal capacity could not be matched by any foreigner. Arnold-Forster drew attention to the modern weapons with which the new vessels would be armed. The hiring rates the Admiralty would pay would be lower than those it laid out during the South African war. In effect, nine-tenths of the costs of crewing and repairing was being met commercially under the agreement; the remaining tenth being provided by the nation as a military contribution. Furthermore, the whole Cunard fleet – not only the two express steamers to be laid down – would be as secure against transfer to or control by foreigners as human ingenuity could make it. [3]

Yet misgiving persisted that vast expense was being incurred purely for considerations of prestige or sentimental patriotism. Either we were in an indecent haste to wrest back the Blue Riband from German halliards or else the government 'has been frightened into the old policy of giving extravagant payments, ostensibly for the post, but really for the maintenance of British supremacy of the seas'. Admittedly the new subsidy would bring faster service. But would not so artificial a stimulus eventually foster inefficiency in Cunard? The patriots, however, carried the day in representing the agreement as a legitimate, nay imperative, national undertaking. Had Cunard succumbed to competition 'the object the American millionaires had in view would have been accomplished'. Technology did not stand still. Let it never be said that 'the time had arrived when the very swiftest steamers, the finest patterns of naval architecture, were no longer to be found under the British flag'. Rear-Admiral Lord Charles Beresford, MP for Woolwich, would have liked to see Britain laying down not two new expresses but four, six or even eight. By the *Quarterly Review* the agreement was applauded as frankly 'an intimation to all the world that the British mercantile marine is a national heritage which in case of need will be guarded by the national arm, even in time of peace, not on economic but on political grounds'.[4]

Of the smaller points of criticism raised in debate, one concerned Cunards's contractual undertaking 'not to unduly raise freights or to give any preferential rate to foreigners'. How, asked Edmund Robertson (MP for Dundee and a frequent contributor to the press on shipping affairs) was 'undue' to be read? Who was to decide whether a rise in freight or passenger charges was duly or unduly reflective of (say) a rise in the price of coal? A more commonsense objection than Robertson's might have been that the whole 'undue' clause was superfluous. For no company would so markedly raise its passenger fares as to drive traffic away to the many second- or third-class boats operating over the same route, nor unduly raise freight charges when so many tramps were ready to take up the slack. Indeed, the ubiquity of the tramp, with its cheap and flexible handling, was a standing rebuttal to the charge that the Cunard subsidy might injure the independent freighter.

However, the objector's second ground for misliking the

'undue' clause, that it represented a peculiar intervention by His Majesty's government into the self-regulation of a private shipping company's own internal finance, could not be brushed aside so lightly. It might not sustain the exaggerated claim of a Liverpool MP, whose shipping interests did not lie with Cunard, that the company had thereby 'surrendered its independence and become virtually a State concern'. But it formed part of a more general criticism that the whole agreement was an unprecedented infraction of the accepted doctrine of *laissez-faire*, in as much as it promised to benefit one shipping company in particular, rather than the maritime trade of the country as a whole. And in so doing it had led us into the grievous error of lesser States who poured out their citizens' money for negligible return. Something like this latter objection Gerald Balfour had already anticipated when first making public the whole scheme in his Sheffield speech of 30th September 1902. The sum to be paid Cunard, he had then emphasised, though large, was unexceptionably so, since it represented

> not more than a fair remuneration for the service to be rendered. To the principle of paying a subsidy in excess of the remuneration fairly due for the services rendered by any shipping company the Government is perfectly opposed. Such subsidy we regard as merely bounty in disguise, and to the principle of giving bounties we are resolutely opposed.

The Cunard subvention was certainly not to be regarded as on all fours with the kind of aid the Americans were seeking and the French already had; but rather, Evelyn Cecil reminded the Commons, as a compensation lying entirely within the permissible field demarcated by his Select Committee on Steam Ship Subsidies.[5]

In a sense, therefore, the Cunard agreement got the benefit of both worlds. Since it could not convincingly be shown to violate the principle of payment solely for services rendered, but merely extended it to cover a new and urgent national predicament, it need not forfeit the support of free-traders. At the same time it wore an aspect of novelty sufficient to gratify the protectionists. For they could recall no precedent for an arrangement whereby the State entered into a working agreement – indeed, virtually a partnership – in which one partner (the government) advanced the capital though without sharing in either the profits or the losses. Not surprisingly the patriotic *National Review* hailed it as 'a nail in the coffin of the laissez-aller system' which signified 'our abandonment of the obsolete shipping policy to which we became committed when the Cobdenite craze was at its climax'.[6]

Sweetest of all praise to British ears, however, must have been those of an envious United States Commissioner of Navigation. 'Two masterpieces of British business statesmanship' was how Eugene Tyler Chamberlain described the Morgan and Cunard agreements. Particularly the latter, he thought, demonstrated that the British government had at long last ranged itself alongside the other major European powers in recognising the usefulness of its merchant marine in time of war, and had at all times secured 'the maintenance of Britsh national supremacy by the best available means'. The episode ought to arouse Congress to the urgency of the choice confronting them. His own government's present mail contract with the American Line would terminate at about the same time as the new Cunarders came into service, and then

> the interesting question will have to settled ... whether or not the United States will definitely withdraw from the North Atlantic except as a War Power ... The new Cunard contract will undoubtedly convince many Americans that again we ought to give up the ocean steamship business, and devote ourselves to farming, and the manufacture of sewing-machines, tin-plates and other industries, for which we have a natural or acquired aptitude ... But the contract is equally sure to convince another considerable portion of the American public, that more than ever the United States should make a respectable showing on salt water ... Undoubtedly, there are just as good national reasons for the United States' maintaining a first-class Transatlantic mail service as for Great Britain's doing so,

and to that end it must be prepared to spend more.[7]

If the preponderance of opinion in Britain welcomed the Cunard contract it was less wholehearted in praise of its twin document governing future relations with the IMM. The *Times* applauded both as 'wise and rational', adding that in particular the terms of the treaty with Morgan 'dispose of nearly all the objections having any kind of validity which have been used against the Combination'. For many, however, it was acceptable only as necessary in order to avoid ruinous rate wars. Some held

that the government, by acting precipitately against an un-
proven threat, had let Morgan out of a tight corner; that his
creature was financially unsound and that he had no real
alternative but to maintain British registry for the lines
affected. We were to blame for licensing, and in a few cases
subsidising, the latter to compete against truly British shipping
in the same area. To such objectors to treat with the transatlantic invader appeared 'a foolish and feeble arrangement',
'unwise and useless', 'legislation in a panic' in response to 'the
silly clamour of hysterical newspapers'. 'Were they so ashamed
of the British flag that they had to bribe companies in order to
induce them to remain under it?' The cry that British shipping
was in danger was unreal, for the 'captured' lines could not in
practice be transferred to the United States register. By continuing subsidies to White Star Britain had merely assisted the
combine to compete with unsubsidised British vessels in whatsoever part of the globe its component units might henceforth be
deployed. Alternatively, since the whole subsidy policy for
cruisers might soon be abandoned by the Admiralty, the agreement with the Americans was 'not worth to the British Government the paper on which it is written ... and it is merely
accepted in political circles as the unnecessary consequence of
the irrational spasm caused by the formation of the Morgan
Combine'.[8]

For a balanced assessment it is worth quoting the views
expressed by Joseph Chamberlain to the Duke of Devonshire
(Unionist leader in the House of Lords) – not merely for the light
they throw on his personal attitude throughout negotiations,
but as seeming to encapsulate and typify what printed evidence
reveals as the tenor of British opinion:

'I agree with you that the proposed agreement (with Morgan) is
vague and probably does not amount to much. But it has the
advantage of meeting the fears of some members of the Cabinet that
we might be engaging in a contest with the United States Government, who would be able to beat us in any subsidy competition. This
arrangement makes us friends with Morgan and prevents anything
in the nature of an international conflict. Personally, I do not share
the fears of my colleagues and I think that Great Britain is never so
weak as when she is afraid to meet any adversary on equal terms.
But then I am a Jingo, and I can never get any real support, from you
or anyone else in the Cabinet, in support of my own convinced

opinion that we ought not to give way to the bluffing of any Foreign Power and that, if the worst came to the worst, we could hold out, as our ancestors did, against the lot of them.

I think the Morgan Combination is a move in a great commercial war, and, if I were dictator, I would meet it with strong measures. As it is, I attach most importance to the agreement with the Cunard Co. which will strengthen them to hold their own in the ensuing fight. The Morgan Agreement is a 'sop to Cerberus', and if we are not prepared to fight for all we are worth, it is the best alternative I can suggest.[9]

So much for the surface turbulence of controversy. But the deeps were stirred also. It scarcely needs remarking that in the Britain of 1900 free trade – what Keynes has called 'the most fervent expression of *laissez-faire*' – was a doctrine still held with quasi-religious fervour by the majority of her office-holders, businessmen and general public. To them its benefits appeared self-evident. In the half-century since repeal of the Navigation Laws our shipping had more than doubled in tonnage, until the quantity deployed in imperial trade was now five times the German figure and ten times the French. That foreigners engaged freely in this trade was held to ensure that freights would be competitive and, to the satisfaction of the manufacturer, prices of raw materials kept down. Though other countries were catching up, yet as an exporter per head of population we still comfortably surpassed any other contender. The shipping interest might be assumed to favour dear freights – though in fact many shipowners were free-traders by conviction. If foreign competitors were excluded or handicapped, however, the shippers and shipowners would have the manufacturers at their mercy: and classical economics did not allow that government policy should favour one single group against the general interest. Ergo, the free-traders were right to reject 'the spacious but shallow appeal to anti-foreign prejudices on which the protectionists trade'.[10] Within our national economy the government should be vigilant against monopolies, differentials, bounties, etc., which were incompatible with the notion of equality of treatment. Internationally, it had no obligation to link commerce with politics – a practice regarded as German and reprehensible.

Hardly less familiar is the minority case of these years. It held that free trade was efficacious only so long as Great Britain continued without challenge to enjoy the pre-eminence afforded by her industrial lead and her network of trading and finance agencies. But this was ceasing to be so; and to cling to a shibboleth was to limit the scope and effectiveness of her commercial diplomacy in an increasingly protectionist world. We must not persist in tying our hands so that we could neither offer encouragement nor threaten retaliation. Only freedom judiciously to apply export bounties, protective duties, and so on, would ensure Britain an equal footing *vis-à-vis* the artificial conditions of trade resorted to by rival nations. Properly speaking, this was not protection but 'fair trade'; and the field *par excellence* in which to pursue it was the Empire.

With this fair-trade movement the figure of Joseph Chamberlain is of course inextricably connected. Bred up to accept free trade as a *chose jugée,* the Unionist leader had of late been drawn away by the writings of Sir Vincent Caillard (an industrialist connected with Vickers) and by his own contact with the colonies and the USA. To Chamberlain's bold and constructive mind some form of imperial tariff would benefit not only the British businessman but the wage-earner too. 'The American working-man believes ... that high wages and a high standard of living are inseparably connected with the tariff.' With Andrew Carnegie he agreed that some degree of protection acted as a stimulus on masters and men to go and produce the article in enormous quantities. The benefits thus accumulated would then be available for social reform. Moreover, 'Free Trade within the Empire' (a far from unpalatable slogan) would bring our widely separated colonies into closer economic, spiritual and eventually political union, with reciprocal enrichment for inhabitants of the mother country also. In particular, if goods at present imported from abroad were made in England, shipping would be more heavily employed in carrying raw material than the finished goods. Hence Chamberlain's demand, voiced in his celebrated Birmingham speech of May 1902, to 'keep British trade in British hands'.[11] In order to educate the British public in these possibilities a number of elections would be required. Meanwhile some existing pressure groups had been infiltrated. The British Empire Union had been persuaded to put imperial preference on its programme, and protectionists had penetrated even that free-trade sanctum, the Imperial Federation League.

The *Daily Express* in the hands of Arthur Pearson provided a platform from which to proclaim that 'Tariff Reform Means Work For All'. And now the industrialists of Chamberlain's native city – in metals, chemicals, glass and building materials – were fathering the Tariff Reform League. Against them were arrayed the shipbuilders, cotton manufacturers, import merchants and financiers. It was Birmingham versus Manchester, with London inclined towards the latter.

Here the impact of the American industrial invasion was important as sharpening this dichotomy, revitalising the debate, and lending strength to the protectionist argument. For the new surge of competition from a highly protected polity compelled us to look again, and much more closely, at the effect of the United States tariff wall – now, at its highest, imposing an average rate of 57·7% tax on imported goods and materials. Suddenly, free-traders found the onus upon them to demonstrate that Britain could hold a commercially expanding USA without herself imitating the latter's fiscal methods. On the other side, and after hopes had been dashed of some tariff reduction when Theodore Roosevelt succeeded McKinley in the White House, Chamberlain and those of his mind redoubled their demand for some bulwark against the flood of American goods arriving or to be expected here. They had the backing of patriotic press organs like the *National Review,* which found that

> The extraordinary power and prosperity of the United States, of which the Shipping Combination is the latest indication, is quite as much due to the fact that she has surrounded herself by a fiscal barrier and refused to be the dumping ground of other countries ... Today, being impregnable at home, the American manufacturer and capitalist is able to emerge and attack the neutral markets and compete in lines of business of which we have previously had a monopoly ... The insular doctrine that we must remain supreme because our ports are open to all surplus foreign produce for which there is no home market, never had any foundation in reason, and has been completely falsified by events ... It is not only the mercantile marine but the whole external trade of the country that is involved in this struggle.[12]

Chamberlain himself was convinced that 'we are face to face with a real danger' in as much as 'the combination which threatens the North Atlantic trade might be extended, and most certainly will be extended, to other parts of the world': for part of the White Star Line's operations were with the Antipodes. Among the shipowners themselves, normally free-traders, some were beginning to have doubts. To David McIver, MP for Liverpool (Kirkdale) the IMM appeared as 'one of the messes in which our Free Trade system has landed us'. More significant was the number of politicians and civil servants who, hitherto free-traders to the core, now expressed a willingness to reconsider their attitude in the face of the American onslaught. One such prominent convert to the 'reciprocitarians' was Dilke, who had of late been chairing the annual conferences of the Shipmasters' Congress. A yet more remarkable *volte face* was performed by the former Assistant Secretary and Controller General of the Board of Trade, Sir Robert Giffen, hitherto an ingrained *laissez-fairiste*. Theoreticians, he told the Select Committee on Steam Ship Subsidies, might demonstrate that countries like Britain gained on the whole, as consumers, from foreign bounties: yet the State could not ignore a threat to its citizens' very livelihood. There were also grounds, if not commercial at least political, for meeting the pressure of the self-governing colonies for colonial preference. 'Protection or no protection,' Giffen wrote in the same year, 'a feeling is growing up that foreign subsidies, and similar hostile attacks on our shipping, must be met by adequate measures of retaliation.'[13]

'Retaliation,' however, subsumed a rich variety of countermeasures: all of them were freely and hotly canvassed in press and Parliament so long as the American threat persisted. When alarm was at its height a formal and somewhat lengthy review, composed by the newly appointed Secretary of the Admiralty, was conveyed swiftly to the highest level. The indefatigable Arnold-Forster had sent his chief the memorandum in mid-June 1902 and Selborne had laid it before the Cabinet by the end of the month.[14] It is interesting both because it takes a full look at the worst that might transpire and because it very carefully juxtaposes the alternative counter-policies available to the government.

Assuming, as then appeared probable, that Cunard would follow Leyland and White Star into the transatlantic combine, the majority of whose shares would be held in America, then Britain (said Arnold-Forster) must be prepared to face a situation where practically the whole of the fast ships in the North Atlantic trade would have passed under American control. How would the latter be used? In all likelihood, politically as well as commercially.

There can be no doubt that it is the intention of the United States government to use the large surplus which it has been compelled by the operation of its tariff to accumulate, for the purpose of destroying the commerce of other nations or promoting that of the United States, and that it is also the intention of the large Trusts to use the immense funds at their disposal to obtain control over the shipping trading with the United States,

first in the Atlantic, but eventually around the world. Assuming also that a subsidy Bill would pass Congress of a nature highly beneficial to the combine, then 'Having once got the Atlantic trade into their hands, it will be their obvious interest to replace every ship which ceases to be effective by a subsidised vessel built in the United States'. The ill effects of the combine would therefore be felt in British shipbuilding as well as British trade, and it must be anticipated that there would be some contraction of business on the Clyde, the Tyne and elsewhere.

What could we do to meet this double threat? We could simply rely upon 'the laws of political economy' to rectify the situation. But the present contingency was peculiar in that the USA had enormous surpluses to get rid of, which represented the proceeds of an immense amount of taxation not required for the ordinary service of that State.

Or we could meet subsidies by counter-subsidies. But from the previous consideration it also followed that the USA would have sufficient reserves to outbid us in any subsidy war. Moreover, the amount of British shipping was relatively so huge that general subsidy would be intolerably costly. The most we could attempt would be 'a judicious rearrangement of our present subsidies'.

Thirdly, we might impose countervailing duties on American shipping. But to do so successfully we would need to preserve a large neutral market comprising areas which neither gave bounties nor imposed such taxes. This we might achieve by agreement upon a common policy within the Empire. Or, fourthly, we might close our coastwise imperial trade to American vessels. The USA could raise no objection to 'what is

195

recognized to be the normal and reasonable practice among civilized nations', including herself. If it were demurred that most Empire trade (amounting to nearly eleven million tons in 1901) was already carried in British bottoms, Arnold-Forster would point out that the fast-growing mercantile marines of other nations were now beginning to attack it. Let us therefore place before the coming conference of colonial Premiers a plan for closing our imperial coastwise trade, or at least for admitting foreign vessels to it only upon purchase of a licence. With the concurrence of its self-governing members – and they had much to gain from adopting such a scheme – our empire would prove the national asset it ought to be. 'We have quite enough to bargain with, even with the United States.' And 'if the British Empire will agree as to its mercantile policy, the threatened attack from Germany and France', at present 'content to play the swordfish to our whale . . . might be crushed within a week'.

Weighing these alternative courses, as they appeared to Arnold-Forster, we note that the second – subsidies to our own shipping – had already been remitted to a select committee, whose report we must for the moment await. His third idea – to impose countervailing duties on foreign shipping – had occurred to others also. Usually it took the form of a proposal that we should levy a tonnage toll or tax on the foreigner up to the level necessary to cancel out the advantage he enjoyed by virtue of his own government's subsidy to him. Some loose comparability might be discerned in the British government's freedom, under the recent Brussels international convention, to levy counter-vailing duties on imported sugar. But applying such a duty to a wide variety of foreign shipping would clearly be a complicated business; and of course it would be irrelevant to United States vessels until such time as Congress acted to subsidise them.

The fourth proposal, to close in certain circumstances our own trade to foreigners, contemplated nothing short of a major reversal of national policy and needed therefore to be very carefully pondered. Was it really true, as some were now coming to believe, that 'the cure for the Navigation Syndicate lies in the navigation laws'? To use access to the United Kingdom and Empire coastal trades (including 'grand cabotage') as a bargaining weapon, and to withold both from those foreign powers who denied us reciprocal access to their own, was a tremendous proposal but a tempting one. Even men who were at heart by no means protectionists were attracted by the notion of reasonable equivalence – or better, since our imperial coastline was the world's longest. It was felt 'not right that any country which reserves its own coastal trade should have at command the coastal trade of other countries: and the real coastal trade of the British Empire is that between all its widely separate members'. The United States in particular, which had extended or was about to extend her 'keep off' policy to dependencies such as the Philippines, Cuba and Samoa, had forfeited any moral right to object. Some MPs accordingly joined hands with journalists and the heads of certain shipping companies in pressing this course of action unequivocally upon the State. 'If the right honourable gentleman,' said Gibson Bowles to the President of the Board of Trade, 'wants a suggestion as to what the government ought to do, let him turn up his Adam Smith.' And a majority of the House of Commons went so far as to order the reprinting, in June 1902, of the report of its select committee of 1847 on the Navigation Laws for further study.[15]

'The question,' Lansdowne warned Chamberlain from the Foreign Office, 'is much complicated by our engagements to some of the Powers, and it will be a big fence to ride at.' Nevertheless he failed to damp the Colonial Secretary's enthusiasm for strengthening the bonds of empire by linking retaliation to a scheme for colonial preference. In his opening speech as chairman of the conference of colonial Premiers in London on 30th June Chamberlain did not hesitate to urge his view that 'the political federation of the Empire is within the limits of possibility'; and the conference responded to the extent of allowing that 'the principle of preferential trade' among the countries represented would offer many advantages. Unanimity was duly forthcoming for the resolution that

it is desirable that the attention of the Governments of the Colonies and the United Kingdom should be called to the present state of the navigation laws in the Empire and in other countries, and to the advisability of refusing the privileges of coastwise trade, including trade between the Mother Country and its Colonies and Possessions, and between one Colony or Possession and another, to countries in which the corresponding trade is confined to ships of their own nationality, and also to the laws affecting shipping with a view to seeing whether any other steps should be taken to promote Imperial trade in British vessels.[16]

It was Chamberlain's cherished design ultimately to link imperial preference with greater co-operation from the self-governing colonies towards imperial defence. Privately, however, he remained sceptical about the possibility of any far-reaching change in this regard. The question of colonial preference was favourably considered at a critical Cabinet meeting in the following November. From this, however, dates the stubborn opposition of Ritchie at the Exchequer which was eventually to prove fatal to Chamberlain's hopes.

There remained the all-important question of shipping subsidies, as debated in Parliament and before its select committee.

Both these audiences heard the standard objections raised again. As to a general subsidy, the prohibitive cost (it was agreed) ruled such a proposal out of court. But, just as clearly, discriminatory subvention would have to be employed with care. It might advance the interest of particular lines to a degree which handicapped others and discouraged them from entering the field competitively. Some lines at present receiving it were members of shipping conferences, always suspected of preserving artificially high rates and of being over-ready to employ 'fighting' ships to starve independent competitors. Not surprisingly the committee noted that 'most shipowners are opposed to subsidies unless they are for services rendered'. And even mail subsidies were thought by some to encourage the favoured lines to raise their freight charges unduly. Furthermore, some shipowners (Pirrie himself was one) argued, with a side glance at French and German experience, that a subvention bred inefficiency in the recipient. One leading maritime historian, indeed, had gone so far as to maintain that subsidies had hindered rather than helped the whole development of steam navigation. A war of bounties, cautioned the *Westminster Gazette,* would rapidly become 'a war of purses, disastrous to the taxpayers, useless to the liners, damaging to the general shipping interest, vexatious to trade – in short, a great folly'.[17]

Fears, notwithstanding, of subsidised foreign rivalry, which had been publicly voiced in Britain ever since the Royal

Commission of 1885 considered the causes of trade depression, flared up again in face of the new American giant. Shipowners like R. W. Leyland told the Commons and its select committee of their conviction that Britain could in future hold its own only by dint of some measure of State bounty. Its 'judicious' use, as one ingredient of a retaliatory policy, was advocated by the chairman of the General Shipowners' Society of London and by officers of comparable bodies in other parts of the United Kingdom. Protectionist MPs joined hands with the shipowners' parliamentary committee, under William Milburn's chairmanship, to lend their weight. The Commons' newly formed commercial committee also appears to have interested itself for a time in the matter. Even the claims of long-voyage sailing ships (i.e. of over 500 g.r.t.) were urged, as a training ground of mercantile mariners. A case was particularly made for subsidies to builders now that, with the reciprocating engine giving place to the turbine, the modern vessel was a thing of such enormous cost and sophistication. Much was made by Lord Strathcona, Rear-Admiral Sir Edmund Fremantle of the Navy League, Lord Charles Beresford, and of course by Chamberlain himself, of the need to link together the Empire by subsidised lines of fast cruisers, with the especial aim of narrowing to four days the sailing time between Britain and Canada so as to encourage the latter to develop her communications system towards the United Kingdom rather than the United States.[18] Dominating every other consideration were Britain's strategic and security needs, and to them we must shortly return.

On 28th May 1902 Sir William Walrond successfully moved in the Commons for reappointment of a select committee 'to inquire into the subsidies to steam ship companies and sailing vessels under foreign governments and the effect thereby produced on British trade'. Such a committee had initially been appointed in the spring of the preceding year upon the motion of Evelyn Cecil (Aston Manor), who was to become its first chairman. Since then it had proceeded with little haste, but got far enough to discover that its scope needed widening to admit consideration of other factors beside foreign subsidies affecting Britain's trade, and particularly of course her shipping trade. Meanwhile the committee had run into cross-winds of criticism. By some MPs it had been accused somewhat *a priori* of displaying too tender a concern for the welfare of the shipowner in particular. Ostensibly the latter was, unlike the trader, interested less in the volume of trade than in the level of freight rates. It was objected that, of the winesses so far called, only two had been connected with trade. On the other hand another objector complained that nine of its fifteen former members had held between them no fewer than forty-two directorships in public companies.[19]

The committee now revived in 1902 was of twelve members, plus Cecil as continuing chairman. They sat from 3rd June to 22nd July, heard evidence from nineteen witnesses, and presented their report, drafted by Cecil during the summer recess, on 3rd December following.[20] This did not fail to recognise the widespread anxiety occasioned by the loss of important British lines to the American combine and could not forbear from reproving the vendors. 'It is to be feared that when business advantages clash with patriotic motives, the British shipowner is not always proof against the enticements of a remunerative bargain, and that if he gets a good offer, foreign or otherwise, for his ships, he is inclined to sell them, however important their possession may be to his own nation.'

By the committee's observation 'we are now meeting with severer competition than we have ever experienced', as more orders were coming to be placed abroad in the expectation of cheaper freight rates or more convenient dispatch. It concluded firstly, that without doubt 'foreign subsidies must exercise a considerable share of influence' in bringing this change about by furthering the transfer of trade away from British ships and in some cases from British manufacturers also. Nevertheless the committee took no exaggerated view of subvention and its effects. Our steam shipping, though unsubsidised, 'creditably holds its own'. And in any case – a second point – subsidies were a minor factor, and commercial skill and industry major factors, in the recent improvement of foreigners' efficiency. Although 'our efforts must be proportionately greater if we are to maintain our supremacy', yet the evidence the committee had heard 'does not warrant the recommendation of any general system of subsidies', which would be 'costly and inefficient'.

Furthermore, the policy of selected subsidies as pursued by

certain other States tended to restrict competition by encouraging the growth of shipping rings. While regarding as 'not proved' the charge that British steamship conferences were injurious to national trade, they could be (the committee thought) in certain circumstances 'contrary to the best interests' of the latter. The government therefore ought not to extend such subsidy to British shipowners unless it was at the same time prepared to limit the extent of their combination and the level of their charges. Even so, the report considered that free competition between them would continue to be more beneficial to country and Empire than dependence on State support and subjection to State control.

Where and if, however, for exceptional reasons subsidy were granted, it should be contingent upon the observance as far as possible of certain conditions. Thus the final stage of negotiating the subvention should be in the hands of a small permanent committee representing Admiralty, Board of Trade and Colonial Office. Further, if the desideratum were rapid communication within the Empire (an object which the committee recognised as laudable), or carriage of food in wartime, or the fulfilment of Admiralty requirements, a high or even very high speed should be a *sine qua non*. Where a line received a subsidy, the majority of its board of directors should be British subjects. So should the officers and a proportion of the crew of a subsidised vessel; and the government's permission should be obtained before it could be sold or hired elsewhere. True, 'the first reason for a subsidy is a political one'. Yet payment should be restricted to value received, e.g. for carriage of mail (at present costing this country about £¾ million a year) for fast merchant vessels as naval auxiliaries, or where absolutely necessary for the creation or development of new trade or (as in East Africa) to offset peculiar handicaps imposed by foreign subsidies. As to the subsidising of sail against steam, the committee tacitly agreed with Lord Charles Beresford in regarding this as tantamount to backing a mail coach against a railway engine.

Much more positive, however, than its treatment of the subsidy question was the committee's pronouncement on the protection issue. 'The occasion,' it concluded, 'has come when the qualified reservation of British Imperial coasting trade might be reserved to British and Colonial ships, and to vessels of those

nations which throw open their coasting trade to British and
Colonial ships.' On this vital point Evelyn Cecil, as chairman,
had been at some pains to sound out Chamberlain personally
and was gratified to find him 'fully alive to the severe handicap
occasioned ... to British trade by foreign subsidies and traffis'.
Cecil was equally relieved to obtain the 'rather hesitating
acquiescence' of the secretary of the Cobden Club, Sir Spencer
Walpole.[21] Of all the committee's recommendations this was the
most significant. For the rest, it agreed that the shipowners
ought to be relieved of payment of light dues, and of a number of
unfair working conditions and restrictions, and that what
Board of Trade regulations were retained should be enforced
against foreign ships equally with British.

Recommendations in this last category were, it goes without
saying, particularly welcome to the shipowners. They had long
been pressing the government to make light dues – then totalling annually about £½ million, of which foreigners paid
roughly £166,000 – a public charge. No less gratifying was the
committee's recommendation in favour of equalising conditions of operation as between all vessels using our ports. Some
owners had been arguing that (for instance) the Board of Trade's
load-line requirements when unilaterally enforced had handicapped our own steamers by 15%–20% of their carrying
capacity. Many other regulations of the Board – about the
number of compartments, of boats carried, manning, etc. – gave
occasion for grumbling. Restrictions of this nature were alleged
to have diverted many cross-Channel steamers from the British
flag to the French.[22]

On the other side, the Board of Trade's reply, as prepared by
its Marine Department for the select committee's benefit, does
not deserve to be ignored. Wrote Howell, 'The cry of "harassing
regulations" is repeated so often that many shipowners have
come to believe it. When any particular case is examined, the
grievance is generally found to be minute or non-existent.'
Admittedly, certain regulations were antiquated in form. But
either they did not hamper in practice or, if they did, the Board
could exercise its discretionary power to waive them. To some
extent they were already incumbent upon all shipping; of the
twenty-nine vessels to be checked in British ports in 1900–01 for
overloading, for example, twenty were foreign. But a more

thoroughgoing application of such regulations to all non-British ships was impracticable and might provoke retaliation. 'It is not the best form of competition to try to injure your opponent.' The Marine Department rebutted with statistical evidence the contention of the Liverpool Shipowners' Association and its chairman, E. A. Beazeley, that rules of this nature had lost us any significant quantity of shipping by transfer to a foreign flag. As for light dues, these were already paid indirectly by the consumer. 'If the shipowners have their way, he will pay twice over,' since the former were unlikely to reduce their rates correspondingly after abolition. All in all, we ought not to be stricken with panic just because some foreign competitor had gained ground. The better course would be to try to improve our own methods, and here State aid would be no answer.[23]

To the Board of Trade also were referred, for comment, the resolutions on subsidies laid by Chamberlain before the Colonial Conference and subsequently carried unanimously, viz. 'That it is desirable that in view of the great extension of foreign subsidies to shipping, the position of the mail services between different parts of the Empire should be reviewed by the respective governments', but that 'in all new contracts provision should be inserted to prevent excessive freight charges, or any preference in favour of foreigners'. To which the Board's reply (through Hopwood and Gerald Balfour) was that it would welcome 'any well-considered scheme' for extending and improving mail services between United Kingdom and Empire. If a subsidy represented payment for services rendered, the government ought not to impose conditions which might handicap the contractor. But if the subsidy represented more than this, then the attachment of certain conditions would be allowable in the taxpayer's protection. It was always hard to decide what constituted an 'excessive' rate; but in any case the insertion of provisions against it, or against preference to foreigners, ought not to constitute grounds for increasing the subsidy. Provisions of that kind were included in the Cunard contract, but there was no question of paying a greater subvention on that account. On this understanding, the Board felt that 'the insertion in mail contracts of some general stipulation of the kind suggested is not unreasonable'.[24] The Board's conservative attitude could surprise no one who considered how many of its officials were ardent members of the Cobden Club. If the department represented any section in particular it was that of the manufacturing industries, with whose interests shipping, alone among the transport services, was fully in line. The shipping industry being normally an inexpugnable stronghold of free competition, and the evidence heard by the select committee being overwhelmingly *laissez-faire,* the few points of difference between the Board and the shipowners are, on the larger view, more remarkable than their general unanimity. As late even as 1918, after experience of world war, a Board of Trade committee on shipping and shipbuilding was to show itself still fanatically attached to free trade and strongly resistant to State intervention.

Even in the crisis of 1902 concern for trade moved the government less powerfully than considerations of national security, the nature of which we have already noticed (p. 120ff above). In the Admiralty's strategic thinking, wartime recourse to merchant cruisers was a corollary of the obsolescence of the navy in the pre-Dreadnought era. In an age of radical alteration in ship design, when technical change demanded the virtual rebuilding of a nation's main sea fighting force every decade, the Royal Navy of 1902, in the words of its principal historian, 'though numerically a very imposing force, was in certain respects a drowsy, inefficient, moth-eaten organism'.[25] The alarms of 1884 and 1888, together with the general disgruntlement during that decade, had elicited the building plans of the regime of Admiral Sir Frederick Richards as First Sea Lord. But for three years prior to the session 1900-01 scarcely any of the money voted for naval construction had in fact been spent. So among the fifteen miles of fleet assembled at Spithead in August 1902 for Edward VII's coronation review, not one new battleship was to be sighted and at least one was thirty-seven years old. We had not a single naval vessel reckoned capable of sustaining twenty knots across the Atlantic. Scarcely one of these ponderous Victorian monsters had fired a shot in anger since the Crimean War, which was incidentally the occasion when, with the introduction of continuous service, rates of naval pay had last been fixed.

This stagnation, however, the new century brought freshening winds to dispel. Passage of the German Navy Acts of 1898 and 1900 threatened to upset the Royal Navy's cherished 'two-power' equilibrium of strength. From 1902 onward this rivalry became the dominating *motiv*, restated at an ever-increasing tempo, of British naval policy. Military humiliation in the South African war, too, administered a psychological jolt. Parliament and public were the readier to lend an ear to the clamour of the Navy League, now at a pinnacle of influence, for the building of an increased number of very fast cruisers mercantile and naval.[26] New stirrings at the Admiralty were manifest in 1900 with the unexpected nomination of Selborne to succeed Goschen as its First Lord, and with the simultaneous (and scarcely more welcomed) appointment of Arnold-Forster as its Secretary. Both were, in Sir John Fisher's eyes, 'good young men'; and Selborne returned the compliment by bringing Fisher from the Mediterranean to Portsmouth as Second Navy Lord. The new and urgent tone of affairs is detectable in the Commons' speeches on the navy estimates of Febuary 1902 and in the debate of the following May on the report of the Admiralty committee set up under Arnold-Forster's chairmanship to consider shipbuilding arrears. As to technical advance, the Admiralty after long discussion resolved to supersede the old cylindrical by the new Belleville water-tube boiler, to experiment with turbine propulsion, and to study the possibilities of oil fuelling. By the end of the year two 22½ knot, 500 ft cruisers had been laid down to the designs of Philip Watts, the Admiralty's newly appointed Director of Naval Construction.

Naturally the Admiralty expressed its official pleasure at the Cunard agreement for the subsidised building of two new mercantile cruisers of the very fastest. Since, however, its current hiring contracts with that company and others were due to expire in 1905, Selborne at the same time stated in the Commons his intention to look ahead with an open mind. The previous government had adopted the hiring policy only as subject to reconsideration, and satisfaction with it was not universal. Critics included a former First Lord, Earl Spencer, who took the opportunity of the debate on the two agreements of August 1903 to voice his beliefs that naval subvention of the merchant marine was 'almost totally' unnecessary and that the Cunard contract in particular was simply one more instance of an ailing government's 'Do Something' policy. Lord Graham, though ardent as any for naval expansion, felt that three years at a stretch ought to be the maximum period of subvention in respect of any mercantile cruiser whatsoever.[27]

Yet – such was the alarm raised by American steamship purchases – the Select Committee on Steam Ship Subsidies heard almost nothing but good of the Admiralty's present hiring policy. Even those eminent witnesses who did not think well of mercantile cruisers as fighters or protectors of commerce nevertheless saw them as fully earning their subsidy in other capacities – as scouts, nurseries of naval seamen, or reservoirs for the navy's engine-room complement. If the navy (Professor Biles, a committee member, had himself written) preferred instead to build its own cruisers of equivalent speed, it would be obliged to reduce their armour to the same degree. Indeed, some of the navy's most recently planned cruisers, such as *Diadem*, were entirely armourless above the upper deck and as vulnerable as any hired merchantman. The select committee was therefore able to report unambiguously. Payment of subsidy to low-speed ships should be discontinued. Subvention was not recommended merely as a retaining fee in time of war, when the government assumed the right to take up any British vessel at fair compensation. But the principle of subsidies by or for the Admiralty was justified for obtaining a limited number of vessels of the merchant marine. Where these were intended to be used as armoured cruisers they should be built to Admiralty specifications, possess the greatest coal endurance, and be capable of twenty-four knots, or no less a speed than the fastest ships of foreign nations. Such a subsidy for any vessel should in time of peace be 'good consideration' for the government's right to prohibit its sale or hire into foreign control. (Parenthetically, the committee did not seek to determine the question as to whether such a right could be enforced.)

Despite this vindication of the Admiralty's current hiring practices, Selborne was not content to remain so largely reliant on them for the indefinite future. In his statement to Parliament of 10th February 1902 the First Lord disclosed the Admiralty's intention to create an altogether new class of vessel, to be denominated Scout, for which he would 'invite the private shipbuilders of the country to give the Navy the benefit of their creative ingenuity by submitting designs to fulfil certain stated conditions', two of which would be exceptional speed and a greater sea-keeping power than any previous navy cruisers had possessed.[28] This innovation was not the least important element in a six-year programme of construction, to begin 1903-04 and to include sixteen new armoured cruisers and sixteen Scouts, four of each kind to be laid down annually for the next four years. And when in October 1904 Fisher succeeded Lord Walter Kerr as First Sea Lord, his notable era of naval development was to carry changes much further. A complete remodelling of the Royal Navy saw the advent of armoured cruisers, turbinely driven, of 15,900 tons and capable of twenty-five and a half kots. Mercantile cruisers thereafter slipped into the background.

Despite the importance of the Cunard agreement, therefore, the influence of the American shipping rivalry of the early 1900's did not operated to prolong unduly an obsolescent dependence of the Navy upon the merchant marine. Rather, it precipitated a rethinking out of which was crystallised one feature of modern naval strategy. The great expresses of the North Atlantic were still found extremely useful during two world wars in ancillary roles, as troop carriers and hospital ships. And to some degree they continued to be available as guardians of commerce. For another immediate consequence of the trans-atlantic threat of 1902 was that Balfour in March the following year established, within a reconstructed Committee of National Defence, a board of inquiry (with the Duke of Sutherland as president) into the use of fast merchantmen for securing the nation's wartime food supply. But nothing in its experience of later years led the Admiralty to believe it had been mistaken in looking to its own resources for auxiliary cruisers. As for the problem of reservists, the First Lord in a memorandum of 25th December 1902 introduced the 'Selborne Scheme' for the establishment of Royal Naval Reserve training colleges, which would provide experience more germane than could the merchant marine to the manning needs of a twentieth-century fighting force.

In thus following the free trade/protection debate, however, we have been running ahead of developments on the North Atlantic itself after 1903. These were not such as to suggest that the fair-traders in pressing their case could rely on an indefinitely prolonged state of national emergency. From the outset (as we noted, p. 93ff. above) the capitalisation of the International Mercantile Marine Co., in both its nature and its timing, aroused on both sides of the ocean serious doubts as to its viability. The promoters had bought the Leyland fleet at a premium of about 50% above the market value of its aggregate components, and for every £1,000 White Star share they had given £1,400. At such seeming extravagance the commercial world had stood aghast. What appeared as speculative over-capitalisation had led commentators to speak of the 'absurd finance' of a 'sky-scraping' combine, 'the most audaciously over-loaded of all Mr. Morgan's creations', which 'contains almost as much water as the Atlantic itself.[29] We must now, by tracing the enterprise's subsequent history, discover how far this scepticism was to prove justified.

As investors the American public had responded to the IMM but poorly; and when in the summer of 1904 the report was published of the company's first working year (ended 31st December 1903) it seemed to justify their caution. For it made apparent that the much-vaunted combine of over 130 vessels valued at more than £38 million, with a bond capital of £14 million and a share capital of more than £20 million, had so far been losing money hand over fist. The surplus, after fixed interest charges had been met, was shown as £71,059, and even this had been achieved by dint of making no provision for depreciation. Seeing that during those same twelve months Cunard, with a fleet of only 191,703 g.r.t., placed nearly £165,000 to depreciation, had the IMM allowed a relatively sufficient sum the oucome would have been an overall deficit of at least £700,000. No steps were taken to redeem debentures, and dividends needless to say were 'postponed'. Despite the US Post Office's mail subsidy to the American Line of £3,000 per voyage, net working profits for the year were a little over £800,000, of which more than £642,000 had been earned by White Star alone. The Leyland and National lines, whose figures were not included in the foregoing, had also made losses. By the end of 1904 the combine's market valuation had fallen to £16·3 million – or some £18 million below its nominal capital-isation. 'Disillusionment,' commented the *Economist,* 'has come with startling rapidity,' and 'the Trust has lamentably failed to achieve the purpose for which it was established'.[30]

Repercussions upon the management of the enterprise were neither unexpected nor slow. Formally the stockholders enjoyed no control over the undertaking, since the whole of the IMM's share capital was held by the five voting trustees who could not be required to deliver the definitive certificates until October 1907. But one of these was J. Bruce Ismay, president of White Star; and the former owners of that line, whose sale of securities had left them owning about 27% of the combine's common stock, were powerfully discontented at the prospect of 'their' profits being used indefinitely to offset the losses of the IMM's American components. Despite Morgan's official denial, early rumours persisted in the British press that a reshuffle at the top was soon to bring a greater measure of control back to this side of the Atlantic. At the end of the combine's first year of operations Baker resigned from the directorate and Ballin revisited New York for some 'rather exciting' discussions during which he roundly criticised the management though himself declining an offer of the presidency. Pressure against Griscom rapidly mounted, and in March 1904 he resigned the headship, becoming instead chairman of the board. The IMM's headquarters were moved from Philadelphia to New York, and there throughout February Ismay came under great pressure to take over the presidency of the concern. He yielded, against his personal inclination, upon receiving certain private assurances from Morgan. To Ismay the great man confessed his belief that it was defective organisation which was losing them money. He proposed that in future the earnings of the subsidiary companies should be allocated to pay the fixed-interest charges, and that any surplus should go to reimburse Pirrie as a prior charge on the company in respect of its indebtedness to White Star as the only profitable component. If fixed charges could not be met, Morgan undertook himself to make good the discrepancy for three years from 1st January 1904.[31]

Late in the latter year there occurred a marked rally in the price of the IMM's common and preferred stock. Partly this was attributable to the re-election of President Roosevelt, who six months earlier had appointed yet another commission to consider legislative aid to his county's mercantile marine. Its report was due early in 1905, and meanwhile Congress had before them yet another subsidy Bill which promised to be peculiarly favourable to the IMM's American components. Partly, however, the rise reflected the termination of a ruinous rate war which had impinged upon the new shipping enterprise at a peculiarly unfortunate juncture and therefore deserves a little notice.

For some time the Hungarian government had been casting around for an arrangement which would secure to itself, rather than to Germany, some part of the material benefit accruing from the emigration of its subjects to the United States. Early in 1904 it announced a contract concluded with Cunard whereby this traffic, instead of moving north to the Baltic ports, was to be officially diverted southward to Fiume. Thence a fortnightly service would run direct to New York, with calls at one or two other Italian ports and Gibraltar. Credible reports were also circulating that the Austrian authorities were prepared to make a parallel arrangement with Cunard for conveying their emigrants via Trieste. Between Cunard and the two great German associations of the IMM – already, and not for the first time, at loggerheads with the British line over the Scandinavian emigrant traffic – a bitter struggle immediately ensued. In a war of rate-cutting the German lines slashed their transatlantic steerage charges to £2 a head from Baltic ports and halved those from Scandinavia. Soon practically every shipping line engaging in the North Atlantic passenger trade was compelled to reduce first its westward and then its eastward rates by 50%–60% of the previous year's.

So fierce a battle could not be sustained for long, and by the end of the year a truce was being negotiated. But six months later a formal termination was still hanging, at Inverclyde's insistence, upon the resolution of all contentious issues; of which a particularly sensitive one for Cunard was that of mail carriage. During 1903 the IMM had begun in effect to perform this twice every week – by White Star and the American Line – instead of only once, to the detriment of Cunard's profit. A satisfactory settlement, since it involved the United States Post Office as well as the warring steamship lines, was delayed. Meanwhile in May 1905 the White Star, American and Dominion lines gave notice of intention to withdraw from the North Atlantic Passenger Conference. If Leyland followed, the only British companies left in would be the Allan and Anchor lines.

But the rate war had produced an effect on net earnings too calamitous for the IMM to risk a renewal of hostitilies. Cunard suffered less, though it passed its dividend for 1904. North German Lloyd reduced theirs from 6% to 2%. Had it not been for the profits accruing to Hapag from the sale of four large steamers to the Russian government it is doubtful whether the Germans could have maintained their rate-cutting for as long as they did. Already obliged to make up the bulk of the losses sustained by the conference as a whole, they had also to fulfil their treaty obligations to their IMM associates. To all participants in the rate war the total cost may have been as high as £1 million.[32]

Yet we should not be misled into attributing the IMM's bad start solely or even principally to this hectic episode alone. Other pitfalls, too, beset its early path. If its passenger trade was demoralised by rate wars, its freight trade was depressed by a foot-and-mouth epidemic necessitating an embargo throughout the summer of 1904 upon all cattle shipments from New England ports. That year's corn crop also was low, and the wheat barely average. If a previously efficient company like Leyland showed losses it was because for months together freights were reduced to a level at which it did not pay to run vessels at all. Internally, too, the combine was failing to realise the saving expected from centralisation of management. Indeed, the assurances exacted by the shareholders of the purchased British companies, that their corporate identities would be preserved, meant that such economies were to some extent foregone. Leyland under Wilding, in particular, was conducting its affairs almost as though it were an independent concern. The IMM's auditors were not slow to point out the problems involved in correlating the accounts of its various component lines.[33]

Larger and more persistent factors, too, were adverse. First – as we have already seen – a period of high prosperity in world shipping at the turn of the century, stimulated successively by the Spanish-American and Boer wars, had now given place to depression in the ocean carrying trade. Several years were to lapse before the boom Griscom foresaw was to be realised, and then in a somewhat unbalanced fashion as between Old and New Worlds. In the interim shipping lines with regular schedules, such as those comprised by his combine, were to sail for much of the time with inadequate cargoes while the more flexible tramps took the cream of the cargo business. The Mercantile Marine Commission of 1904, which heard Bernard Baker's renewed plea for subsidies at the rate of $5 a ton for ten years, was bluntly told by the IMM's western agent that 'our business today is in a very wretched condition, as far as freight is concerned'.[34]

Secondly, the American enterprise was launched at a juncture when the market for new issues was rapidly becoming congested. The public's buying power, it seemed at last, had been exhausted by the multitude of such combinations, and the IMM's securities had little chance of a favourable reception. Indeed, all securities issued by the House of Morgan were showing price declines. In the United States popular hostility was sharpened by the 'silent' or 'rich men's' panic of 1903, and by the somewhat scandalous failure of the US Shipbuilding Trust, and was certainly not allayed by the decision of the Supreme Court in the Northern Securities Co. case the following spring.[35] Over here the press, hostile to the IMM from the outset, gladly relayed the warnings of New York newspapers that its condition was 'desperate', 'a dismal fiasco', Morgan's 'one big failure', etc. British vendors naturally sold the stock they had received in payment for their interest as soon as they could.

The strain on the promoters was therefore both early and heavy. Within a week of Morgan's announcement of the formation of his syndicate the call went out (as we saw) to the underwriters to put up 25% of their commitments. From then until the end of 1902, when the new company's operations officially began, a series of further applications brought this percentage up to eighty – a demand which compared most unhappily with the maximum of 25% called from the US Steel's syndicate and one which obliged not a few of the underwriters to make heavy sales of choice corporate bonds ouside New York in order to meet. Stock quotations opened – preferred at 55 and common at 15 – well below the prices anticipated at the time the shipping lines and other properties had been purchased. Even so they were thought unlikely to attract the investing public at large, indicating as they did a general conviction, persistent throughout 1903, that the company's equity was worth little. In late November that year the life of the underwriting syndicate was renewed until 1st March 1905. By then 100% of its commitments had had to be called upon and it was clear that the bulk of the bonds would remain on its hands for the foreseeable future. 'Even the organizers', commented a European observer in January 1904, 'must have been surprised at the depreciation which has taken place in the value of the securities of the International Mercantile Marine Co. since they were issued.' The market quotation for a $100 share of common stock was then down to $4, for the preferred $19, and for the 4½ collateral trust debentures 75. On this basis the depreciation of securities from their face value could be calculated at about £18 million.[36]

If the IMM's annual report for 1903 had been deplorable, that for 1904 was disastrous. Net earnings decreased by £425,000 and fell short of interest charges by roughly the same amount. Again the extent of the loss was masked by transfer of the surplus in the insurance account. Again no provision was made for depreciation: an adequate one would probably have brought the company's overall loss to the million pound mark. And again, despite some slight revival in Atlantic freight, Leyland's cargo element of the combine showed a loss. Though some small improvement was perceptible during the trading year 1905, in the following March, after a further renewal of the syndicate's life, the bond issue was reconisged as a failure and the bonds and the common and preferred stock bonuses were distributed to the underwriters. 'The future of the undertaking', said informed comment in London, 'as at present constituted does not look particularly hopeful'; and reconstruction of its capital, so as to write it down to a figure approximating the value of its assets, was confidently awaited.[37] But by 1909, after six years of struggle, the IMM had still paid no dividends and its bonds had not risen to par. In 1912, a boom year for world shipping, 122 British companies between them paid an average dividend of 7%. That earned for its investors by the IMM's fleet of over 130 vessels, many of them in first-class condition and all enjoying the use of their own terminal facilities on both sides of the ocean, was precisely nil. And this although from 1900 to 1915 the average annual increase in the total of American waterborne foreign trade was reckoned at around $160 million.

The rest of the IMM's history can be briefly told. The two

213

German lines, after their ten years' agreement had run its course, declined to renew the association. Loss of the *Titanic* caused even White Star's earnings to fall. Ismay himself was among the few to be saved, but thereupon resigned in disgrace and was succeeded by one of his White Star vice-presidents, H. A. Sanderson, who reorganised the whole of that line's management. The uncertainties caused by the outbreak of World War I for a time reduced world demand for shipping and reduced the combine to a state of technical bankruptcy. The voting trust was dissolved and the courts appointed as receiver one of the IMM's vice-presidents, P. A. S. Franklin, manager of the New York office of the Atlantic Transport line before its merger in the combination. But it was less his skill that prolonged the IMM's life than the rapid expansion of wartime demand, which in the following year brought it out of bankruptcy with Franklin as president. Although its financial interest in the shipping of a belligerent power prohibited the combine initially from acquiring any of the numerous liners of which the United States government suddenly found itself the owner, yet neutrality placed its American components in a very advantageous position. The years 1916 to 1921 were the great years, when in an effort to meet accumulated past obligations to holders of its preferred stock the IMM declared dividends ranging from 11% up to 21%. Even so, and unlike the leading British companies, it paid none on its ordinary shares.[38]

The end of World War I saw IMM's management pursuing simultaneously policies of dispersal and concentration. Even before the return of peace, wartime profits had enabled Holland—America to recover its alienated capital and independence. Soon after hostilities ceased the decision was taken to dispose of the combine's other foreign holdings, which over the next ten years were gradually shed in a series of deals which require only brief notice here. The Dominion Line had been the pricipal sufferer from the pre-war policy of building up the profitable White Star component of the combination, to which it very nearly lost its Boston trade and tonnage. In 1921, though Dominion continued to fly its own flag, its eight remaining vessels were transferred to the management of the Leyland line, and by 1926 it had been completely absorbed. But Leyland, too, had been quietly diminishing, though to the last it continued to be predominantly a freighter fleet. In 1932 the IMM sold its interests in the line, whereafter Leyland vessels went one by one to the scrapyard. During the late 1930s the residue of the Red Star Line, which had already suffered piecemeal dispersion of some of its fleet to White Star and the American Line, was finally disposed of, two of its remaining ships being bought by Holland-America. Negotiations for British repurchase of White Star, at first abortive, were resumed in the early 1920s, and at one stage it looked as though a syndicate led by Furness Withy & Co. might be the successful bidders. Then in November 1926 it was suddenly announced that the line would, after all, go to the Royal Mail Company. Thus control returned to British hands under the chairmanship of Lord Kylsant; and since Kylsant was chairman of Harland & Wolff also, the historic relationship was to be preserved, at least for a few years more.

Having shed its foreign interests, the American rump of the IMM proceeded to reorganise. War had brought the Atlantic Transport Co. enormous profits. But many of its biggest freighters were requisitioned by the United States government for troop-carrying and had become casualties, and much of the remainder of its fleet had by 1920 become hopelessly obsolescent. In 1924 it was wound up. Four years later Franklin acquired on very favourable terms a number of vessels which the United States government had been operating as the US Mail Line. Early in 1931 control of the reshaped enterprise passed to the Roosevelt Steamship Co. – its executive head was the son of Theodore Roosevelt – which had acquired 51% of its stock. Twelve years later, on America's entry into World War II, the IMM suffered its final transmogrification into United States Lines. Only thus, and after many vicissitudes, did the IMM's begetters achieve their objective of a shipping line whose capital, flag and fleet should be wholly and solely American.

But at what cost to themselves meanwhile? For Baker and Griscom, who had demonstrated their faith in the enterprise by engaging heavily, the losses must have been fairly considerable, since both had had to put up 100% cash for their underwriting commitment. Whether either would have fared better had he remained an independent operator is, however, doubtful. Of the other underwriters in general, those who liquidated their holdings before World War I must have forfeited up to one-third of their investment: whereas those who hung on to their securities until World War II eventually received par after a long period of illiquidity. In view of Morgan's personal undertaking to Ismay, his House did not withdraw when the underwriting syndicate was wound up in 1906, and a credible assessment of its eventual losses could vary from $1 million to $1½ million.

As for the stockholders, those of Frederick Leyland & Co., who had been bought out wholly in cash and at the peak of the market (1901), came very well out of the transaction, particularly if they then reinvested in Ellerman's new line, which from the first declared dividends of around 6%. Holland-America prospered for the next ten years, with dividends averaging 10%; and when that line in 1917 bought back from the IMM its controlling interest and independence, it was at a figure not substantially above what it had originally been paid for it. Stockholders in the two American companies, Atlantic Transport and International Navigation, continued to do very poorly until the 1914 world boom in shipping. On the other hand, they might have fared even worse had not White Star's profits been available to offset the American vessels' losses.

This latter circumstance naturally displeased White Star stockholders, who would have been much better off had they not sold. Part of their remuneration (it will be recalled) was in the form of $112 million of stock and $50 million in bonds of the IMM. While these securities rapidly slumped to three-quarters of their real (and about half their new nominal) value, the line's dividends went to shore up the combine as a whole. Traffic-wise, the broad policy of the IMM's management under Ismay's presidency was (not surprisingly) to nourish White Star, as its most profitable member, at the expense of the other lines. In 1908, by arrangement with the Canadian Line, White Star extended its passenger activities into the St Lawrence. From about this period, too, the type of new vessels it ordered from Harland & Wolff showed that its management was turning its back, for the time being at any rate, on the ocean greyhounds of record-breaking standards. At the onset of war in 1914 the *Oceanic* and her sisterships of the same class – *Teutonic, Celtic* and *Cedric* – were immediately taken up by the Admiralty as armed merchant cruisers. The *Adriatic, Baltic* and *Olympic* were commandeered for troop-carrying and the *Britannic* as a hospital ship. Towards the war's close a syndicate headed by Lord Pirrie and Sir Owen Phillips (later Lord Kylsant) made an offer of £27 million for all the 3IMM's British flag tonnage and other assets. When everything had been prepared for completion, President Woodrow Wilson for *raison d'état* vetoed the deal by cablegram. As a member, after 1926, of the Royal Mail group the line suffered heavy losses in consequence of corporate policies which Kylsant's removal from the chairmanship came too late to correct. In its altered form the White Star Line Ltd was absorbed by Cunard in 1934.

For Cunard itself the future was to be comparatively bright. While the agreement of 1903 was under negotiation with the government the company decided to experiment with two new ships (the 'Pretty Sisters') from John Brown. The *Carmania*, fitted with turbines, convincingly excelled the *Caronia*, with reciprocating engines. The commission appointed to look into the design of the new subsidised flyers therefore, and with the Admiralty's cordial approbation, opted for turbine propulsion. Contracts were placed in May 1905, and proceeded so rapidly that the *Lusitania* was launched from Clydebank in June 1906. The *Mauretania* followed, from Swan & Hunter on Tyneside, on 20th September. During her trials she averaged 26·04 knots, over the measured mile reached 26·75 knots, and after less than a year from completion regained the Blue Riband from the Germans, which she was to hold for twenty-two years.

As Cunard's directors explained, the formation of the IMM left the company with no alternative but to withdraw from its rate agreements on the North Atlantic and resume its freedom of action, which in June 1903 it did. Cunard had always resented the Germans' use of frontier control stations as collection points for Central and East European emigrant traffic, and took the treaty between Hapag, NGL and the IMM as aimed at itself. The rate war of 1904 quickly, though temporarily, transformed Cunard's posture of independence to one of rivalry. In consequence the company's working expenses rose throughout the latter year by over £223,000 while its earnings fell by some £187,000 and its share quotation from 19½ (in 1902) to 12¾. No dividend was declared in 1904, and £75,000 was transferred to depreciation from a reserve fund which in 1903 had stood at

£550,000 – figures which clearly refute the allegation of some German authorities that in its struggle over rates the Cunard company was fortified by its new contract with the State.[39] On the other hand it is hard to say that the company lost anything by its rather vacillating attitude towards the Atlantic conference, always a very unstable arrangement and covering as a rule only articles essentially requisite as ballast cargo.

In retrospect it is possible to see the rate war of 1904 as the last engagement between the American challenger and its remaining British rival. After hostilities had ended in March the year 1905 saw a considerable recovery, with Cunard's net profit reaching up to only £672 below the record year of 1900. The Hungarian and Austrian contracts helped to raise the line's Continental passengers from 1,267 in 1902 to 35,705 in 1906, accounting in the latter year for nearly 39% of its total passenger trade.[40] So by the time the Atlantic pool was revived in a slightly more durable form Cunard had secured, in addition to its Fiume service, nearly 14% of total westbound traffic – too strong a position for future rate-cutters to assail when next the emigrant traffic fell off, as it did in 1907-08 with the USA's economic crisis. In 1913 Cunard went on to create a 'unification of interest' which included the Anchor, Brocklebank and Thomson lines, bought a half-interest in the Donaldson service to Canada, and formed its own Mediterranean business.

After the vicissitudes of world war the United States abandoned its open-door policy, imposing in 1922 a quota system on immigration. All steamship traffic in European emigrants slumped disastrously. When, therefore, Cunard in 1929 had matured its plans for a new liner, to be capable of 28·94 knots, it felt compelled to sound the government as to their willingness to bear the additional burden entailed by special insurance. The latter's response took the form of the Cunard Insurance Act of December 1930. But there was a complicating factor in the circumstance that negotiations were, under governmental pressure, at the same time being opened for the purchase by Cunard from the Royal Mail Company of White Star's ailing Atlantic fleet. One of the conditions mooted for the transfer was that the Treasury should virtually repeat the financial terms of the 1903 agreement under which the *Mauretania* and *Lusitania* had been built.

But both Treasury and Bank of England hesitated; and without their support no offer Cunard could afford to make was satisfactory to the government of the day. However, after the latter had received the confidential findings of Lord Weir's inquiry into the trading and financial position of British shipping companies (passenger and mail) on the North Atlantic, negotiations were more hopefully resumed. The agreement reached in 1933 envisaged a State loan to Cunard of £9½, of which £8 million was for completion of the new ship and construction of a sister vessel. Cunard and White Star merged in 1934. Although international depression was to delay the eventual implementation of plans for the *Queen Mary* and *Queen Elizabeth*, no one who studies the Weir report – its arguments so uncannily reminiscent of the debate of thirty years before – can doubt the crucial influence exerted upon the government's final decision by the great precedent of 1903.[41]

Up to the first world war – putting the matter into perspective – Cunard's mounting prosperity was a very fair reflection of the growth of British shipping as a whole. In terms of tonnage of all kinds the national figures reveal a rise from 10 million g.r.t. in 1890 to 15 million in 1905 to 18 million in 1910, by which last date 42% of the world's tonnage flew the British flag. On the eve of hostilities in 1914, 52% of the world's cargo by volume, and 71% by value, was being carried in British bottoms, and 60% of world tonnage was being built in United Kingdom yards. On the North Atlantic not only Cunard but British (including Canadian) lines altogether maintained their relative position better than the Germans, who lost ground to their non-British rivals.

It was not that the latter failed to grow, but that the gap widened, German steam tonnage in 1903 aggregating 1¾ million g.r.t. to the British 8½ million; whereas in 1912, by when the latter had exceeded 11 million, the German figure was still at only 2¾ million. The performance of the two great German lines, though mutually uneven, was better than their nation's average. Over the ten years while their treaty with the IMM's was in force the annual earnings of the NGL averaged only 4% and on several occasions it failed to pay a 6% dividend: but Hapag's earnings reached almost 7¼%. Hence at the end of ten seasons the profit-sharing accounts very nearly cancelled out, Hapag owing the IMM under the joint treaty almost as much as the latter owed NGL. When the treaty was allowed to lapse NGL turned down a suggestion from Ballin that his own company should supply a similar mutual guarantee in its place. By then Hapag had for several years been turning over to new steamships, such as those of the *Imperator* class, whose design showed the company's main reliance to be on the cabin trade. In 1914 Hapag and NGL were respectively, and by a comfortable margin, the world's first and second biggest lines, Hapag's 430 vessels totalling more than $1\frac{3}{4}$ million tons against the 800,000 g.r.t. of NGL's fleet of 170 ships. After heavy losses during World War I both companies managed to re-establish themselves with the aid of American capital, and in the mid-1920s began once more to lay down Atlantic record-breakers.

And what, meanwhile, of the Americans themselves? It would be pleasant to be able to record that the dramatic episode of the shipping combine had shaken Congressional thinking into a new pattern, and one loose enough to permit the emergence of a mercantile policy more in accordance with the realities of twentieth-century international competition on the high seas. Candour compels us to recognise that it did not. In April 1904 Congress responded to President Roosevelt's prodding by creating another commission – five Republicans and five Democrats – on the nation's merchant marine, which at once began to look at the North Atlantic. Its report of the following year, having noted that the equivalent costs of American shipbuilding remained as much as 40% above European, repeated certain old proposals, viz. bounties based on tonnage for native-built or registered vessels, plus a mail subvention. The commissioners pointed out that Americans were now paying foreigners £30 million a year for transport of passengers, cargo and mails, and reckoned that a sensible subvention policy would save two-thirds of this. They also recommended, however, the levying of a tonnage tax on certain classes of foreign vessel using United States ports. And this was a sign of a new trend. For the attention of the shipping lobby after 1905 was being redirected, and not only topographically, away from the Atlantic towards the South American and Oriental trades. Many leading builders and owners, coming at last to recongise that Democratic opposition to 'unconstitutional' subsidy was unshakable, now began to divert their main pressure from direct to indirect aid and especially to discriminatory duties. A typical Bill of 1904–05 proposed an extra tonnage duty on foreign vessels entering American ports to load for any other foreign country; a tariff rebate on all foreign goods imported in American bottoms; restriction to American bottoms of carriage of all stores for the United States Army and Navy; additional tariff imposts on all articles hitherto imported duty-free in foreign vessels; and export premiums, varying with distance, upon the value of all native products sent abroad in American vessels. Demand was revived for the extension of America's monopoly of coastwise trade to include the Philippines, as it already did Puerto Rico. The IMM promoters, and especially Griscom, had believed that a growing seaborne commerce would rouse the American people and Congress to patriotic support of their merchant marine. But by 1905 it had become clear that any such support would not take the form of a direct subsidy, and without that they believed the IMM was crippled. Further tariff discrimination, as now proposed, would do the combine no good and might wreak it harm by provoking international retaliation. So henceforth, though Republicans continued until 1911 to press for federal aid, the IMM's attitude was ambivalent and lukewarm.

Not until 1912 was the aim of the 'free ship' advocates achieved, when Congress attached to the Panama Canal Bill a provision admitting to the United States register foreign-built ships purchased by Americans, so long as they were not used in the protected coastwise trade. A further proviso that they be not more than five years old was removed by the Ship Registry Act of two years later.[42] This *volte face*, however, came too late. Before a single foreign-built vessel reached the register war broke out in Europe, and the United States government was to find itself willy-nilly the owner of a mounting quantity of tonnage. Many decades of delay in tackling its merchant marine problems at the roots was to the cost it dearly. Upon America's entry into the war a $3 billion federal building programme was put in hand which, together with other acquisitions, nearly trebled the size of the merchant fleet and, by historical irony, left Washington the largest shipowner in the world. To encourage dispersal of this fleet into private hands the government after the war offered more attractive mail subventions to contractors over liner routes, and to stimulate shipbuilding extended loans at rates as low as ⅛%. Both policies foundered on the old troubles – high cost of domestic building and lack of supervision over execution of contracts – the latter reviving inquiries into corruption and inefficiency. An Act of September 1961 set up a wartime board of shipping commissioners (of which Bernard N. Baker was a promoter and for a very few months a member) with extensive powers in both foreign and domestic trade to build or acquire vessels and sell or charter them to United States citizens. But not until the depression year of 1936 did Congress at long last enact subsidies on a worthwhile scale and couple this with some kind of public utility regulation. Nothing less would avail, as the US Maritime Commission confessed: 'It must be admitted that, despite the millions of dollars lavished on the American merchant marine during the past fifteen years (including a quarter of a billion dollars in mail contracts and other subsidies) the effort has been a failure.[43]

Enough has been said to show the venture of the International Mercantile Marine Co. as an attempt to escape from the dilemmas created by the United States government's longstanding failure to create a viable mercantile marine policy. That this failure was thereafter to prove long-continuing, also, was one of the factors that likewise contributed to the IMM's lack of success. By hindsight it is easy enough to see that the protectionist climate of America, however much it might foster other of her industries, was fatal to her shipping. For in the absence of a subsidy policy, or of a navigation system, or of access to the United States registry for foreign-built vessels, no serious possibility existed of attracting capital on a large enough scale for investment in a fleet for foreign trade save through trustification. Having burnt its fingers in the 1850s by indiscriminately supporting a rival line (Collins) in the Atlantic without securing efficiency, it refused thereafter for more than eighty years to experiment again with adequate and flexible subsidy. By the late 1880s, just when a burgeoning nationalism might have aided its achievement, the mood of at least half the country was adamantly against it. Vacillation gave the United States the worst of every alternative – her shipowners had no protection, her shipbuilders had no business, and the national defence was impaired.

By hindsight, too, it is easy to distinguish the main features of what would have been the most desirable policy for the United States to pursue in the interest of her mercantile marine. The first objective ought to have been to secure the best at the lowest cost. Accordingly, access to the registry should have been allowed much earlier for American owners of foreign-built vessels. Either all tariffs on shipbuilding materials should have been unconditionally removed: or else the Attorney General should have used the anti-trust laws to attack the artificial price structure of the nation's steel industry, which by the 1890s had ceased to merit 'infant industry' consideration. In addition, domestic shipbuilders for the foreign trade could have been subsidised in a selective and flexible manner, so as to extend to them the same advantages as the railroad builders had earlier received, but with safeguards against extravagance. It should have been recognised that contract services rendered to the government by shipping lines were of the nature of a public utility, requiring careful and constant planning, regulation and support. Overall, the country should not have had to await the New Deal before the establishment of a commission to administer a stable shipping policy in the national interest.

In one particular area of shipping policy, it is worth noting, the government displayed a coincidentally similar concern to that of the British. Another of the many consequences of the American shipping trust was to stimulate in both countries closer attention to the effects, for good or ill, of shipping conferences in general. In Britain the rate war of 1904 was soon followed by the appointment of a Royal Commission on Shipping Rings and Deferred Rebates. This body, which commenced its sittings in 1906 and reported in 1909,[44] was very widely representative of relevant interests in both mother country and colonies. A majority and a minority report were therefore found necessary, and these reveal a considerable divergence of opinion about the relative weight to be accorded the alleged advantages or abuses of the shipping conference as a co-operative device. The minority of commissioners were concerned to stress the danger of allowing pools freedom to charge 'what the traffic will bear', and saw less evidence of compensatory benefits such as rate stability. The majority did not think this monopoly power excessive, but recommended that the Board of Trade be charged with the duty of trying to conciliate disputes and investigate abuses. Inverclyde was one of those who signed the majority report, but did so with the reservation that he objected to the Board of Trade's being granted this supervisory power and to the compulsory publication of steamship tariffs. But in fact neither of these proposals was acted upon, and in the matter of State regulation the effect of the Royal Commission was to leave matters precisely as they were.

Strikingly similar evidence was given to a committee set up by the US Senate five years later under the chairmanship of Senator Alexander. Here a single report was brought in, recommending that a stronger line be taken against the monopolistic activities alleged. In the American case, action followed in the form of the Shipping Act of 1916 – still the basic statute governing certain commercial practices in United States shipping today. This declared both the 'fighting ship' and the deferred rebate illegal. But it permitted the general practice of preferrred rates to continue and exempted shipping conferences from the operation of the anti-trust laws so long as they had received the prior approval of the federal government. In the same year the Interstate Commerce Commission investigated, at the Senate's request, the financial transactions of the New York New Haven & Hartford Railroad, and drew attention in its report to the quasi-monopolistic influence of the ancillary steamship lines of certain railroads, mostly in the United States coastwise trade.[45] On several occasions thereafter the shipping conference has been the subject of investigation by United States federal agencies, but none has recommended disturbing its use of the contract rate system by which it offers a lower rate to shippers using its lines exclusively. By the middle of the present century more than 120 such conferences were in effect on United States trade routes alone, although the North Atlantic remains the area where they are weakest.

NOTES

1 *P. Debs.*, 4 series, 127:1090 and 1096, 12 Aug. 1903; Royal Meeker: *History of Shipping Subsidies* (1905), p. 22.

2 *P.Debs.*, 139:687, 2 Aug. 1904; 127:1080–110, 12 Aug. 1903; *Economist* 59:1599–1600 (1902).

3 *P.Debs.* 127:1090–8 and 1103, 12 Aug. 1903; B. Taylor in *North American Review* 179:245–8 (1904).

4 *P.Debs.* 127:1090–3, 12 Aug. 1903; 'The British mercantile marine', *Quarterly Review* 98:353 (Apr. 1904).

5 *P.Debs.* 127:1080 ff., 1095 and 1098, 12 Aug. 1903.

6 Fremantle in *National Review* 40:328 (1902).

7 E. T. Chamberlain: 'The new Cunard steamship contract', *North American Review* 177:533–43 (1903).

8 *Times*, 1 Oct. 1902; *Quarterly Review, loc. cit.*; B. Taylor, *loc. cit.*; *Economist* 60:1600 (1902); *P.Debs.* 139:835, 3 Aug. 1904.

9 Chamberlain to Devonshire, 22 Sept. 1902, JC 11/11/10.

10 *Westminster Gazette*, 20 Jan. 1906, leader.

11 Chamberlain's own notes at JC 16/3, pp. 6 and 7; JC 18/18/18 and 119.

12 *National Review* 39:521–2 (1902).

13 Chamberlain to Seddon, 22 July 1902, JC 17/1/1; *P.Debs.* 107:492, 1 May 1902; *Report* of Select Committee on Steamship Subsidies, Minutes of Evidence, P. P. 1902 (385) ix, q.180, and Giffen's introduction to the 2nd edit. of Farrer: *The State in its Relation to Trade* (1902).

14 'Memorandum with respect to the Transfer of Certain Atlantic Steamship Lines to American Control', 11 pp. 13 June 1902, published for the Cabinet 24 June 1902, *Selborne Papers* (Ministry of Defence).

15 'Calchas' (J. L. Garvin) in *Fortnightly Review* 71:956 (1902); Taylor in *North American Review, loc. cit.*;*P.Debs* 107:470 1 May 1902; *Fairplay* 40 (5 Mar. 1903).

16 Lansdowne to Chamberlain, 7 June, and the latter's reply of 10 June 1902, JC 11/21/18 and 19; abstract of Chamberlain's notes on the Colonial Conference at JC 17/1/1.

17 Select Committee on Steamship Subsidies, *Report* xxiii, Sect. v and Pirrie's evidence, pp. 116–17; *Westminster Gazette*, 13 June 1902, p. 1.

18 Royal Commmission on the Depression of Trade and Industry (1886), *3rd Report*, C. 4797, xxiii, 10,830, p. 136, evidence of A. Scholefield, representing North of England Steam Ship Owners' Association; Select Committee on Steamship Subsidies, Minutes of Evidence, p. 93; *P.Debs.* 107:484 and 946; *Times*, 2, 16 and 21 May 1902; 'Bounties for British sailing ships', *Shipping Gazette*, 30 May and 2 Aug. 1902, and resolutions of Liverpool Shipowners Association; *National Review* 39:524 and 592 (1902); Chamberlain to Ashley, 24 Oct. 1903, JC 18/18/9; E. C. Burgis, 'A new route to Canada', *Nineteenth Century* 51:88–93 (1902).

19 *P.Debs.* 107:949, 108:846 and 852–4.

20 P.P. 1902 (385), ix; E. Cecil to J. L. Garvin, 23 Oct. 1920, JC 17/5/7.f

21 *Idem*

22 Fremantle, 'The outlook for our merchant marine', *National Review* 39:581–96 (1902).
23 MT9 697/M147/02, 718/M3677/02 and 730/M9283/02.
24 BT 11/2, C4099/02.
25 A.J. Marder: *Fear God and Dread Nought* I:147 (1952).
26 *National Review* 39:693 and 944–8 (1902).
27 Statement of First Lord of the Admiralty explanatory of the Navy Estimates 1903–4, Cd. 1478 (1903), p.7; *P.Debs.* 127:1137–48; *National Review, loc. cit.*
28 Statement of First Lord of the Admiralty explanatory of the Navy Estimates 1902–3, Cd. 950 (1902), p.8.
29 C. Duguid in the *World*, 1 Oct. 1902; E. Crammond in *Financial Times*, 28 Nov. 1902; 'Calchas' in *Fortnightly Review* 71:949 (1902); *Economist* 60:645 (1902); *Daily Telegraph*, May and June 1902 *passim.*
30 *Economist* 62:1227–8 and 1857 (1904).
31 *Fairplay* 42:366, 405 and 688 (1904), quoting chiefly the *Daily Express* and *Daily Telegraph*; *Economist* 62:692 (1904); Huldermann: *Albert Ballin*, p.63: W.J. Oldham: *The Ismay Line*, pp.144–59, contains family correspondence throwing light on this episode.
32 D.H. Aldcroft, 'The depression in British shipping, 1901–14, *Journal of Transport History* 7:20 (1965). See also Inverclyde's letter to the *Times* of 10 May 1904 and Ballin's reply of 14 May. The course of the struggle may be followed in the *Shipping World* and *Fairplay* throughout these months.
33 Price Waterhouse's report for the year ending 31 Dec. 1903, quoted in Navin and Sears, *loc. cit.*, p.320.
34 Senate Doc., 58 Cong. 3 Sess., *Report* No. 2755, 11:723 and 111:1873.
35 *Northern Securities Co. v. US.*, 193 US 197 (1904). For the fiasco of the US Shipping Trust see Arthur S. Dewing: *Corporate Promotions and Reorganizations* (1902), ch. xvii.
36 *United States Investor*, 27 Dec. 1902, p.2529; *Economist* 62:83 and 672 (1904).
37 *Ibid.*, 62:797 and 1707–8; 63:797 (1905) 64:1085 (1906).
38 Abraham Berglund: *Ocean Transportation* (1931), p.332.
39 *Shipping World*, 19 Apr. 1905, p.405; *Economist* 64:633 (1906); Herschel: *op. cit.*, p.115.
40 Murken: *op. cit.*, p.331.
41 Neil Potter and Jack Frost: *The Mary* (1961), ch. 5; W.J. Reader: *Architect of Air Power* (1968), ch. 8. Students of the Weir papers are indebted to Dr Reader for his indexing.
42 38 US Stat. 698 (18 Aug. 1914), amending US Stat. 562 (24 Aug. 1912).
43 US Maritime Commission, *Economic Survey of the American Merchant Marine* (1937), p.79.

44 *Report* of the Royal Commission on Shipping Rings and Deferred Rebates, P.P. 1909, xlvii and xlviii.
45 US Interstate Commerce Commission, *Report* No. 6569, xxxi:33–43 (11 July 1914). For a study of the Alexander committee see Daniel Marx, Jr.: *International Shipping Cartels* (1953), pp. 48–67.

Epilogue

The dramatic maritime and political events of 1900–03 having
been scrutinised in detail, it is now appropriate to stand back
and reappraise their position in the wider historical sequence of
those countries involved.

First, in the history of Anglo-German relations. Here the
North Atlantic episode marks a watershed in at least two
respects. Firstly the popular alarm generated by the IMM and
its German component ensured, as never before, that the
British public were aware in some detail of the nature of the
German threat. Thereafter the change in tone manifested itself
in various ways, of which the sensationalism of the press was
only one. When visiting his dying grandmother at Windsor in
mid-January 1901 the Kaiser had been cheered by British
crowds. On his visit to her son at Sandringham at Christmas
1902 he confessed himself shocked at the hostility shown openly
to himself and his government.

In this public alarm the tariff reformers saw their opportunity, and something of a vicious circle ensued. For Chamberlain's proclamation of a crusade had upon German agrarians
the effect of raising pressure for a commercial war out of the
conviction that a Unionist government would soon be further
blocking their country's path by introducing tariffs. And indeed
the North Atlantic scare during the recession of 1902 helped to
ensure that when trade revived generally thereafter, free trade
never again enjoyed the same popularity with the British
public, whereas protectionism began its slow conquest of the
Conservative Party.

Secondly, there was the reaction of those in official quarters.
German participation in the IMM can be said to mark the
approximate point at which self-conscious Anglo-German
antagonism – the belief that German hostility to Britain was
implacable and therefore irreversible – became for the first time
a settled feature of international politics. Hitherto, mistrust of
the new nation had rested on certain identifiable grounds – her

228

attempts to isolate Britain diplomatically, or to foment quarrels among the powers; or what seemed to be her policy of global self-advancement by a kind of *chantage*; or simply the authoritarian Hohenzollern tone of administration in a country only recently unified. But after about 1902 mistrust was more sharply focused on the image of a rival attempting to wrest maritime hegemony from the Royal Navy. By comparison the threat from French and Russian navies sank into second place.

For the Anglo-German naval race escalated. At precisely the same juncture when they were pondering the IMM and Cunard contracts, Selborne, Balfour, Lansdowne and Chamberlain were conferring on 'certain naval matters' in consequence of which they accepted the proposal of the First Sea Lord, Sir Walter Kerr, for the secret purchase of land necessary for a North Sea naval base, the size of the battle fleet to be stationed there to 'be practically determined by the power of the German navy'.[1] In the following spring it was publicly announced that land for this purpose had been secured at Rosyth. Thenceforward the Royal Navy's resources could be regrouped so as to form a powerful new North Sea fleet. This redeployment, shifting weight from the Mediterranean to home waters, was to render Tirpitz's strategy (though its author was unwilling to recognise the fact) too risky.

Selborne himself, originally one of the advocates of Anglo-German *rapprochement*, had before 1902 been proposing abandonment of the 'two-power' standard against all other navies, and greater reliance on their self-restraint. But after 1902 he made it a condition of remaining as First Lord of the Admiralty that the Treasury support his demand for an adequate margin of battleships over and above the two-power standard 'in view of the rapid expansion of the German navy'. To this expansion Arnold-Forster as Parliamentary Secretary was shortly to testify on his return from Wilhelmshaven, and in due course Selborne himself after viewing the Kiel regatta of 1904.[2]

Then, on Trafalgar eve 1904, John Arbuthnot Fisher came back to the Admiralty as First Sea Lord, and the '*Dreadnought* leap' was taken to a class of vessel which, carrying an armament to ten 12 in. guns and virtually no secondary armament, rendered all earlier battleships obsolescent. Within two years Germany had retaliated with the first of the *Nassau* class, based initially on the Elbe and German Bight until the Kaiser Wilhelm Canal could be widened. In 1909 Lloyd-George's budget provided for eight new capital ships. Reciprocally, and despite the strains already placed by the Navy Laws of 1906 and 1908 upon her economy, Germany proceeded to a further stage of Tirpitz's immense scheme for sixty large warships, replaceable at the rate of three per year.

Despite its internal logic, this deadly duel had a certain futility. On the one side, no naval increase could restore to Britain her erstwhile maritime ascendancy. On the other, Germany had succeeded in alarming her rival without improving her own relative position at sea. Tirpitz's *Risikoflotte* could never be effectively used for its original purpose: indeed, his expansionary vision remained incompletely realised when the assassin struck at Sarajevo. Yet mutual limitation was inconceivable so long as British and German maritime aims reained mutually incompatible. Our competitor was striving for access to the ocean: our Admiralty must be able, before all else, to repel aggression in the home waters he must first cross. Britain would give no assurance of neutrality in the event of a Continental war: without it, Germany would not scale down her naval expansion, any limitation upon which would appear tantamount to recognising the existing ratio as valid.

Just as the possibility of Britain's introducing tariffs agitated businessmen on both sides of the Atlantic and the North Sea, so the prospect of a naval war spread horror among Europrean financiers. Unfortunately men of finance, merchants and industrialists composed but a relatively small proportion of the Reichstag. Men like Cassell might enjoy close private relationships with private banks such as Warburg's, and indeed with Ballin himself, and he and Dawkins might place their services at the disposal of the Deutsche Bank in the endeavour to promote joint Anglo-German enterprise, but the British government would pull out of such projects as the Baghdad railway. Ballin was convinced that what Tirpitz was doing was driving Britain into the camp of his country's foes. After world war supplanted his own schemes for international 'community of interest' in maritime affairs, in November 1918 he took his own life.

Next, the place of the North Atlantic episode in the sequence of Anglo-American relations. And here we meet a contrast indeed. That opinion, both popular and official, in Britain should have feared the consequences of German rivalry so much more than of American is not merely a matter of geography, of the proximity of the one and the remoteness of the other. The distinction comprehends a contrast in national images which went much deeper. It was well expressed, a few years after the events of this study, by the future Lord Lothian:

> The ideals of the United States, like our own, are essentially unaggressive and threaten their neighbours no harm. But Germanism, in its want of liberalism, its pride, its aggressive nationalism, is dangerous, and (Britain) feels instinctively that if it is allowed to become all-powerful it will destroy her freedom, and with it the foundation of liberty on which the Empire rests.[3]

To the United States Britain was prepared to make very considerable concessions of power and territory which at least one student of Anglo-American relations at this period has gone so far as to describe as 'appeasement ... the natural, if belated, conclusion of a policy which Great Britain had long since adopted in the interests of her security'.[4]

But in fact by the end of the 1900's the particular transatlantic threat concerning us here was felt to have diminished, even though not as suddenly as it had grown. Partly this was attributable to a lull in American trustification itself as signs appeared of public abstention from buying and of overstrained credit. A severe money squeeze was perceptible even in 1903 as evidence that the underwriting syndicates which had guaranteed the Wall Street promotions hitherto were now caught with a burden of undigested and indigestible securities. Many began to liquidate their reserve investments of older high-grade stocks and bonds in a heavy unloading for what they could get – sometimes very little, for the market broke under the selling.

Partly, too, the shift in commercial equilibrium around the turn of the century was a consequence of the Boer War, which had laid a quite unforeseeably severe strain upon British taxpayers both private and corporate. They had met it in many cases by the sale of fixed assets, and a large number of the ready stock purchasers were American. The war, too, damaged British overseas markets, and from this circumstance Americans were among the foreign enterprises who gained. With the return of peace it was to be expected that this trend would be stabilised and in due course reversed as Britons acquired fresh assets elsewhere to compensate for the assets which Americans had obtained from them.

This stabilisation, again, was abetted by an eventual steadying of British opinion as orthodox explanations for American expansion were found, of a kind to satisfy and reassure industry and public. Thus commercial circles were brought before long to abandon the erroneous assumption that in purchasing industrial undertakings in this country American capitalists were acting in pursuit of some co-ordinated and deeply laid scheme of commercial subjugation. On the contrary, explained the economists, United States capital in seeking new markets for a growing volume of investment was merely obedient to universal economic laws governing the balance of trade. That balance would swing again. But until it did the Americans had no option but to seek investments ouside their own country as a means of taking payment for a portion of the commercial debts due to them. And meanwhile this 'invasion' was no unmixed evil, in that the fund of American capital being devoted to the purchase of British securities might be deemed to have exerted a salutary and reassuring effect on international markets. When, before long, American securities were sold freely on the London stock exchange, Britons would be able to regard the transatlantic threat as a thing of the past. Europe, in the words of one commentator, was

> growing accustomed to the formidable competitor who has sprung so suddenly into the centre of the industrial arena ... Foolish panic had changed to rational curiosity as to the true significance of a strange phenomenon.[5]

Subsidence of national alarm, furthermore, weakened *pro tanto* the thrust of the protectionists' attack. The boost given the fairtraders by the American shipping challenge was to prove no more than a single shot in the arm. The Prime Minister, to be sure, made a remarkable speech in the Commons in May 1903 in favour of preference, and in a lengthy memorandum to his colleagues (published the following August) argued a limited and highly sophisticated case for retaliatory tariffs as a means 'to get rid of bonds in which we have gratuitously entangled ourselves' in a world of protectionist nations toward whom we ought to 'use fiscal inducements which they thoroughly understand.'[6] And by occupying this central ground Balfour did in fact contrive to hold a reconstructed Cabinet together for longer than anyone had thought possible. But Ritchie's stonewalling at the Exchequer, under the influence of Sir Francis Mowat (permanent Under-Secretary of the Treasury) delayed implementation of the government's new line until the impetus behind it had flagged. Chamberlain departed in September 1903 to mount his 'raging, tearing campaign' for fair trade. In December 1905 the Liberal leader Campbell-Bannerman promised unequivocally that his party if returned would defend free trade. Chamberlain failed to carry the working-class voters with him, and after the electoral revolution of 1906 the majority Liberal view was to prevail for ten years. United Kingdom trade markedly revived during 1905; whereas the American financial crisis of 1907 had a further muting effect upon British tariff reformers.

For free-traders in national administration the Board of Trade was to remain the traditional haven until, in the 1920s, mistrust of *laissez-faire* became general. Even as late as 1929 a select committee on industry and trade was to view shipping subsidies and flag discrimination as undesirable.[7] Particular administrative trends continued after 1904 in the direction favoured by shipowners still alarmed at the transatlantic competitor. In March 1906, for example, Lloyd-George moved to amplify merchant shipping legislation so as to apply Board of Trade regulations to foreign vessels with more rigour. The Merchant Marine Act of that year set up a merchant shipping advisory committee, and before long Bonar Law's committee on statutory regulations for foreign shipping proposed additional safeguards and sanctions. Yet the advance of State control over the merchant marine was unobtrusive and pragmatic, whereby 'each successive step' (it has been well said) 'so far from being the product of doctrinaire theory, was forced on reluctant governments in spite of current doctrines by the stern pressure of practical necessity.'[8] In retrospect there appears some irony in the circumstance that at a period when *laissez-faire* seemed predominant, the foundations were nevertheless being laid for a new and elaborate code of regulation by the State over its most traditional and characteristic industry.

To return, finally, to the International Mercantile Marine Co. itself. That alarming phenomenon demonstrated beyond doubt the availablilty, indeed pressure, of capital on a very large scale for shipping promotion in the USA. Historically the IMM remains the most vigorous attempt by American capitalists to evade the burdensome restraints of the registry laws while taking advantage of the working economy and legal security which combination seemingly provided. Yet, since the type of combination chosen failed to take into account the nature of the commercial medium in which it was to operate, the early story of the IMM is a chapter of misconceptions.

In Morgan's eyes it was a virtue of the combine that it would eliminate 'wasteful' competition. To one whose name and fortune had been made by doing precisely that for American railroads, the analogy between the two types of steam loco-motion must have been irresistible. Indeed, in his country the two were often conjoined, and until 1914 railroad companies still owned nearly 50% of the entire United States tonnage engaged in domestic trade.[9] Moreover shipping lines, Morgan could not help but infer, were now suffering from the very same malaise as had afflicted the trunk-line railroads and their investors before his 'rationalising' skill had been applied to their financing and management. Nor was there anything in-appropriate *per se* in the notion of 'community of interest' as applied to shipping. It was the postulate of all conferences; and so experienced a director as Ballin was for pressing the concept wherever he could. Where Morgan went wrong was in pushing his dislike of competition to the point of amalgamating lines in the hope of eliminating it. Virtual monopoly might be achiev-able by the owner of a railway system, even if that meant buying off a 'blackmailing' rival. A combination of carriers on the high seas, by contrast, cannot be welded into any such monopoly over trading routes on an international ocean free to all comers. A rail right of way is by its nature exclusive and grows in value *ceteris paribus* as the territory it serves increases in density of population. But nothing can prevent a man of means from introducing a new line of steamships whose parallel operation may well cut into the trade of those already plying there.

From this vital difference certain consequences naturally follow. The international shipping business is liable to notorious irregularity, not merely from cyclical alternations of world prosperity and depression but from sudden fluctuations in rates and traffic which are entirely without analogue in any other branch of trade. Despite all attempts by conferences to impose some stability through self-regulation, charges continue to be set by the haggling of the market and vary from route to route and port to port to a degree which the railroad traffic manager could neither conceive of nor cope with. To these variations Morgan left himself peculiarly vulnerable by the unwarranted emphasis which – to judge from his only considerable public utterance on the subject (p. 78 above) – he proposed to lay upon rationalising freight in particular. For liner services across the North Atlantic, freight had long been of secondary importance. Rapid development of tramping in the 1870's and '80's, to fill the vacuum left by the obsolescent sailing ship, had left liners there with cargo capacity in excess of demand. Probably by the 1900's nearly two-thirds of the world's ocean freight was being carried by tramps of 2,000 to 8,000 g.r.t., which made up perhaps one-third of the entire mercantile fleet of Great Britain. The liner's service was relatively inflexible: its route, as Kipling observed, is cut and dried. The tramp on the contrary, with a McPhee or MacAndrew at her boilers, would move in anywhere to undercut. Any hope Morgan may have nurtured about resting the profitability of his amalgamation of companies on raising and stabilising freight rates was therefore doubly misconceived.

From all these considerations the wise shipping-line owner pursues a cautious policy in fleet aggregation and a niggardly one in profit distribution. The IMM, however, was conceived and born in euphoric mood and in an *annus mirabilis* of maritime prosperity. World shipping had come out of its recession of 1893–96, and the Spanish-American and Boer wars had successively raised the largest demand for tonnage that had been known for more than a generation. But precisely because it saw a commercial climax, 1900 was a dangerously abnormal year for the IMM's promoters to take as an exemplar when capitalising a line's annual earnings and still more so to base their offers of purchase upon. Even allowing for the ingrained optimism of speculative American capitalism in that epoch, the prices paid were over-generous to a fault. In applying to the shipping industry the same principles of consolidation which had succeeded on land, Morgan and his colleagues imposed upon their new marine enterprise at the outset an unwarrantably heavy burden. In addition to an amount of bonds fully sufficient to absorb the maximum earnings of the combine for the calculable future, a liability of $54·6 million of cumulative preferred stock was assumed, all of whose dividends must be paid before the common stock received a cent. So far, then, from being free to pursue a correct – that is to say, conservative – policy in distributing earnings the directors at the very start tied their hands as to any distributive discretion whatsoever.

In this light it now becomes possible to see Morgan, not as the wily and dominating master of capital, but as the victim of his own inexperience in an unfamiliar medium – a tyro, not a tycoon. He had been caught in a web not of his own spinning. His House, purely as bankers, had scrutinised the plans of Griscom – a shipping magnate, and as such credibly supposed to possess the necessary expertise – and had presumably deemed it a financially worthwhile proposition. Then, unforeseeably, they had been confronted by Ellerman's demand for full payment for Leyland in cash. Once they had advanced the necessary money the Morgan company's position was transformed in as much as its own funds, and its depositors', were involved in the virtual ownership of a freight line. Willy-nilly the House of Morgan was henceforth in the shipping business, and at the mercy of circumstances which no intra-national force could fully control.

And here yet another misconception became evident – that as a controlling device the holding company, which had been resorted to as best suiting the legal exigencies of industrial organisation within the United States, was the most appropriate device for international trade also. It is an unexamined belief, in part fostered by the textbooks of American economic history, that the progression from pool to trust to holding company (p. 00, ff. above) is the story of natural, inevitable and desirable advance in sophistication of management. But in fact the holding company type of control, based on stock ownership at not one but several removes from management, was too remote and rigid for the shipping industry, whose nature requires an almost day-to-day flexibility of operation. Even for the

American tobacco industry (as we have seen) it was not a happy day when the financiers moved into the seats of power. *A fortiori* the shifting complexities of international commerce soon presented the IMM directorate with a dilemma. Either one centralised the management in a trust where influence resided with men who lacked the necessary knowledge of shipping, and perhaps saw it as analogous to the railways that a number of them simultaneously owned. Or else one permitted the manager of each unit of the combine to do what seemed to him best in an ever-changing situation – in which event the economics of central management were negligible.

Had earlier successes betrayed Morgan into reposing blind faith in the magic potency of consolidation *per se*? For the first time failure attended one of his great schemes. Thereafter he attempted no more trustifications. The IMM's great fleet proved unable either to stifle competition or to control rates, and did not perceptibly raise productive efficiency in the trade. Instead of being a dominant influence, its share of the trans-atlantic business never reached 40% and constituted no more than one element in future shipping conferences in that area. It did not, as we saw, become even a paying proposition until dowered with the somewhat artificial profits of world war. Morgan's goal of traffic rationalisation was to be approached not by aggregation of but by intenser self-regulation among competing lines, where equilibirium, as always, depended on institutional factors such as bargaining power at the conference table.

Would it have thriven if the subsidy Bills of Senator Frye and others had come to fruition? For Griscom and his colleagues, we are bound to conclude, misconception on this point amounted to a patriotic delusion. Revival of nationalism in the late nineteenth century had as its concomitant a kind of neo-mercantilism very hospitable to the belief that the prosperity of one's country in foreign trade was a direct function of the size of the merchant marine on its register. Efficient nationalism, both in commerce and in war, was thought to be bound up with the widest possible flying of its own flag, and to that end a subsidy was regarded as the *sine qua non*. The political balance within Congress in the 1890s, however, repeatedly prevented a subvention policy from emerging; and on this deficiency Griscom and his fellow promoters blamed their creature's ill success. But they had not sufficiently studied the case with regard to the maritime powers of continental Europe. Otherwise they might have observed that, of their two German associates North German Lloyd, which drew a moderate subsidy from the imperial government, was outstripped by Hamburg-America, which (at Ballin's insistence) took none; and that within NGL furthermore those of its services which received no subvention were more profitable than those which relied on one. Griscom's hopes from Congressional aid were doubly illusory.

If the transatlantic titan had feet of clay, were the British government wise to take it seriously? On the whole we may allow they were. The American combine could never have secured a monopoly of North Atlantic freight. But it could have achieved at least a near-monopoly of passenger traffic if it had succeeded in adding Cunard to its strength. And is it possible to say with certainty that, had the government not contrived to delay the deal until the right moment had passed, Cunard would have resisted purchase? The question, even if answerable with conviction in the affirmative, still leaves one unexplained residue. Why did a nation and empire as puissant as the British, with its oceanic trade in a position of unassailable dominance, allow itself to be so deeply perturbed by a shipping threat of relatively minute dimensions? With the swings of fashion in historical study the Edwardian era is at the moment attracting very detailed attention from historians both political and economic. Yet none has so far shed any light on the sense of insecurity in terms of which alone can be explained our national nervousness as the new century broke. Perhaps it is time for the social, or sociological, historian to take up the investigation.

NOTES

1 *Selborne papers* 44, Kerr to Selborne, 28 May 1902, enclosing memorandum 'On the Strategic Position in the Mediterranean' from Sir Reginald Custance, head of Naval Intelligence.
2 AC 16/6/3, Appendix B to the printed Cabinet report on 'The Morgan Shipping Contract': Arnold-Forster papers, Add. Mss. 50287, 'Notes on a Visit to Kiel and Wilhelmshaven, August 1902'.

3 Quoted in P. M. Kennedy: *The Rise of the Anglo-German Antagonism* (1980), p. 399.
4 K. Bourne: *Britain and the Balance of Power in North America, 1815–1908* (1967), p. 410.
5 W. R. Lawson: *American Industrial Problems* (1903), pp. 1 and 2; for orthodox economists' reassurances see Walter F. Ford in *Contemporary Review* 81:401–8 and 780–7 (1902).
6 A. J. Balfour: *Economic Notes on Insular Free Trade* (1903).
7 *Final Report* of the Committee on Industry and Trade, P.P. 1928–9, Cd. 3282, Sects III, IV and VII.
8 H. L. Smith: *The Board of Trade* (1928), p. 122.
9 US Interstate Commerce Commission, Proceedings and Investigations of Shipping Combines, IV:404 (1914), testimony of House of Representatives Committee on Merchant Marine and Fisheries.

Appendix I

Excerpts from letters of Sir Clinton Dawkins to Sir Alfred Milner, April to October 1902 (*Milner Papers*, vol. 40, Bodleian Library, Oxford). Milner, of whom Dawkins was an intimate friend, was for most of that period occupied with peace-making in South Africa.

Folios 40–43, 25th April. Ships are serious. Govt. very unhappy, particularly Selborne & Joe. I don't like it BUT on the whole the White Star and other lines have done the best and inevitable thing. I don't like it and wish it were we who exported across the Atlantic and controlled the transportation from a vast hinterland to the coast ...

But the key of the situation is this. Under Morgan's auspices the great railways & growing shipping lines in the US have become as thick as thieves. The railways control all the Atlantic ports except New York which remains an old-fashioned entrepôt port. Consequently the railways had begun to give, and threatened to go further in giving, preferential rates to cargo taken in American boats, & our own boats might have been squeezed out of all ports but New York, where they would have to fight subsidised Germans & Americans indirectly subsidised by advantages in other ports.

The White Star line appealed to Govt. for subsidies in these circumstances. Goschen refused on the old grounds. The lines were left to shift for themselves ...

The new Company starts with a majority of its shareholders British, but of course the Americans with their thoughts turned to the sea might buy them out & then place the whole tonnage of the Company under the Stars & Stripes if Congress passed an Act enabling foreign-built ships to pass on to the American Registry . ...

The Germans take a different attitude. But then there is a Kaiser over there, and an organized patriotic opinion, while we?

Folios 44–48, 9th May. The Atlantic! Oh, haven't we had a hooroosh & a scramble & everything else. Personally, I think our shippers might have fought it out for a long time yet, and were too frightened and ready to accept this accommodation or surrender ... And from a national point of view of course the American control, when in course of time it passes out of Morgan's hands, *may* be used against us.

The Govt. admit that the English lines have secured certain immediate advantages, but are furious with them for not fighting it out longer (when Goschen's last act was to refuse to increase subsidies) and see the contingent distant danger written up in Belshazzar letters. I have myself spoken with Joe, Selborne and Gerald Balfour, and with old Sarum who is very little disturbed and takes the purely business view. The other three wanted the contract modified so that there should be no exchange of shares. They *might* have achieved this if they had come along earlier, but I have had to tell them at the eleventh hour when all contracts are sealed & options declared and *money raised*, nothing can be done. The fact is they *ought*, if they moved at all, to have moved earlier. They are naturally sore at the White Star & other lines not having taken the Govt. into confidence. I think they are right, but the shippers were very sore with the Govt. over subsidy questions.

Personally, I warned Selborne in confidence weeks ago and advised him to extend his cruiser contracts with the White Star – which he did – as all ships carry their contracts into the new concern. But he did not do more and Chamberlain did not awake to the importance of the subject until all arrangements were completed & in the papers. It is a disagreeable business in many ways. But I think I did everything I could to advise them in time, more than perhaps I ought to have done as a partner ...

The King indeed got me to explain the matter and after professing satisfaction tried to intervene through Cassel or rather I think Cassel tried to intervene, using the King's name but without his knowledge, to have a dainty dish – if he succeeded – 'to set before the King' ...

This incident will produce a great revulsion in opinion as regards the use of our national financial strength. We have to tear up a good many old notions. The fact is private money *cannot* fight Govt. money. Welsh tin plates cannot fight protected American tin plates ... Nor can our unsubsidised steamers compete with German subsidised steamers ... Govt. money can only be fought by Govt. money.

Joe is immeasurably the strongest of all these fellows. It is a pleasure to discuss with him. He is so clear and takes such broad views. His face is delightful, in spite of his beastly nose, it is so lit up with intelligence. Gerald Balfour not much good. Makes little subtle academic or semi-legal points quite off the big lines. He has no force. In Selborne, whom I like personally, I experienced some disappointment. He labours under half suppressed emotion the whole time – he is far too emotional – and this doesn't help him in a discussion. He cannot *master* his emotion and let it give steam to his reason. It floods his reason.

Folios 50–53, 23rd May We have had fearful ructions, since I last wrote, about the shipping business. I am sorry to say that the man who is most violent and unreasonable is Chamberlain, for the most, though Selborne is so emotional that he cannot be reasonable. The Cabinet is seriously exercised and there is great division of opinion. Old Sarum takes a perfectly rational and tranquil view: so does Lansdowne and Arthur Balfour is inclined the same way. Beach also is doggedly on that side. But Chamberlain has taken the question up very hotly, partly I think out of resentment at the reticence practised by the ship-owners towards the Govt., partly out of chagrin at the Germans having secured a better arrangement on paper and taunting our Govt. with sleepiness and ineptitude, partly from a desire to appear the chief protector of any menaced British interest.

I had an interview with him, when he made his point with great emphasis that the control *might* become American, might therefore transfer the ships to another Register, and might clear off the British sailors. I pointed out to him that it was equally possible that the control would be *British* – the majority of the shareholders at the outset being British, that both the dangers he apprehended were equally imminent without the Combine, as the lines, like the Leyland line last year, could be bought up in detail and that indeed the Combine might be taken advantage of to get assurances which could not be so if the lines were left exposed in detail. Finally I told him he had better see Morgan, got them to dinner and fixed up an interview.

Morgan met his difficulty by offering there and then to bind the new Company for fifty years not to transfer any British ship in the combination to any foreign register without the consent of the Board of Trade, to hold any ship as a subsidised cruiser on the same terms as other lines, to accept any terms agreed on with other lines for the maintenance of a proportion of British sailors among the crews.

To my astonishment Joe replied by further asking him to bind the Combine to use no ships outside of the trades they were in, and to build a certain percentage of new vessels in the UK for 50 years. Morgan replied he accepted the first if other lines were also restricted to their trades, and also the second provided that if, at any time, it should become cheaper to build elsewhere the Govt. should make up the difference on ships built here at a greater cost.

Joe would have none of these provisions, but intimated that the Govt. thought of exercising an option it has to buy out all the fast White Star boats. To this Morgan replied that the Govt. would, if it did so, be paying 30 or 40 p.c. on the fixed values rather than the real values of the boats, that it would only be putting money into our pockets for building better and faster ships, and that we should not even be temporarily embarrassed as our allies the Germans and Dutch would lend us their fast boats. And he went on to say impressively that while no formal alliance between us and the United States could take place, nothing would do more to establish a good understanding and feelings between the two countries than community of business interests, that in time of war the fact that wheat was coming across to us in British vessels, it is true, but vessels in which the Americans had a very large interest would be of no small moment, and that if the Govt. did buy out the ships the action would be taken in America as proving that the British Govt. was, in spite of its professions, actuated by suspicion and hostility, and that the United States Govt. in turn would be called on to exert itself.

Chamberlain was courteous, but merely repeated his threat, leaving Morgan to go away very sore and astonished and inclined to withdraw all his offers. I cannot bring myself to believe that Joe will really drag the Govt. after him into so insane a measure. But I could never have believed he would be so unreasonable and unbusinesslike! Never.

Folios 54–55, 13th June. I am still struggling with ships and hoicked my old man over from Venice to dine with Edward Rex whom, I think, he quite reassured and comforted for the moment. But to bulldoze E.R. for the moment is perhaps no great feat.

I have talked my tongue nearly off with Joe, 2 Balfours, Lansdowne, Rosebery, Grey, Haldane, Harcourt and tutti quanti. And the situation has had a new element introduced into (it) by Pauncefote's last words from the US warning the Govt. that but for the Morgan combine an avowedly hostile combine would have been formed in the US (backed by all the great moneyed people) to run our ships off the Atlantic and squeeze them, as was possible by cooperation with the railways, out of US ports.

Landsdowne is a good deal impressed by this; by the fact that if food supplies come to us in British vessels (still British) in which the Americans have a large interest we go a long way to secure our food supplies. Rosebery, Grey and Haldane all take that view very strongly, and so also does Arthur Balfour. Morgan goes still further and believes he could get the United States to enter into an Atlantic Convention with us to guarantee against third parties all vessels in Anglo-American companies engaged in commerce. Out of this, which I think is no chimaera, might grow a wider alliance or accord.

Morgan has also offered to contract for an indefinite time that no British ships built or to be built in the combine shall be transferred to a foreign Registry without the written consent of H.M. Govt, that they shall carry a fixed proportion of Royal Navy men, that they shall be available as cruisers and transports at 30 hours notice at any time, that a percentage of combine ships shall always be built in British yards. In fact I think he has met every serious point and as Grey says we had better go into partnership with him, and through him with the American people

I am sorry to say the only unreasonable man is Joe, who exasperates Morgan and threatens to get up a rival combination helped with British (which Parliament won't vote) and

Canadian subsidies (the Americans will buy up the Canadian Pacific if tempted) which can have no other effect than to create bad blood between the countries and bring on a regular subsidy war. He may be stopped – I *think* his colleagues will stop him, but Joe is unreason itself.

Folio 56, 20th June. I am becoming a most regular correspondent. But I won't bother you about ships. Joe still continues raging mad. The rest of the Govt. appear sane, and such different authorities as our old Goschen and Spencer Wilkinson consider it inconceivable that the Govt. does not close with Morgan and assist towards laying the foundation of an Anglo-American maritime convention in the Atlantic.

Folios 57–58, 6th October ('aboard SS Celtic'). As you may imagine my short time in New York was entirely taken up with the organization of this shipping business, over 1,200,000 tons with another 1,000,000 tons German and Dutch tied up in a close alliance and pool.

I was able to take over in my pocket and get ratified in New York an arrangement with H.M. Govt. which I had drawn up with the brothers Balfour at Whittinghame. It is an arrangement of reciprocity. We guarantee not to change the flag on the British companies in the merger, to build at least ½ our new tonnage in England, to carry British crews on British ships, and to hold all our British ships at the disposal of the Admiralty. The Govt., on their side, promise to give our British lines equal facilities with other British lines for the carriage of mails and any services wanted by Govt.

I think this ought to allay the national irritation especially as the Govt.'s reciprocity is by no means absolute, in so far as the Govt. is specially lending money to the Cunard to build two *very* fast ships.

This is Joe. Balfour frankly told me he did not like it. I think he is right. Joe has been influenced by some very speculative gentlemen like Alfred Jones and C. Furness who will make money out of this and make occasions for misrepresenting Joe. Moreover, and this is serious, I think the action of the Govt. will pass the American Subsidy Bill.

The ostensible pretext is that we must have two ships at least as fast as the two great German greyhounds. But we have endured this situation for five years; the German ships are being worn out, and the Germans have decided to build no more.

The commercial advantages for Great Britain of the whole combination are great. We secure the cooperation instead of the antagonism of the great American railways who can control or direct freight. And, politically, to have our food supplies carried in British vessels in which there is a powerful American interest may prove very important.

The real management of the 'Combine' will be on the British side, conducted by the British Directors in the International Co., five of us, all, except myself, practical shipping or shipbuilding men. I had to promise to go on the Board partly as Morgan's representative, partly because Balfour wished it. I looked forward to taking a rather nominal part and indeed had got Morgan to designate a Chairman on the British side. But much against my wish and much against Morgan's this arrangement was upset in New York, as both the British and American directors made it a sine qua non to have me in the British chair. We had to give way.

Appendix II

(a) Expansion of United State foreign trade, 1891–1901 ($)

Exported to:	1891	1901	Increase
United Kingdom	499,315,332	631,177,157	131,861,825
British North America	44,885,988	107,746,519	62,860,531
British West Indies	9,038,376	10,190,059	1,151,683
Australia	11,386,677	30,726,687	19,340,010
British South Africa	3,464,765	21,654,458	18,129,693
British East Indies	3,674,307	6,251,804	2,577,497
Hong Kong	4,894,049	8,009,848	3,115,799
Total, British Empire	576,659,494	815,756,532	239,097,038
Austro–Hungary	1,527,980	7,222,650	5,694,670
Belgium	48,785,117	49,389,259	604,142
France	99,126,707	78,714,927	(20,411,780)*
Germany	105,521,588	191,780,427	86,258,839
Italy	14,317,782	34,473,189	20,155,407
Netherlands	43,917,984	84,356,318	40,438,334
Russia	6,698,835	8,084,228	1,385,393
Spain	11,528,424	15,480,288	3,951,864
Norway and Sweden	6,579,381	11,844,152	5,264,771
Total, Continental Europe	338,003,798	481,345,438	143,341,640
Mexico	14,293,999	36,475,350	22,181,351
Cuba	17,953,570	25,964,800	8,011,230
Central America	6,122,046	6,707,465	585,419
South America	33,147,614	44,400,195	11,252,581
Africa, non-British	1,596,500	3,888,160	2,291,660
China	5,663,497	15,259,167	9,595,670
Japan	3,290,111	19,000,640	15,710,529
Dutch Indies	1,372,035	2,064,765	692,730
Total	87,625,462	158,426,256	70,800,794

* (decrease)

Global figures

Exported to:	1901	% of whole	Increase 1891–1901	% of total increase
British Empire	815,756,532	56	239,097,038	53
Continental Europe	481,345,438	33	143,341,640	31·5
Elsewhere	158,426,256	11	70,800,794	15·5
	1,455,528,226	100	453,239,472	100

Source: US Bureau of the Census, decennial reports.

(b) *International Mercantile Marine Co.: initial distribution of cash and stock, 1902*

Company	Cash($)*	Stock ($100 par) Preferred	Stock ($100 par) Common
International			
Navigation	–	9,205,000	2,500,000
Atlantic Transport	450,000	9,000,000	3,000,000
F. Leyland & Co.Ltd	11,964,275	–	–
White Star Line	15,131,651	24,502,358	12,251,179
Ismay Imrie & Co.	2,491,923	2,469,206	1,234,603
Dominion Line	1,916,890	2,524,305	1,262,153
Richards Mills & Co.	611,681	464,186	232,093
Organisation expenses	652,429	–	–
Balance for new ships	16,781,151	–	–
Bonus to shipper-promoters	–	1,701,138	4,453,069
J. P. Morgan Co. commission	–	500,000	5,000,000
Bonuses to bond underwriters	–	2,000,000	20,000,000
Stock not issued	–	7,683,807	10,066,903
Total	**$50,000,000**	**60,000,000**	**60,000,000**

* Cash proceeds from sale of bonds to underwriting syndicate.

Source: Price Waterhouse & Co., auditors to J. P. Morgan Co., quoted in *Business History Review*, 38:311 (1954).

(c) *British steamships sold to foreigners, 1896–1901*

Steam vessels	Sold in 1896		Sold in 1897		Sold in 1898		Sold in 1899		Sold in 1900		Sold in 1901	
	Number	Gross tonnage	Number	Gross tonnage	Number	Gross tonnage	Number	Gross tonnage	Number	Gross tonnage	Number	Gross tonnage
Built prior to 1875	47	69,190	31	44,895	59	79,992	49	62,480	30	35,183	21	20,525
Built 1875 to 1879	26	36,318	27	24,928	20	36,058	37	53,742	19	25,043	18	23,525
Built 1880 to 1884	59	89,018	76	119,624	59	88,918	59	85,627	58	112,046	37	73,737
Built 1885 to 1889	24	40,219	32	41,881	43	76,031	58	90,790	62	88,924	18	19,723
Built 1890 to 1894	18	15,741	29	36,802	51	109,165	76	125,649	76	139,004	23	45,753
Built 1895 to 1896	16	10,703	} 19	} 18,665	} 28	} 44,551	} 59	} 87,423	} 50	} 84,212	} 40	} 62,390
Built 1895 to 1897	—	—										
Built 1895 to 1898	—	—	—	—								
Built 1895 to 1899	—	—	—	—	—	—						
Built 1900	—	—	—	—	—	—	—	—	5	6,719	} 24	} 32,737
Built 1900 to 1901	—	—	—	—	—	—	—	—	—	—		
Total	190	261,189	214	286,795	260	434,715	338	505,711	300	491,131	181	278,182

Source: Returns of the Registrar General of Shipping and Seamen, as compiled by the Board of Trade for the Select Committee on Steam Ship subsidies, *Report*, P.P. (385), p. 256, Appendix No. 25.

(d) *The Cunard company's fleet as at 1st June 1902*

	Name	G.T.R.	Built	Builders	Horse-power	
					Effective	Nominal
Retained	Saxonia	14,280	1900	J. Brown	10,000	1,700
,,	Ivernia	14,057	1900	Swan Hunter	10,000	1,668
Subsidised	Lucania	12,952	1893	Fairfield	30,000	3,191
,,	Campania	12,950	1893	,,	30,000	3,191
,,	Ultonia	8,844	1898	Swan Hunter	4,750	863
,,	Umbria	8,127	1884	J. Elder	14,500	1,559
Retained	Etruria	8,119	1884	,,	14,500	1,559
,,	Aurania	7,268	1883	J. & G. Thomson	9,500	1,170
,,	Sylvania	5,598	1895	London & Glasgow Shipbuilding Co.	4,400	723
	Veria	3,228	1899	Armstrong Whitworth	1,800	361
	Pavia	2,945	1897	Workman Clark	1,800	354
	Tyria	2,936	1897	,,	1,800	347
	Cypria	2,945	1898	,,	1,800	356
	Samaria	2,558	1868	J. & G. Thomson	1,530	346
	Aleppo	2,146	1965	,,	1,255	237
	Saragossa	2,166	1874	,,	950	282
	Cherbourg	1,614	1874	,,	803	185
	Skirmisher tender	607	1884	,,	800	168
	Plus six barges and tenders (total)	981	from 1848	(Various)	350+0	–
	Total	114,421			140,538+	
Building:	Carpathia	12,000 (approx.)			7,500 (approx.)	
		12,000 (approx.)			7,500 (approx.)	

Source: Cunard documents prepared by Messrs Hill Dickinson & Co., vol. 2, No. 99, p. 61, Memorandum of 14th June 1902.

APPENDIX II

(e) *Estimated first cost of ships (1902) having a speed of 20–26 knots*

Average ocean speed (knots)	*First cost building, etc. (£)*	*Engine (i.h.p.)*	*Annual subsidy (£)*
20	350,000	19,000	9,000
21	400,000	22,000	19,500
22	470,000	25,500	40,500
23	575,000	30,000	67,500
24	850,000	40,000	110,500
25	1,000,000	52,000	149,000
26	1,250,000	68,000	204,000

Source: Report of the Committee on Mercantile Cruisers, 1902, Cd. 1379, Admiralty, 9th July, p. iii.

(f) Westbound North Atlantic passenger traffic (excluding Mediterranean) of selected lines

	1883 Cabin	1883 Steerage	1891 Cabin	1891 Steerage	1903 Cabin	1903 Steerage	1913 Cabin	1913 Steerage
North German Lloyd	7,228	66,474	16,629	68,239	34,908	161,946	50,738	195,718
% of total	12·3	17·1	11·1	15·3	23·9	23·9	12·9	19·3
Hamburg–America	3,706	53,057	11,016	75,835	22,941	109,523	45,377	148,523
% of total	6·3	13·7	7·3	17·0	11·4	16·2	11·6	14·6
Cunard	9,153	11,647	14,769	27,341	23,686	61,528	43,812	86,176
% of total	15·6	3·0	9·8	6·1	11·8	9·0	11·2	8·5
Anchor	6,380	24,545	7,323	15,082	8,820	11,909	16,970	16,190
% of total	10·9	6·3	4·9	3·4	4·3	1·8	4·3	1·6
White Star	5,842	27,994	13,193	35,502	27,712	45,957	42,095	61,970
% of total	9·9	7·2	8·8	7·9	11·3	6·8	10·8	6·1
Total of *all* lines	58,596	388,267	15,023	445,290	200,972	677,403	391,148	1,016,356

Sources: For 1883, *Glasgow Herald*, 31st January 1884; for remainder, Murken, *op. cit.*

Index